Carmen Astrologicum

with charts, tables and index

translated by David Pingree

Astrology Classics Publishers

2005

On the cover: From the Dead Sea Scrolls: Part of a page of prayers and hymns, discovered in Cave 1.

Thanks to Rob Hand for his assistance.

ISBN: 1 933303 14 X

Published, 2005 by:
Astrology Classics

The publication division of:
The Astrology Center of America
2124 Nicole Way
Abingdon, MD 21009

on the net at www.astroamerica.com

Contents

(Page numbers are according to the 1976 Pingree edition.)

The first book of Dorotheus:
FROM THE STARS ON THE JUDGMENTS CONCERNING NATIVITIES

On the upbringing and condition of the native

The second book of Dorotheus:
FROM THE STARS ON THE JUDGMENTS CONCERNING NATIVITIES

On marriage and children

THE THIRD BOOK OF DOROTHEUS WHICH HE WROTE WITH RESPECT TO THE HAYLAJ AND THE KADHKHUDAH, WHICH ARE THE GOVERNOR AND THE INDICATOR OF THE TIME OF THE YEARS OF LIFE.

THE FOURTH BOOK OF DOROTHEUS ON THE TRANSFER OF YEARS.

THE FIFTH BOOK OF DOROTHEUS, ON INTERROGATIONS.

Index of Charts

*(Numbers/titles are as given by Pingree, who sorted the
first eight charts in chronological order.)*

To Victor Stegemann
Most excellent investigator of Dorotheus

PREFACE

Learned men[1] have very often examined the poem of Dorotheus, to which end they have used it as a foundation of the science of astrology, but who nevertheless were relying to a great extent only on Greek, Latin and Arabic fragments. In this volume, kind reader, you will find a new version, never made accessible until now, I mean the Arabic text from a Pahlavi source. The Pahlavi work, composed in the third century, was transmitted together with other similar books on Greek astrology to educated Persians in the Sassanid kingdom.[2]

Dorotheus, in the preface of his book, calls himself the king of Egypt and Hermes his son;[3] however, we have testimony of both Firmicus Maternus and Michael Italicus[4] that Dorotheus was certainly from Sidon, though in fact Hermes Trismegistus is also called the king of Egypt in Book 2.[5] It is plain that Dorotheus, therefore, was speaking in Greek hexameters to his son Hermes, that is, his student, by which name disciples are denoted not only in the collected writings called the Corpus Hermeticum, but also in mystical and astrological books. We know in fact that Dorotheus was named as king of Egypt in a Pahlavi work made from a translation of the Pahlavi book of Zoroaster dating from about 750.[6]

However, eight nativities preserved in Book 1 inform us about the time in which Dorotheus lived.

1. *Prima.* I 24, 15-16. About the 11th hour before noon, 29 March 7 B.C.

	chart	computed longitudes[1]
Saturn	Pisces	15 Pisces
Jupiter	Pisces	9 Pisces
Mars	Virgo	11 Virgo
Sun	Aries	7 Aries
Venus	Taurus	23 Aries
Mercury	Aries	13 Pisces
Moon	Pisces	23 Pisces
Ascendant	Gemini	ca. 11 a.m.

2. *Secunda.* I 24, 12-14. About the 10th hour after noon, 31 October, year 12.

	chart	computed longitudes
Saturn	Scorpio	8 Scorpio
Jupiter	Libra	4 Libra
Mars	Leo	18 Virgo
Sun	Scorpio	7 Scorpio
Venus	Virgo	2 Libra
Mercury	Scorpio	25 Scorpio
Moon	Libra	9 Libra
Ascendant	Cancer	ca. 10 p.m.

3. *Tertia.* I 24, 5-6. About noon, 26 January, year 13.

	chart	computed longitudes
Saturn	Scorpio	17 Scorpio
Jupiter	Libra	15 Libra
Mars	Scorpio	9 Scorpio
Sun	Aquarius	5 Aquarius
Venus	Pisces	15 Capricorn
Mercury	Aquarius	13 Aquarius
Moon	Sagittarius	17 Sagittarius
Ascendant	Aries	ca. noon.

Venus was placed on the other side of the Sun.

4. *Quarta.* I 24, 17-19. About the 2nd hour after midnight, 25 November, year 14.

	chart	computed longitudes
Saturn	Scorpio	1 Sagittarius
Jupiter	Sagittarius	28 Scorpio
Mars	Capricorn	17 Libra
Sun	Scorpio	2 Sagittarius
Venus	Sagittarius	9 Sagittarius
Mercury	Scorpio	25 Scorpio
Moon	Gemini	5 Gemini
Ascendant	Virgo	ca. 2 a.m.

Mars was placed in square to itself.

5. *Quinta.* I 24, 7-8. About noon, 30 March, year 22.

	chart	computed longitudes
Saturn	Pisces	29 Aquarius
Jupiter	Cancer	10 Cancer
Mars	—	15 Cancer
Sun	Aries	7 Aries

Venus	Virgo	21 Aquarius
Mercury	Aries	11 Aries
Moon	Cancer	22 Cancer
Ascendant	Cancer	ca. noon

Venus was placed opposite [to its position].

6. *Sexta.* I 21, 14-20. About noon, 2 May, year 29.

	chart	computed longitudes
Saturn	Taurus	27 Taurus
Jupiter	Aquarius	29 Aquarius
Mars	Gemini	29 Taurus
Sun	Taurus	10 Taurus
Venus	—	19 Taurus
Mercury	Taurus	22 Taurus
Moon	Taurus	10 Taurus
Ascendant	Leo	ca. noon

7. *Septima.* I 24, 9-11. About the 8th hour after noon, 2 April, year 36.

	chart	computed longitudes
Saturn	Virgo	28 Leo
Jupiter	Virgo	16 Virgo
Mars	Aquarius	5 Pisces
Sun	Aries	11 Aries
Venus	Taurus	27 Taurus
Mercury	Pisces	1 Taurus
Moon	Scorpio	17 Scorpio
Ascendant	Scorpio	ca. 8 p.m.

Mercury was placed on the other side of the Sun.

8. *Octava.* I 24, 2-4. About the 2nd hour after midnight, 2 August, year 43.

	chart	computed longitudes
Saturn	Scorpio	19 Scorpio
Jupiter	Taurus	18 Taurus
Mars	Aquarius	9 Scorpio
Sun	Leo	7 Leo
Venus	Leo	6 Leo
Mercury	<Virgo>	4 Virgo
Moon	Scorpio	11 Scorpio
Ascendant	Gemini	ca. 2 a.m.

Mars was again placed in square to itself.

From all of these it appears that Dorotheus flourished from about the year 25 to the year 75. One must not believe Simon of Phares, a 15th century astrologer from Lyon, who relates that our Dorotheus was one and the same as the son of Nathanael whom Josephus (Ant. Iud. 20, 14) included among the envoys sent by the Judaeans to the Emperor Claudius in the year 51.[1] We will pass over other stories about Dorotheus related not only by Simon but by other writers of the middle and more recent ages; we are examining here only genuine Dorotheus.[2]

Dorotheus affirms that his doctrines are drawn from Babylonian and Egyptian sources.[3] Yet it is evident that he owes all his doctrines to a science which is said to be of the Hellenistic age, and not more ancient. We have learned that he cited Hermes Trismegistus, under whose name books on astrology were widely known in the 1st and 2nd centuries B.C.; but about Qitrinus (Cedrenus?) al-Sadwali[4] we have been informed neither about the man himself, nor his city, nor his generally unknown iatro-mathematical work [i.e. astrological medicine]. In two places also, opinions of Vettius Valens, astrologer of Antioch at the end of the 2nd century, have been inserted;[5] these are not found in his *Anthology* which has been handed down to us unfinished, but seem to be interposed by some learned man who has either translated the Greek text into Pahlavi or already read a translation; for it is easy to perceive that he has used the work of Vettius Valens.[6] Therefore we have little for sure about the sources of Dorotheus, but at this time we will consider many which are derived from his work.

Manetho, born 80 A.D.,[7] tried in his poem on astrology[8] to explain in many verses the doctrines of Dorotheus; they will not be noted here since his poem, edited first by Koechly, may have to be corrected. Somewhat later, the elegiac poet Anubio copied the work of Dorotheus, of which an ancient paraphrase of the verses composed on the aspects and places of the planets was published later. In about 350, Firmicus Maternus turned the greatest part, it seems, of Anubio's poem into Latin in Books 5 and 6 of the *Mathesis*.[1] Third in order, Maximus, a poet of uncertain timeframe, follows Dorotheus primarily in his book entitled On Inceptions (*Peri Katarch M´n*).[2] All fragments of the work of Dorotheus from these three poets will be found preserved in a new edition, now begun, of their poems.

Hephaistio of Thebes composed three books of Apotelesmatics about 415,[3] in which he transmits very many fragments of Dorotheus which are collected for us in this volume. Likewise the most expert astrologer Rhetorius, falsely called the Egyptian, in my opinion, followed the trail of Dorotheus closely.

His work, in very many hand-written codices is inscribed "Explanation and narrative of every astronomical craft from the Thesaurus of Antiochus," and in only one, more recent copy, "Exposition and explanation of Rhetorius concerning the aforesaid twelve zodiac signs and other different things from the Thesaurus of Antiochus"; we are using the purest text preserved to us in Codices L and R to make an almost complete edition.

In chapter 110 a nativity of 24 February 601 is found.

	chart	computed longitudes
Saturn	26 Scorpio	14 Scorpio
Jupiter	3 Taurus	6 Taurus
Mars	19 Taurus	21 Taurus
Sun	20 Pisces	9 Pisces
Venus	27 Gemini	2 Aquarius
Mercury	17 Pisces	17 Aquarius
Moon	24 Virgo	0 Libra

Venus is trined by its own place.

Rhetorius therefore seems to have flourished at the beginning of the 7th century; they err who assert that he lived in the 6th century.[1] Also, many chapters of "Rhetorius" were inserted, translated into Latin, in the Liber Hermetis,[2] a book we judge was translated from Greek in the 13th century.

Among Byzantine astrologers of the 10th, 11th and 12th centuries who read the work of Dorotheus, two primarily must be mentioned: one discussed the geniture of Constantine Porphyrogenitus, born 3 September 905,[3] the other computed a natal chart and return of the same person, the latter on about the 10th hour after noon, 13 October 1011, and the former on about the 9th hour after noon on 11 October 984.[4]

Geniture: Saturday, 11 October of the year of the world 6493 ind. 13.

	chart	computed longitudes
Saturn	15; 9 Scorpio	19 Scorpio
Jupiter	22; 54 Virgo	26 Virgo
Mars	1; 51 Leo	29 Cancer
Sun	20; 17 Libra	24 Libra
Venus	9; 33 Virgo	15 Virgo
Mercury	22; 26 Libra	29 Libra
Moon	19; 9 Aries	11 Aries
Dragon's Head	5; 1 Aquarius	20 Aquarius

Ascendant	7; 28 Gemini	ca. 9 p.m.

Return: 13 October, 6/7 hour, year of the world 6520

	Chart	computed longitudes
Saturn	20; 17 Libra	25 Libra
Jupiter	5; 11 Sagittarius	16 Sagittarius
Mars	11; 12 Scorpio	17 Libra
Sun	20; 17 Libra	25 Libra
Venus	Virgo	9 Virgo
Mercury	11; 43 Libra	9 Scorpio
Moon	3; 40 Aries	8 Aries
Ascendant	21; 59 Sagittarius	ca. 10/11 a.m.

Mars was put in the place of Mercury and Mercury in the place of Mars.

Two learned men of the 12th century, John Tzetzes[1] and Michael Italicus,[2] who mentioned Dorotheus, were followed only by Eleutherius Elius, concealed under the name of Palchus,[3] in about 1388; still yet another genuine fragment[4] repeated the many Pseudo-Dorothean ones drawn from Arabic sources.

On the Arabic Text of Dorotheus

Ibn al-Nadim informed us of the Arabic translation of 'Umar ibn al-Farrukhan al-Tabari[5] when he wrote:[6]

"From the books of Dorotheus, his great book comprising a number of books, which is called the Pentateuch. And to it is joined as I say: the 1st book on nativities, 2nd book on marriage and children, 3rd book on the prorogator and the lord of the domicile, 4th book on the revolution of years of nativities, 5th book on the beginnings of actions, [6th book - - -, 7th book on interrogations and nativities; and there is also a 16th book on the revolution of the years of nativities.] Which books 'Umar ibn al-Farrukhan al-Tabari translated."

Therefore it is evident that 'Umar translated the text of Dorotheus from Pahlavi into Arabic; all agree that in the book of Zoroaster the work of Dorotheus was cited. Ibn al-Nadim refers[7] to a history composed by Ibn Nawbakht: "Mesopotamia until the reign of Ardashir ibn Babak lacked science. It was he who first sent envoys to India, China, Rome, so that they could copy, and thereafter translate into Persian, works which had been destroyed in his own kingdom; which work Sabur ibn Ardashir also supported. Among the books written in antiquity and then translated were works of Hermes of Babylon former King of Egypt, Dorotheus of Syria, Cedrus (Cedrenus?) of Greece, from the city of Athens, illustrious in science, Ptolemy of Alexandria, Farmasb of India; which works Kisra Anushirwan afterwards elaborated."

The Pahlavi work of Dorotheus is confirmed also in Persian words employed in Books 4 and 5, and in two genitures inserted in Book 3.

Geniture, about the 7th hour before noon, 20 October 281 (III 2, 19-44)

	chart	computed longitudes
Saturn	12 Sagittarius	21 Sagittarius
Jupiter	28 Gemini	19 Gemini
Mars	7 Virgo	17 Virgo
Sun	22 Libra	26 Libra
Venus	28 Leo	27 Libra
Mercury	29 Libra	15 Scorpio
Moon	6 Cancer	6 Cancer
Ascendant	6 Scorpio	ca. 7 a.m.

Geniture, about 1 and a half equinoctial hours, 2 Mihr (that is Phamenoth), year 96 (read 97) of Darinus (that is Diocletian), or about the 8th hour before noon, 26 February 381[1]) (III 1, 27-65).

	chart	computed longitudes
Saturn	4; 34 Taurus	7 Taurus
Jupiter	20; 10 Libra	27 Libra
Mars	24; 55 Taurus	27 Taurus
Sun	6; 50 Pisces	9 Pisces
Venus	26; 50 Pisces	29 Pisces
Mercury	19; 55 Pisces	21 Pisces
Moon	19; 7 Virgo	20 Virgo
Ascendant	18 Pisces	ca. 8 a.m.

It is evident, then that 'Umar rendered a Pahlavi translation into Arabic. However the Persians, who reshaped the text, seem to have added nativities to its 3rd book, small parts of Vettius Valens to the 4th book (IV 1, 15) and 5th book (V 5, 15) and, finally, the doctrine of the novenaria of the Indians to the 5th book. We do not know what they contributed in the end to a certainly incomplete text.

Preface

It is commonly known that Arab astrologers at the end of the 8th century used the work of Dorotheus; here we mention those such as Masha'allah,[1] 'Umar ibn al-Farrukhan,[2] Sahl ibn Bishr. In another place we will discuss in greater detail doctrines of Dorotheus cited by writers of the middle and more recent ages.

On the Codices

The Arabic text of Dorotheus is transmitted to us in two codices, of which one, C = Constantinopolitani Yeni Cami 784 folia 1-69, the other, B = Berolinensis or. oct. 2663 pages 2-133 from C described above, pages 88-89 destroyed, the 5th book omitted, preserve the work of Dorotheus. In preparing our edition we have used Codex C, whose corrections, added from C^2 are also found in B. The folia of the original Codex C now appear to be disordered from V 33, 23, V 36, 6-7 and V 36, 77 – (80b). Certain Arabic words seem to be nevertheless retained no matter how corrupted, since vestiges of the Pahlavic translation remain.

Now my greatest thanks gladly go to my most learned friends F. Haddad and E.S. Kennedy of Beirut, and B.R. Goldstein of Pittsburgh who assisted me in many ways in reviewing the Arabic text; and also G. Chr. Hansen of Berlin and Ae. Boer of Dresden, who read through each version and the fragments most diligently.

D. Pingree

Oxford, 16 Feb 1976.

[list of codices omitted by the translator]
[list of Persian words, list of fragments, both omitted by the publisher]

(Footnotes)

Page vii:

[1] Primarily V. Stegemann, Die Fragmente des Dorotheus von Sidon (Quellen und Studien zur Geschichte und Kultur des Altertums und des Mittelalters, Reihe B, Heft 1), 2 parts, Heidelberg 1939-1943. I have taken care of photocopying an example of the extent of this unpublished work, i.e. fragments 58-134; Victor Stegemann's manuscript volume is itself preserved among the manuscript books of the public library of Berlin.

[2] D. Pingree, Masha'allah: Some Sasanian and Syriac Sources, Essays on Islamic Philosophy and Science, ed. G.F. Hourani, Albany 1975, pp. 5-14.

[3] I pr., 2; see also V 1, 1.

[4] Firmicus Maternus II 29, 2 (App. I); Michael Italicus (App. III E 1); fr. ad V 20, 1-8 cit.; App. III A.

[5] II 20, 1; see Ibn Nawbakht p. XV below.

[6] G. Toomer and D. Pingree are presently preparing an edition of this most valuable book.

Preface

Page vii:
[1] B. Tuckerman, Planetary, Lunar, and Solar Positions: A.D. 2 to A.D. 1649 at Five-day and Ten-day Intervals, Memoirs of the American Philosophical Society 59, Philadelphia 1964.

Page x, top:
[1] E. Wickersheimer, ed., Recueil des plus celebres astrologues et quelques hommes doctes, Paris 1929, p. 44; see also pp. 134-135; 147; 148.
[2] The reader must be advised not to accept the mistaken opinion that S. Weinstock, in CCAG 9, 1; 138-140, has alleged about the mansions of the Moon; see D. Pingree, Isis 54, 1963, 230, n. 10.
[3] I pr., 4; IV 1, 8 and 85; V 1, 3.
[4] V 41, tit.; perhaps he is the same as Cedrus (Cedrenus?) called the Athenian by Ibn Nawbakht (p. XV below).
[5] IV 1, 15 and V 5, 15.
[6] C.A. Nallino, Tracce di opere greche giunte agli Arabi per trafila pehlevica, A Volume of Oriental Studies Presented to Professor E.G. Browne, Cambridge 1922, pp. 345-363; also in his Raccolta di scritti editi e inediti, vol. VI, Roma 1948, pp. 283-303.
[7] O. Neugebauer and H.B. van Hoesen, Greek Horoscopes, Memoirs of the American Philosophical Society 48, Philadelphia 1959, p. 92.
[8] Ed. A. Koechly, Lipsiae 1858.

Page x, bottom:
[1] S. Weinstock, A New Anubio Fragment, Chronique d'Égypte 26, 1951, 210-217; see also V. Stegemann, Dorotheos von Sidon und Firmicus Maternus. Ein Betrag zur Bewertung der Quellenexcerpte in der Mathesis, Hermes 78, 1943, 113-131. However, folia 1 - 27 of the Codex Lugdenensis Batavorum Orientalis 891 have included another recension of the 2nd book of Dorotheus, chap. 14 sqq., which was written at the end of the 8th century; see D. Pingree, JAOS 82, 1962, 501.
[2] Ed. A. Ludwich, Leipzig, 1877.
[3] Ed. D. Pingree, 2 vol., Leipzig 1973-1974.

Page xi:
[1] F. Cumont, Astrologues romains et byzantins, Mélanges de l'École Française de Rome, 1918, 33-54, esp. 38-54; and CCAG 8, 4; 174, n. 1.
[2] Ed. W. Gundel, Neue astrologische Texte des Hermes Trismegistos, Abh. Bayer. Akad. Wiss., Philos.-hist. Abt., NF 12, Munich 1936.
[3] D. Pingree, The Horoscope of Constantine VII Porphyrogenitus, Dumbarton Oaks Papers 27, 1973, 210-231.
[4] At IV 1, 1-30 cit.

Page xii:
[1] Fr. at V 24, 6 cit. and App. III F.
[2] App. III E.
[3] D. Pingree, Dumbarton Oaks Papers 25, 1971, 203-204.
[4] At V, 16-17 cit.
[5] D. Pingree in Dictionary of Scientific Biography; it will appear.
[6] Kit´b al-fihrist, ed. G. Flügel, 2 vol., Leipzig 1871-1872, p. 268.
[7] Ibidem, p. 239; D. Pingree, The Thousands of Abk Ma'shar, Studies of the Warburg Institute 30, London 1968, pp. 9-10.

Preface

Page xiii:

[1] This geniture demonstrates that the Handy Canons were known to the Sassanid astrologers; see D. Pingree, JAOS 93, 1973, 35.

Page xiv:

[1] On nativities cf. E.S. Kennedy and D. Pingree, The Astrological History of Masha'allah, Cambridge, Mass. 1971, pp. 145-174.

[2] On nativities cf. N. Pruckner, Iulii Firmici Materni ... libri VIII, Basileae 1551, vol. 2, pp. 118-141.

The first book of Dorotheus
from the stars on the judgments concerning nativities:
on the upbringing and condition [of the native]

p. 3

In the name of God, the merciful and compassionate. May the lord be rich in compassion towards you.

I pr.

This is the first book of Dorotheus the Egyptian, on the judgments concerning nativities. He chose it and selected it and picked it from the books which were before him, and he wrote it for his son Hermes.

1

2

He said to his son at the time of his testament: I shall relate to you, oh my son, and I shall explain to you so that you may depend on and be confident in your heart about what I shall show you of my work and words according to the stars which indicate for men what will pertain to them from the time of a native's birth till his leaving the world, if God wills. I have traveled, oh my son, in many cities, and I have seen the wondrous things which are in Egypt and in Babylon, which is in the direction of the Euphrates. I collected the best of their sayings from the first [authorities] who were before me like the bees which gather [honey] from the trees and all kinds of plants; for from it there is the honey of medicine.

3

4

5

Chapter 1. The knowledge of the seven in longitude and latitude, and the triplicities of the signs and their lords.

I -1

Always, my son, before everything [else] understand the seven [planets] in longitude and latitude, divide the four cardines by their degrees, and know with this the triplicities of the signs. As for the triplicities: Aries, Leo, and Sagittarius are a triplicity; Taurus, Virgo, and Capricorn are a triplicity; Gemini, Libra, and Aquarius are a triplicity; and Cancer, Scorpio, and Pisces are a triplicity. Know the lords of the triplicities of the signs: the lords of the triplicity of Aries by day are the Sun, then Jupiter, then Saturn, by night Jupiter, | then the Sun, then Saturn; the lords of the triplicity of Taurus by day are Venus, then the Moon, then Mars, by night the Moon, then Venus,

1

2

3

p. 4

then Mars, and in Virgo is also a share for Mercury; the lords of the triplicity of Gemini by day are Saturn, then Mercury, then Jupiter, by night Mercury, then Saturn, then Jupiter; the lords of the triplicity of Cancer by day are Venus, then Mars, then the Moon, by night Mars,

4 then Venus, then the Moon. I tell you that everything which is decided or indicated is from the lords of the triplicities, and as for everything of afflictions and distress which reaches the people of the world and the totality of men, the lords of the triplicities decide it, in an eclipse of the Sun or Moon in which they indicate the things which happen

5 and for how long it will be and of what kind it will be. If the Sun is eclipsed, its eclipse is for two hours and each hour is a year; as for what an eclipse of the Moon indicates when its eclipse is for two hours,

6 each hour is a month. If the Sun is eclipsed in Aries, I say that this distress and affliction is among sheep; if it is in Sagittarius, I say it is among work-horses and horses; if it is in Leo, I say it is among lions; and similarly is it said in all the sorts of signs.

7 I know, oh my son, to which of the seven [planets] each sign belongs, and I understand the signs crooked in rising and straight in

8 rising. Know the houses of the planets: Cancer is the house of the Moon, Leo the house of the Sun, Capricorn and Aquarius the houses of Saturn, Sagittarius and Pisces the houses of Jupiter, Aries and Scorpio the houses of Mars, Taurus and Libra the houses of Venus, and

9 Gemini and Virgo the houses of Mercury. Saturn rejoices arriving at Aquarius, Jupiter in Sagittarius, Mars in Scorpio, Venus in Taurus, and Mercury in Virgo.

I-2 **Chapter 2. The exaltation of the planets.**

1 The ascent of the Sun, which is its exaltation, is in nineteen | degrees of Aries, of the Moon in three degrees of Taurus, of Saturn in twenty-one degrees of Libra, of Jupiter in fifteen degrees of Cancer, of Mars in twenty-eight degrees of Capricorn, of Venus in twenty-seven

p. 5

2 degrees of Pisces, and of Mercury in fifteen degrees of Virgo. The descent of each one of them is opposite to its ascent.

I-3 **Chapter 3. Judgment about the case of the native or his difficulty to his mother.**

1 If a woman gives birth, if the native is a male and you find the Sun and the Moon and the ascendent in male signs, then the native of his

birth escapes what frightens him, and trouble does not strike his
mother nor does misfortune. If the native is female and you find the　2
Sun and the Moon in female signs and the ascendent also a female sign,
[it happens] similarly; and so speak about the goodness of her giving
birth and of her deliverance. But if it is contrary to what I say it　3
indicates misery and death, then especially when you find Saturn,
[who is] difficult [and] slow, in a cardine [which is] a female sign because it is more intense for its power with respect to evil and misfortune of birth. If you find Mars in a cardine, and especially in a female　4
sign, say that the woman will give birth heedless of what is happening,
and giving birth will not be unbearable for her because Mars begins to
cut, and sometimes [the time] comes upon her in the bath or on the
road or like this. Look concerning the signs [which are] straight in　5
rising and [which are] crooked. If you find the Moon in [those] crooked　6
in rising and in the aspect of the malefics, there is no good for the woman who is wretched in this indication. If you find both malefic [pla-　7
nets] in signs [which are] crooked in rising and the Moon in a cardine
aspecting them, it indicates injury and misfortune [for] the woman.
Similarly, if you find the malefic [planets], both of them, in a cardine　8
and the two luminaries, which are the Sun and the Moon, not aspecting
the ascendent, this is an indication of evil [for] the woman.

| **Chapter 4. Judgment concerning the matter of the upbringing of**　I-4
the native.　p. 6

Now I will tell you the matter of the upbringing. Take care that　1, 2
you are not afraid nor interrupt your expectation from the native
because you find a malefic for him in a cardine because you desire that
the first, second, and third lords of the triplicity of the ascendent
aspect. If you find one of them in its term and a cardine or in what is　3
equivalent to this from among the places in which they are strong,
then this increases his life, if God wishes, and strengthens him. If the　4
three of them are together in strong places, it is best. If two of them　5
are in a strong place, then the strength in their indication is complete,
and this is better if the first of them is in a good place. If they are　6
together in one strong place from quartile or trine and one of them
aspects the other, this indication is best. If they also aspect one of the　7
two luminaries, this is stronger for them.

8   If you find Saturn or Mars or both of them in the ascendent and the
lords of the triplicity of the ascendent in places in which they are
strengthened and not under the rays of the Sun but coming out in
9 their light, decree for him upbringing. But if you find the lord of the
triplicity of the ascendent in a sign of misfortune, either the sixth or
10 the third, make use of the lord of the triplicity of the lot of fortune. If
you find it aspecting the lot of fortune or in a good place and aspecting
11 the Sun by day or the Moon by night, it is good. If you find Jupiter in
the ascendent or in the triplicity of the ascendent or in what follows
12 the cardine of the ascendent, then he will be brought up. If you find
the Moon and Mercury together in the ascendent and Jupiter in the
cardine of the earth, it indicates life, if God — He is exalted! — wishes.
13 If you find Saturn and Mercury and Jupiter by day in the cardines,
14 they indicate the goodness of the upbringing. If you find Saturn by
day in a cardine and in his own triplicity, he will be brought up, if
God wishes.

I-5   **Chapter 5. On the superiority of the places.**
p. 7

1   Keep what I tell you of the places and the superiority of one of them
2 over another in power. So the best of the places is the ascendent, then
the midheaven, then what follows the midheaven, which is the eleventh from the ascendent, then the opposite to this eleventh place
from the ascendent, which is the fifth from the ascendent which is
called the house of the child, then the opposite to the ascendent,
which is the sign of marriage, then the cardine of the earth, then the
3 ninth place from the ascendent. Thus these are seven places which are
preferred to the places which are not recognized as good: the third
from the ascendent because it is said that it is the place of the joy of
the Moon, and the second from the ascendent, then the eighth from
4 the ascendent, which is the sign of death. Of these places which I told
5 you, the first is the strongest. There remain equal to this two places
which are the worst of the worst, and they are the sixth and the twelfth.

I -6   **Chapter 6. The power of the seven planets.**

1, 2   Now I will tell you the power of the seven planets. Each planet is
benefic when it is in its house or in its triplicity or its exaltation so
3 that what it indicates of good is strong, increasing. A malefic also,
4 if it is in its own place, its evil becomes lighter and decreases. Say how

Saturn harms one who is born by day and Mars one who is born at
night — then especially if Mars is in a feminine sign and Saturn in a
masculine sign. They are better if they are in one of their dignities. 5
The planets, if they are under the rays of the Sun towards the west, 6
their power disappears and they have no power. If it is retrograde in 7
motion, there is difficulty [and] misfortune in the natives and others.

Chapter 7. The upbringing of natives, and for whom there will be I-7
an upbringing or for whom an upbringing will not be known. p. 8

Now I will tell you the matter of natives, and for whom there will be 1
a good upbringing and for whom an upbringing will not be known.
This is known from what I wrote for you without trouble and without 2
pain. Look concerning this at the seven places [about] which I inform- 3
ed you that they are the strongest of them — the four cardines, the
triplicity of the ascendent, and the eleventh place. If the nativity is 4
diurnal and you find diurnal planets in one of these places, he will be
brought up. If the nativity is nocturnal and nocturnal planets are in 5
one of these places, it indicates similarly concerning the matter of
upbringing. If a benefic is in one of these places, it is beneficial. If you 6, 7
find a planet [such that there are] fifteen degrees between it and the
ascendent, then, even if it is in the second sign from the ascendent,
reckon its power as if it were in the ascendent. But if it goes beyond 8
this, it has no strength in the ascendent and it is an indication of those
who will have no upbringing. If you find the lord of the triplicity of the 9
ascendent eclipsed under the rays of the Sun or in a bad place, this
indicates a diminution of life, and especially if with this first lord of the
triplicity of the ascendent is also the second. There is no good for the 10
native in the matter of his upbringing if Saturn and Mars strike the
Moon, then especially when the Moon is in a cardine and one of the
two malefics aspects it from opposition and the degrees of the ascendent from the degree. This is the indication of ruin, and retain this. 11
If the Moon is in the seventh place from the ascendent free from the 12
benefics and a malefic is in one of the cardines, then the women give
birth to what has no escape from ruin. Similarly if the Moon is in the 13
cardine of the earth and Saturn and Mars aspect from opposition or
are with it, this is a corrupting indication for the upbringing. If the 14
Moon is as I told you and is in its own triplicity and the benefics
aspect the malefics from trine, he is not ruined but he is brought up in

another house than his parents' because he is expelled and is brought up in the house of strangers, and sometimes he will be a slave and will be employed and will be miserable.

15 | I will tell you which of them and to whom it happens concerning
p. 9
16 slavery and that they are cast out. But however it is, if you find the Moon between the two malefics [and] one of the malefics casts its rays
17 upon it, then the livelihood of the native is little. If the Moon with this is decreasing in its light, it indicates fate and shortness of life.
18 If you find a benefic with this it indicates his escape from what I told
19 you, but if it is a malefic ruin. If you find the Moon with a malefic in a cardine or what follows a cardine and benefics aspect it, the native
20 will be brought up but his parents [will cast him out]. If you want to know which of them will desire this, if you find the Sun aspecting the malefics say that his father favors his expulsion and believes in him
21 a belief of misfortune. If you find the Moon injured, his mother fa-
22 vors and desires this. If you find the Moon and the Sun both injured,
23 he departs from his house learning from his parents who they are. If you find Mars by day in a cardine or in what follows a cardine in oppo-sition to the Moon, and the Moon in another than its own house and not its place, or aspecting the Sun similarly, the native is cast out
24 while he is young. Similarly say thus if you find Saturn in a nocturnal nativity aspecting the Sun and the Moon.

25   If you find one of the two malefics in the ascendent and the other opposite to it and the Moon in the midheaven or in the seventh sign,
26 the native has no upbringing. If you find the Moon in a term of the malefics and a malefic in a cardine and the Moon not aspected by the
27 benefics, there is calamity for him. It does not stop unless they aspect the lord of the triplicity of the Sun in a diurnal nativity and the lord of the triplicity of the Moon in a nocturnal nativity because these two indicate upbringing and other than that because a benefic, if it aspects
28 a malefic, removes its evil. If we do not find for the native one bene-fic in a cardine and not [in] the sign of fortune and not in the triplicity of the ascendent and the malefics aspect the Sun and the Moon and the conjunction and the fullness [of the Moon], all of this is an evil indication, and this is also a misfortune if it [the Moon] is injured, and worse if the Moon and Venus are both injured as Venus and the Moon
29 indicate the matter of his mother. If it is thus, it indicates injury to his
p. 10 condition and injury | to the condition of his mother unless we find a

benefic aspecting the ascendent and the Moon as the ascendent indicates the native and the Moon and Venus his mother.

Chapter 8. Knowledge of the masculine and feminine "hours" of the nativity. I-8

Know the masculine and feminine "hours" as, if the Moon is in a 1
masculine dodecatemorion, he [the native] is masculine. If the Sun 2
and the ascendent and the Moon are in masculine signs, then, even if
the "hour" of the nativity is double [i. e., even], males are born in it.
If the Sun is in the ascendent in a masculine sign and the "hour" is 3
double, males are born in it. If the ascendent is a two-bodied sign and 4
is masculine and a masculine planet is in it, then, even if the "hour" of the
nativity is double, males are born in it. If you find a masculine 5
planet in the ascendent and another masculine [planet] in the seventh
sign and the "hour" is double, males are born in it. If the Moon is in 6
a masculine sign and the Sun also is in a masculine sign and the ascendent is what it is and the lord of the ascendent is Jupiter, similarly
males are born. Count the dodecatemoria according to this manner: in 7
a masculine sign two and a half "days" [i. e., degrees] masculine and
two and a half "days" feminine, and in a feminine sign: two and a
half "days" feminine and two and a half "days" masculine.

Chapter 9. The matter of bringing up again. I-9

Look concerning the matters of bringing up at the lot of fortune and 1
the lot of the demon. If you find the Moon with one of them or aspecting 2
them in trine, this is a good indication in the matter of bringing up,
and this is an indicator of the beauty of his face and the perfection of
his limbs and the sprouting of his teeth without discomfort. If the 3
Moon is free from these two, say the contrary to what I said.

| Chapter 10. Knowledge of what indicates whether the native and his mother are slaves or free. I-10
p. 11

If you want to know whether the native is a slave or free, look first 1
thing at the Moon. If you find the Moon in the twelfth or in the sixth 2
[place] and the lord of the triplicity of this sign is not in a good place,
then the native is a slave. If you find with this the first lord of the 3
triplicity of the Moon or its participant by night and the first and the

second lords of the triplicity of the Sun by day in a good place, this
indicates that the native is born from free [parents] but according to
4 this his parents are poor. If you find the Moon in the degrees of the
end of the sign, his mother is bad in descent unless Jupiter is with it.
5, 6 If a sign other than his sign is bad, the misery is removed. If you find
Venus with the Moon in its [Venus'] house, it indicates the disappear-
7 ance of the evil. If you find a malefic in his cardine and you find Mars
by day or Saturn by night aspecting the Sun or the Moon without the
aspect of Jupiter, the reputation of the free will leave the native and
8 he will be a servant. It is worse than this if the Moon is in a feminine
9 sign, and [even] worse than this if Venus is injured. Look: if you find
the Sun and Saturn in the sixth or twelfth or eighth or fourth [place],
10 judge for his father misfortune in his condition. If you find the Sun
and the Moon in term[s] of the benefics and [in] the aspect of the lords
of their houses, judge goodness in the condition of his parents, and
11 length of their survival and goodness of their house. It is better than
this if the Sun or the Moon is lord of the lot of fortune or is in a cardine.
12 But if you find the Moon in a cardine or in what follows a cardine
[and] supervising it one of the malefics, it will strike him even if he is
13 free. His descent is destroyed if [one] malefic is with the Moon and
14 the other supervises it. Similarly, if you find the Moon when the nativity is nocturnal in the seventh or fourth sign in the aspect of the
malefics, judge for him destitution and slavery and difficulty in liveli-
15 hood. If you find the lot of fortune in the sixth or twelfth | [place],
p. 12
16 this is an indicator of service. If you find the lord of the lot of fortune
in the sixth or twelfth [place and] not in its term, it indicates [some-
17 thing] similar to this. If you find the Moon when the nativity is
nocturnal in a masculine sign while the ascendent is feminine, or the
Sun in a diurnal nativity is in a feminine sign while the ascendent is
18 masculine, the native is like a slave. You want to look at the term[s]
of the Sun and the Moon and the ascendent, so that it is known whether the lord of the term is masculine or feminine (the feminine planets are Saturn, Venus, and the Moon, the masculine ones the Sun,
19 Jupiter, and Mars). If you find the Moon with the malefics free from
20 the benefics, it indicates slavery. If you find a malefic in a cardine or
Mars is aspecting the Moon while the Moon is coming into conjunction
21 with Saturn or the reverse, it indicates that the native is a slave. If
you find the Moon at the end of a sign and in the aspect of Saturn or

Mars, it indicates that the native sometimes is cast out [aborted] and
sometimes [his] birth is hard. If Jupiter or Venus aspect the Moon 22
with this, he is born [but] then he grows up in the house of strangers.
If you find the lord of the triplicity of the ascendent cadent and you 23
find the Moon [with] a malefic opposing it and the Sun in an evil
place, the native's parents are slaves.

I command you, concerning the one who is born in a conjunction, 24
to see that you observe the degree of the conjunction so that it is
known which is the lord of the triplicity of this sign, and [concerning]
one whose nativity occurs in the fullness [of the Moon] so that there
is known the lord of the triplicity of the sign in which the fullness
occurred. You look at these two signs [and] which [planet] aspects 25
them. If you find the first lord of the triplicity in an evil place and 26
the second in a good place, these will release him from slavery to
manumission. If you find the first lord of the triplicity in a good place 27
and the second in an evil place, say that he is free in the beginning of
his age and at the end of his life poverty and contempt and service
will come to him. The evil places are the sixth, the twelfth, the eighth, 28
and the third except that the Moon rejoices at its arrival in the third.
If you find the first and second lords of the triplicities of the con- 29
junction and the fullness [of the Moon] in an evil place, the one who is
born in this does not cease being a slave or a servant from the be-
ginning of his life till the end of his life. | If both of them are in a 30
good place, he is free from the beginning of his life till the end of his p. 13
life. If you find a malefic in the sign of the conjunction or of the full- 31
ness [of the Moon] and you find another malefic aspecting it, he will
experience his fate and evil will overcome him. If you find the lord of 32
the term of that degree in which the conjunction or the fullness [of the
Moon] is in an evil place or in the seventh sign or the fourth from the
ascendent, it indicates slavery and poverty. But if a benefic planet 33
is aspecting it and the lord of this term is in a good place when the
conjunction or fullness [of the Moon] is in an evil place and [in] the
aspect of the malefics, then the father of the native is of noble birth
and his mother is bad in her lineage.

If you find Jupiter in the nativity of a slave in a cardine in any sign 34
except Capricorn, [whether] you find it with malefics or with benefics,
it indicates his manumission and escape from slavery. If Jupiter 35
aspects the Moon from wherever it aspects or is uninjured, the pains

36 of slavery are completely loosened for him. If in the birth of a slave
Venus is in a cardine without the aspect of the malefics, this is an
37 indicator of manumission. If you find Venus also with the Moon in the
38 seventh [place], it informs [you] about his escape from slavery. If
you find the Sun and Mercury and the Moon in cardines or you find
the Sun and the Moon in one [and the same] triplicity, they indicate
39 manumission. If you find the Moon in Taurus or in Cancer when they
are cardines, without the aspect of the malefics or in the aspect of the
40 malefics and the benefics together, he is freed from slavery. He who is
born when Jupiter is with the lot of fortune or in quartile from it, the
41 misery of slavery will depart from him. But if Jupiter aspects the lot
of fortune and they are both in evil places, this indicates that he will
be manumitted but he will not escape from servitude which is like
42 slavery. He who is born while Jupiter is in the eighth sign from the
43 ascendent or the second, as for him it indicates what is like slavery. If
it is in the sixth or twelfth, it is more evil and worse.

I -11   **| Chapter 11. The knowledge of how many will own the native if he is**
p. 14 **a slave.**

1   If you wish to know how many will own the native if he is a slave,
look in the day-time from the Sun to the lord of the triplicity of the
lot of fortune, then [at] whatever of the planets is between these two,
2 and count these planets as rulers. If the nativity is nocturnal, [look]
from the Moon to the lot of fortune, then [at] whatever of the planets
3 is between these two, and then the number of these is ruling. Look,
and if you find the Moon above the earth, then you count what is
between the sign of slaves, which is the sixth place, to the twelfth
place, and then whatever of the planets is between these two, that is
4 the ruling number. If the Moon is under the earth, then mark off from
5 the twelfth sign to the sixth [and proceed] as I told you. Whatever
6 planet you find in a sign having two bodies, double it. If you wish
to know how many will own his father, then mark off from the Sun
to the lord of its [the Sun's] triplicity, and whatever of the planets is
7 between these two, that is the number which will own him. Mark
off from the Moon to the lord of the triplicity of the Moon for his
mother.

Chapter 12. Consideration concerning the upbringing of the native, his condition, and his livelihood.

It is necessary also to look at the sign which the Moon enters on the 1
third day from the birth of the native as you will know this from the
place [of the Moon] and the lord of [its] exaltation and which [planet]
is associated with it and from its lord and from [the planet] aspecting
it. It indicates the native because, if benefics aspect this sign, it indi- 2
cates first thing the goodness of [his] upbringing and [his] good fortune. If it is evil and malefics aspect it, it indicates his misery. Look 3, 4
also at the lord of the house of the Moon on the third day, and mark it
off, but if you find it in a good place shining in its light or benefics
aspecting it, then the native is middling in condition and livelihood,
and he is in this neither happy nor destitute. If it is different, then this 5
is misery. If you find the dodecatemorion of the Moon with malefics 6
or they aspect it, then this is an indication of misfortune for the native.
If you find the Moon void of all the planets, [and] none of them aspects 7
it, and none is in the ascendent | or aspecting the ascendent, then this p. 15
native is void of good in livelihood, possesses pain and hardship in the
pursuit of what he needs. If you find the Moon increasing and Mars 8
aspecting it from opposition or quartile or [Mars] is with it, or [if] it
[the Moon] is decreasing and Saturn is aspecting it, then there is no
good for him in [his] livelihood. If the Moon is increasing in the di- 9
rection of North, he attains good at the end of his life, and if it is
cutting from the direction of the South to the direction of the North
and is ascending, then he attains good at the beginning of his life and
at its end. Know that the Moon is best of all if it is increasing, rising in 10
the sphere of heaven toward the North. This is an indication of pros- 11
perity and manly virtue for the native.

Look at the tenth place from the Moon; if you find a benefic in it, 12
it indicates splendor and good for the native, but if a malefic is there,
a diminution of this and injury. If the Moon is injured and Saturn is in 13
the tenth from it, it indicates misery and misfortune. If the malefic is 14
in other than its house and its place is not on this side, this is an indication of great harm, but if a benefic is in the tenth from the Moon in
its own place, then this native attains wealth and gains in right and
honesty.

If you wish to consider the parents of the native, look for his father 15

from the Sun and the lord of its triplicity because from these planet[s]
are known the lineage of his father and his livelihood [respectively].

16 If you find the lord of the triplicity, [whether] benefic or malefic, in a
good place, and the Sun also strong in its place, then this is an indi-
17 cator of wealth and praise and fame for his father. If the Sun is in the
terms of the benefics, then it is better, and it indicates with this that
18 the native will inherit this from his father. But if you find with the lord
of the triplicity a malefic, it indicates a decrease in the property of
19 his father and injuries and calamity. If you find the Sun and the lord
of its triplicity in bad place[s], then this indicates that his father is not
20 noble and poverty and necessity have overtaken him. If you find the
Sun in a good place and the lord of its triplicity cadent, then this indicates that his father is noble, but he will not keep his property and
21 his honor because the Sun's indication is thus. If you find with this
the Sun in the terms of malefics, say that his father has no splendor
22 because [this is] an indication of service for him. If with this the male-
p. 16 fic aspects the Sun, you | will find illness, putrefaction in his father. If
23 with this you find the Sun in a bad place and the lord of its triplicity
in a good place, then say that the father of this native increases the
good, and they are elevated afterwards over those whom they meet of
24 equal position. If you find the first lord of the triplicity of the Sun in a
strong place and the second is in a bad place, then his father at the
beginning of his birth attains goodness of condition, but this does not
persist till the end, and if it is the opposite, then reverse it.

25   Look concerning the matter of his mother from the Moon and, in
lineage, from its place and its term and its right side and its left side
and from its place in the South and its position relative to the ascending node and the descending node because, if you find it descending
toward the South or in an eclipse or in [its] dejection or in the terms of
the malefics, then all of this is bad for his mother, then especially if
26 the malefics aspect it. If you find the Moon in the term[s] of the benefics descending toward the South or in a constellation with what I
told you of its malefic or its dejection, then his mother is noble, but
27 ignominy and disdain and humiliation have struck her. If you find
the Moon in the cardine under the earth, then a chronic illness will
strike his mother or his mother will be harmed in [her] reputation.
28 And especially if the Moon is in the cardine of the West or in the cardine under the earth in the term[s] of the malefics and the lord of

its house is cadent, then the livelihood of his mother is in slavery. If   29
you find the Moon in a cardine and it is in quartile of Saturn or Mars
or [in] opposition to these two or conjoining with them, then his
mother will die a terrible death.

If you find the Sun, and the lord of its triplicity is in a bad place,   30
[its] dejection, in other than its [the Sun's] sign, then it indicates
death in a terrible place for his father. If with this the malefics   31
aspect it from quartile or opposition or are with it, all the property of
his father and his mother will be squandered. If [the nativity] is in the   32
daytime and the Moon and the lords of its triplicity are in a bad place
while the Sun and the lords of its triplicity are in a good place, then
this is something with respect to his mother and her end, and similarly in a nocturnal nativity. If the Sun is in the place of the Moon, it   33
indicates the father in a diurnal nativity. If you find the Sun and the   34
lord of the triplicity | of the Sun in a cadent sign in a bad position, then   p. 17
judge for the native and his father affliction and misery, and [that]
sometimes his father will desire his expulsion and his ousting from
his house, and his nursing will not reach weaning at the whim of his
father till the time he is cut off, because in a diurnal nativity the Sun
and the lords of its triplicity indicate the father, and the Moon and
the lords of its triplicity [indicate] the matter of the native and of the
mother. If you find the Moon and the lords of its triplicity in a noctur-   35
nal nativity in a bad place, then it indicates misfortune in the condition of the mother and the native, and so on. Say in a diurnal nativity   36
that the Sun and the lords of its triplicity indicate the matter of his
father and his end, and so the Moon in a diurnal nativity indicates the
matter of his mother. If you find the Sun and the Moon and the lords   37
of its [the Sun's] triplicity in a bad place, then judge for these two
together what is mightier than he has strength for of misery, and little
livelihood, and with this that the native will not be brought up, but
will be harmed by his parents, but if you find one of the benefics in a
cardine, this misery is withheld from him until a rotation of that planet which is in his cardine has passed. If you find the Sun shining in a   38
good place and the aspect of the malefics while the benefics aspect,
this indicates his father's doubling in what there is in him of property
and wealth, but it indicates also the diminution of the property of the
native. If you find the Moon thus, say [the same] about the matter of   39
his mother. It is worse than this if the lord of the cardine, the fourth,   40

41 is injured because it is the indicator of the matter of the parents. If
you find the Sun in a cadent and the malefics aspect, it indicates the
slavery of his father, and if the Moon is thus it indicates the slavery of
his mother and their poverty and their need for nourishment day by
42 day. If with this you find the lord of the ascendent cadent like this,
then the native is not brought up out of misery and expulsion because
he is a slave or a pauper or one in need of nourishment.

I-13 | Chapter 13. Knowledge of the lot of the father.
p. 18

1   Do not leave aside the consideration concerning the lot of fathers
2 and so on. Calculate it by day from the degree of the Sun to the
degree in which Saturn is, and by night from Saturn to the Sun, and
add to it the degrees of the ascendent [by day] and subtract it from
the ascendent [by night] thirty [degrees at a time], and look where its
3 lord is situated. If you find its lord in a good place, it indicates the
good of his father, and the condition of his father is known by means
4 of the fate of its [the lord's] location. Prevent that it be the sixth or the
5 eighth or the third or the twelfth as these four places are bad. From it
6 [the lord] is also known the character of the father. If you find Saturn under the rays of the Sun, then mark off the lot of the father from
Mars to Jupiter, and add to it the degrees of the ascendent [by day] or
subtract it as you subtracted previously; then [you find] the lot of the
7 father. Look from the lord of the sign in which the lot of the father is,
and if you find it aspecting the lot or you find the lord of the lot in
what follows its own house, or [if] the lord of the sign opposite the sign
of the lot is aspecting the lot, then the native is summoned to [some-
one] other than his father.

I-14 | Chapter 14. The lot of the mother.

1   Calculate the lot of the mother in a nocturnal birth from the Moon
to Venus and in the daytime from Venus to the Moon, and add to it
the degrees of the ascendent [by night] or subtract [it] from the ascendent [by day] thirty [degrees at a time]; wherever it ends, there is the
2 lot of the mother. If you find the Sun and the Moon in tropical signs,
and the ascendent is a tropical sign, then the parents of this native are
not from one race, and especially if the malefics aspect them or are
3 with them or in quartile of them or in opposition. It is also thus if
you find one of the two luminaries not aspecting the other and not

174

aspecting the ascendent, or [if] one of the two is under the earth and the other above the earth with the malefics, or [if] the ascendent is a tropical sign in which there are more planets than one, and especially if these planets are malefic and one of the two luminaries is with them, as it is an indicator that his parents are not from one race. If you find the Sun in the seventh sign, it indicates the separation | of his parents, one of the two from his companion. If with this it [the Sun] is in the term[s] of the malefics, it indicates the squandering of his father's property. If you find the Moon in this position, then say [something] like this concerning his mother. If you find Mars and Saturn with the Sun or in quartile to it [the Sun] or opposition without the aspect of the benefics, it indicates the squandering of his father's property and its dispersal. If you find the Moon in this position which I described, this is concerning his mother, and his parents are separated, one of the two from his companion, in the youth of the native, in life or [in] death, so that he is not about by mistake to become an orphan — and sometimes he is a needy orphan. If you find Saturn in a cardine (and this is worst if it is in the cardine [which is] the seventh) without the aspect of Jupiter, while Jupiter is cadent, then this indicates the separation of his parents. Say similarly if you find Mars in a cardine without Venus. If you find one of the two luminaries cadent from the sign of the West [and] the other opposes it from the twelfth, then this also is an indicator of the separation of his parents. If you find both luminaries in one of the two places which I mentioned, and the two of them are together in one place and the conjunction is in it, then it is an indicator of the separation of his parents. Similarly it indicates the separation of his parents if you find the lot of the father and [that] of the mother together in one place. The aspect of the malefics also indicates separation from his parents. Similarly [does it happen] also in a nativity in which one of the two luminaries does not aspect the other or the ascendent. If you find the two lots, each one of them, in a sign at its term[s], and the malefics are also injuring them from the sign, then this is an indicator of the destruction of what is between the parents.

Look at the cardine, the fourth. If you find Venus and the Moon aspecting the cardine, the fourth, then predict regarding his mother an increase of good and a goodness of condition. If you find the Sun and Jupiter and Saturn are opposite the house of the father, it indicates

20 praise of the father and the goodness of his condition. If they aspect
together, then judge for his two parents together good fortune and
21 wealth and fame. If you find | Mars and Saturn aspecting the cardine,
p. 20 the fourth, in opposition to it or in quartile or [if] they are in it without
the benefics, then predict concerning his parents misfortune and mis-
22 ery and slavery. If the position of the Moon is in the cardine, the fourth,
then predict regarding his mother the aggregate of this evil, but if the
position of the Sun [is in it], then regarding his father.

I-15   **Chapter 15. Knowledge of the death of the parents of the native, one
of the two before his companion.**

1   If you wish to know which of his parents will die before his companion, then look at the lots of these two; that in which the malefics are or which they aspect from opposition or quartile, that is the
2 one who will die first. If you find Mars in quartile to the Sun on the
left side, then say that his father will die before his mother so that she
3 will become a widow. If you find Mars in the second sign from the
Sun, then similarly [will it happen]; say also: if you find the Sun in
quartile with a malefic or in opposition to a strong malefic, then his
4 father is dead. If you find the Moon approximately as I told you
about the Sun, then predict concerning his mother in the way you
5 predicted concerning the father. If you find the malefics aspecting
both of the lots but [the two lots] not aspecting any of them [the
malefics], then look after this at the two luminaries, which of them
more quickly will enter the cardine under the earth — not by the
6 proper motion of the stars, but [by] the rotation of the sphere. If you
find [that] the Sun will precede [the Moon] to that place, then his
father will die first; but if the Moon is quicker to that place, then the
7 mother [will]. If you find the two luminaries, both of them, injured
from opposition or quartile, then look from the conjunction or the
fullness [of the Moon] as this will indicate to you whatever of that
8 you wish. If you find the Sun under the earth and the malefics aspect
9 the ascendent, then his father will die first. If the Moon is in this posi-
10 tion, then the mother [will die first]. Look also at the conjunction of
11 the Moon. If you find Saturn in opposition to Mars or [if] you find
Mars in right quartile from Saturn, then this is an indicator of the
12 destruction of his father's property. As for the time of death of these
13 two, that is made clear from the lot. If Saturn transits that lot and

Jupiter is in a cardine, then predict thereupon [that] the native will
inherit his father's wealth at his [the father's] death. If Saturn and   14
Mars transit the sign in which the two luminaries are, then it indi-
cates the death of them both.

| **Chapter 16. Knowledge of whether the native will inherit his par-**   I-16
ents' property or not.   p. 21

If you wish to know whether or not his father's property will reach   1
him, look at his father's property from the Sun and Saturn by day.
If you find them both in a place good in luck for them, then this is an   2
indicator that his father's property will reach him and of [his] holding
on to it. If Mars does not aspect from quartile and is not with the   3
Sun, you will succeed [when you predict thus] because Mars is an indicator of the squandering of property. But if you find the benefics   4
aspecting the Sun and Saturn or the Sun alone, then he will inherit
his father's property and will hold on to it. But if this is reversed, and   5
you find Mars in a cardine, and especially by day if Saturn is not in his
dejection, then he will waste the property of his father during his
father's lifetime and after his death. If you also find the Sun in the   6
sixth or the twelfth, then similarly it indicates the loss of his father's
property. If with this Jupiter aspects, the grief which strikes him   7
because of the property will be diminished.

Look concerning the mother's property from Venus and the Moon   8
and from their lords because if these two are in the West in a bad
place and the Sun also is in a cadent, and [its] rays do not relieve
these two nor the bad place, then predict that the native is from poor
[and] needy [parents] and [that he himself] is needy. If you find the   9
lord of the lot of the father in a bad place and a malefic aspects from
the fourth or the seventh, then his father will die a terrible death. If   10
you find the lord of the lot of the father in a bad place while the lord
of the Sun and the Sun are not aspecting the ascendent, this indicates
a terrible death for his father. If you find Jupiter overcoming Saturn,   11
it indicates miseries of the father because of his son. If you find Saturn   12
in opposition to Jupiter, it indicates misery and misfortune in what
is between son and father. But if you find Saturn in the triplicity   13
of Jupiter, it indicates the love of son and father and with this the
seeking of affection, and that the son will inherit the property of his
father.

I-17
p. 22 | **Chapter 17. Knowledge of how many will be born to the mother of the native.**

1   If you wish to know how many will be born to his mother before she bears [them], then look at the ascendent and at the lord[s] of
2 its triplicity, and consider which lord of its triplicity is the stronger. If you find the stronger of these two in the ascendent, then say that this child is the first, if you find it in midheaven, then say he is the fourth or the first, and if you find it in the seventh, then say he is the seventh
3 or the first because the cardines indicate the beginning. If [the two
4 lords] are in cadents, then sometimes nothing is allotted. If [the two lords] are in the vicinity of the left side from the ascendent under the earth, then mark off from it to the ascendent, and from it it will be
5 clear to you how many were born before him. If you find a malefic between this [and the ascendent], then say that he is a miscarried fe-
6 tus or one having a [birth]mark or a defect. If you find a benefic [there], then say that there will be more than that number which you predicted if that benefic is direct in [its] motion [and] is brilliant in its
7 light. If you find the lord of the triplicity above the earth, then count from the ascendent to it, and the rest of the consideration is as I wrote
8 for you; he who considers [correctly] is a master. If you don't find a malefic or a benefic in what is between the ascendent and the mid-heaven, say that this [native] is the first-born, but if he is not the first-born, then the one who is before him will not be counted and there is no good in him, [but he is] a miscarried fetus or [something]
9 like that, or it indicates the death of the one who is before him. If you find a malefic in what is between that [ascendent and midheaven], then say that there is no use in him who is before him, and he will die.
10 Look from the ascendent to the cardine under the earth; if you find a planet in what is between that [ascendent and cardine], then say that
11 a child will be born to his mother. If that planet is a malefic, it indi-
12 cates the death of him who is after him [the native]. If you then find nothing, then say that there is none who is [born] from his mother after him.

I-18   **Chapter 18. On the matter of brothers.**

1   I am showing you the matter of brothers: know that he for whom the Moon is in Leo or Sagittarius or whose ascendent is one of these

two signs will have few brothers. If you find Mercury in a term of   2
Mars aspecting the Moon or the ascendent, then | this is harmful to   p. 23
the brothers. Whoever has Scorpio or Cancer or Pisces for his ascend-   3
ent, know that his mother will bear numerous children.

Chapter 19. The lot of brothers.   I-19

If you wish to compute the lot of brothers, count from the degree   1
of Saturn to Jupiter and add to it the degrees of the ascendent [by
day] and subtract it from the ascendent [by night]; wherever it comes
to, then [there is] the lot of brothers. If you find a planet in it or   2
aspecting it, then from this the matter of brothers will be made clear
to you. If the lot happens to be in a sterile sign, then there is no good   3
in his brothers (sterile are Leo, Virgo, Capricorn, and Aquarius, while
great in number are Cancer, Scorpio, and Pisces because some of them
are signs of water and the rest of them keep the middle). If you find   4
Jupiter and Venus aspecting the lot of brothers, then it is a good indication in the matter of brothers. If they, aspect from quartile, then   5
according to that they are beneficial. If you find Mars and Saturn   6
aspecting the lot from quartile or opposition, then this will injure the
brothers and diminish them, and sometimes their death will be seen.
But if the malefics aspect from trine, then there is no great calamity   7
for them.

Chapter 20. Knowledge of the love of the brothers.   I-20

If you wish to know what of love and other than that there is be-   1
tween him [the native] and his brothers, then look from the lord of the
lot of brothers. If its lord aspects it from trine, it indicates love   2
between them, and if it aspects from quartile, it indicates a medium
amount of that love. If you find it in opposition to the lot, then it is   3
an indicator of enmity and separation. If it [the lord] does not aspect   4
it [the lot], it indicates the estrangement of one of them from the other.

| Chapter 21. Knowledge of the number of brothers and sisters.   I-21
                                                                        p. 24

Count from the degree in which Mercury is to Jupiter, and add to it   1
the degrees of the ascendent [by day] or subtract it from the ascendent
thirty [degrees at a time] [by night]. Whenever the counting comes   2
to an end, look at the number of planets which aspect that place, and
in their number will he have brothers. Whenever Venus and Mercury   3

aspect [that place] from a good place, then if the sign is feminine they
4 are feminine, but if the sign is masculine they are masculine. If one of
these two is in a masculine sign and the other in a feminine sign, then
5 the brothers are feminine and masculine. If those planets which aspect
the lot are in bad places, then it indicates [that] the brothers [have]
no good in them or have sicknesses, or [that] there is enmity between
them, and bad and evil [are their] opinion and thought [of each
6 other]. If you find Saturn and Mars and the Moon and the Sun in
7 houses not their own, then they indicate the loss of the brothers. If
you find some of them in their house or their own places, then he has
brothers who do not love him and are not his friends or who have no
use for him because what the malefics indicate is not complete.

8   Look from the third sign from the ascendent about the matter of
9 brothers. If you find it [a sign] having two bodies, or its lord is in a
sign having two bodies, then it indicates [that] the brothers are
mixed [in their parentage], sons of concubines, [born] from his father
10 and his mother and others than them. Look in the matter of brothers
as I told you: Saturn and the Sun indicate older brothers, Jupiter and
Mars indicate middling ones, Mercury younger ones, the Moon older
sisters, and Venus younger sisters.

11, 12   Look in the matter of brothers from Mars. If you find the first and
second lords of the triplicity of Mars in a bad place, it indicates a small
13 number of brothers. If you find one of the two in a good place and the
other in a bad place, then he has brothers, but it is inevitable that he
will see their death.

p.25

"Sexta"

Virgo Libra	Ascendant Leo	Cancer Mars Gemini
Scorpio		Sun Moon Saturn Mercury lot of brothers Tenth Taurus
Sagittarius Capricorn	in it Jupiter Aquarius	Aries Pisces

It is the nativity of a man when midheaven is Taurus, in which are   14
the Sun, the Moon, Saturn, Mercury and the lot of brothers, and Mars
is in Gemini, Jupiter is in Aquarius, and its ascendent is Leo. The   15
indicator[s] of the matter of brothers are Saturn and Mercury because they are the lords of the triplicity of Mars. Because they both   16
happen to be above the earth you count from them to the ascendent,
but if they were below the earth you would count from the ascendent
to them. Thereupon you predict that the native will have five brothers   17
because from Taurus, in which are the two lords of Mars' triplicity, to
Leo, which is the ascendent, are three signs and [one] sign having two
bodies; so this [makes] five. But if you did not find both of them in   18
one sign, it would be necessary for you to separate them. Whichever   19
of the two is eastern and in a strong place, count [from it]; but if both
of them are in the same strength, then the first is the better, and so on.
Predict to whoever asks you about the like of this nativity which I   20
mentioned to you: the lot of brothers is in midheaven, and because the
sign is feminine and Saturn is in it his sister will die, and because the
Sun [is in it] then also because of this a brother who is older than he
will die, and because Mercury is there another who is the youngest of
them will die, but what is equal to this [i. e. its full effect] will be
rejected because Jupiter aspects this place.

| There are some experts who consider in a diurnal nativity how   21
many planets are above the earth, in a nocturnal how many below   p. 26
the earth, then in accordance with that number they predict the
[number of] brothers. If Jupiter aspects the Moon from right trine and   22
the lot of brothers is with Jupiter, then it indicates that he has brothers older than he is. If you find the Sun aspecting the Moon in [a   23
case] like this, then it indicates brothers who are older than he is. If   24
you find Mercury in the ascendent, then predict that he has no brothers older than he is, and if there were, they are dead. If you find   25
the Moon leaving Saturn, especially by night, then predict that he
will have no benefit from his brothers who are before him because they
will die, but a reputation of eminence will remain for them. If the   26
Moon leaves Mars, it indicates [something] like this. If it leaves Venus,   27
then he has a sister older than he is, and he will love the acts of Venus,
and in old age he will be better with respect to his property and his
medical treatment than he was in his youth. If the Moon leaves Mer-   28
cury, then this native is not older than his brothers, and he is gentle,

integral in mind and character for things, and he will be praised con-
29 cerning this. Look also with this at the varieties of signs as the ac-
tualization of this will be made clear to you in them.

30　　If you find the Sun in the ascendent, then there is no good in this
31 with respect to brothers. If you find Mars and Saturn in the ascendent
or midheaven or either what follows the ascendent or [what follows]
the tenth, then this is the worst thing in the matter of brothers as
sometimes he will see concerning them [things] like this: he will have
no brothers, or whatever of them he does have will not survive or will
32 be enemies, each one of them to his companion. If you find Mars in the
twelfth or in the cardine under the earth or in the cardine, the seventh
[place], then there is no good in the matter of brothers, especially if
you find the lord of the ascendent or the lord of the Moon with Mars
33 or Mars aspecting Mercury. It is worse than this if Mars in a nativity
like this is the lord of the ascendent or of the Moon as this indicates the
34 enmity of some of the brothers to others. But if Mars is in the place of
Mercury or aspects it, then a quarrel will occur between the brothers
until they bequeath this terrible quarrel [to their heirs] and it will
come to be a momentous affair, especially if Mars aspects the Moon or
Mars aspects the lot of brothers.

35
p. 27 　 | If you wish to know what benefit will be his from brothers or what
36 loss will be his from them, then look at the lot of fortune. If you find
the lot of fortune and the lot of brothers together, then he will benefit from his brothers and, if they die, he will inherit their properties.
37 If you also find the lord of the lot of fortune with the lot of brothers
or the lord of the lot of brothers [at the same time] the lord of the third
from the ascendent [and] with the lot of fortune, then similarly it
indicates benefit from them.

38　　Look concerning one who will see the death of his brothers, look at
these two lots, and count from the degree of the lot to the degree to
which Saturn casts its rays in quartile or opposition or presence, as
according to this the native will see the death of his brothers, espe-
39 cially if Mars aspects or is stationary in this place. If it is stationary,
then it is a calamity, and worse than this if Jupiter does not aspect.
40 If Saturn and Mars in the place of the lot aspect Mercury, it indicates the death of his younger brothers, but if it is Venus [that
they aspect], then females [i. e., sisters]; all this is according to this
manner.

Chapter 22. Knowledge of the matter of the fortune of the native I-22
and [his] property and his illness.

Look concerning the matter of fortune and property and what is the 1
utmost limit of this fortune and its stages in rising up. If the nativity is 2
diurnal then look at the Sun and the lords of its triplicity, if it is
nocturnal then look at the Moon and the lords of its triplicity. If you 3
find the first and second lords of the triplicity, both of them together
or each one of them separately, in a good place, then his condition
will not cease from the beginning of his age to the end of his life to be
in excellence and elevation and wealth. If you find the first lord of the 4
triplicity in a good place and the second in a bad place, then his condition will be better in the beginning of his age, but will degenerate at
the end of his life. If you find the first in a bad place and the second in 5
a good place, then it indicates middling good in his life, but this will
not last in him so that it will abate. But if | the second lord of the 6
triplicity is under the earth or in a bad place and the first is in a good p. 28
place, then some misfortunes reach him and he does not have every
desire, but some forbearance against calamity and grief and loss in
livelihood is inevitably his. If you find both of these [lords] in cadents 7
in it [the nativity], then this will not cease being in misery and poverty,
especially if the malefics aspect these two from quartile or opposition
and the malefics are in cardines; whoever is thus will not find bread to
fill his belly or clothes in which to clothe himself. If you find the lord of 8
the triplicity under the rays of the Sun and in the place of Saturn, then
whatever of good it indicates is not stable, and his property will not
increase, and he will be more learned in meditation than he is in work.

Chapter 23. Knowledge of the division of the planets with regard to I-23
good and evil.

If you find Jupiter in a bad nativity in a cardine, then it will drive 1
off the evil for twelve years, but if it is in what follows a cardine, then
it will obstruct the calamity until it reaches a sign in which Jupiter
indicates calamity. Venus will obstruct [evil] for eight years if it is in 2
a cardine. Saturn will obstruct [evil] for thirty years if it is in a car- 3
dine and dominant in that nativity (and its dominance is when by day
it is lord of the Sun's triplicity or by night the lord of the Moon's
triplicity), but if it does have these credentials it is not beneficial. Mer- 4
cury will obstruct [the evil] in a nativity like this for twenty years if it

is in a cardine and it has a share in the nativity like what I told you
5 with regard to Saturn. Mars will obstruct [the evil] for fifteen years
6 if it is thus. If the Sun in a diurnal nativity is in a cardine or in its own
triplicity, it will drive off the evil for nineteen years, but this will not
7 happen to it [the Sun] in a nocturnal nativity. If the Moon is in a cardine which is a feminine sign, it will drive off the evil for twenty-
five years, but in masculine signs for twenty-five months.

| **Chapter 24. In it are judgments concerning the matter of fortune
and property in nativities.**

1	Now I will cause to pass by you [in review] the things in which I
showed you [what to do] if you wish to judge the nativity with regard
to property and fortune.

2	A native was born when the ascendent was Gemini and the posi-
tions of its [the nativity's] planets in the sphere were according to this
diagram.

"Octava"

		Taurus	
Cancer	Ascendent	Jupiter	
Leo	Gemini		Aries
Sun Venus			
Virgo			Pisces
(Mercury)			
Libra			Aquarius
Scorpio	Sagittarius		Mars
		Capricorn	
Saturn Moon			

The nativity was nocturnal, and I found the first planets in the ³
matter of fortune to be Mars and Venus because they are the lords
of the triplicity of the sign in which the Moon is; and both of them
are in cadents so that this man should be needy, poor, not finding
his daily bread, miserable. And this was in him more evident than ⁴
what I told you.

"Tertia"

Taurus Gemini	Ascendent Aries	Pisces Venus Aquarius Sun Mercury
Cancer		Capricorn
Leo Virgo	Jupiter Libra	Sagittarius Moon Scorpio Saturn Mars

| This nativity was diurnal, and Aries was becoming visible at that ⁵
hour in the East from out of the depths of the sea, and the lord of the p. 30
Sun's triplicity was Saturn, then Mercury. Saturn was in what follows ⁶
the cardine of the West and Mercury in what follows the cardine of
midheaven, which is the place of fortune, so that the native should be
wealthy, rich, powerful in business affairs, great in property, seizing
eminence and fortune and increasing in them.

"Quinta"

Leo Virgo Venus	Ascendant Cancer Jupiter Moon	Gemini Taurus
Libra		Mercury Aries Sun
Scorpio Sagittarius	Capricorn	Pisces Saturn Aquarius

7   This nativity was diurnal, and the first lord of the [Sun's] triplicity is the Sun, the second Jupiter, and both of these are in cardines in their own exaltations, so that the native should be praised with the 8 praise of kings and nobles and wealthy men. Because Saturn is the third lord of the triplicity and is cadent from a cardine and Jupiter aspects it in its [Jupiter's] house from trine, so for that reason he will be praised with the praise of kings.

"Septima"

Sagittarius Capricorn	Ascendant Scorpio Moon	Libra Virgo Saturn Jupiter
Aquarius Mars		Leo
Mercury Pisces Aries Sun	Taurus Venus	Cancer Gemini

| Another nativity: its ascendent rising up from the earth is Scorpio, and the nativity is nocturnal, and the positions of the planets are according to what is in the diagram. The lord of the Moon's triplicity is Mars, then Venus, then the Moon. Because the three of them are in cardine[s] this man is mighty in eminence, powerful in leadership so that crowns of gold and silver are placed on him and he is praised.

9
p. 31
10
11

"Secunda"

Virgo / Venus	Leo / Mars	Ascendent / Cancer	Gemini	Taurus
Libra / Jupiter Moon				Aries
Saturn Mercury / Sun / Scorpio	Sagittarius	Capricorn	Aquarius	Pisces

This is a second nocturnal nativity, and the first lord of the triplicity of the Moon is Mercury, the second Saturn. Because both of these are in a cadent in the vicinity of [the cardine] under the earth, the man will be needy with respect to property. But because Jupiter is the ruler of part of this nativity and is with the Moon in a cardine, he will have the closest thing to living out [his] days in poverty except that he will have the danger of the hand of misfortune.

12
13
14

187

"Prima"

Cancer / Leo	Ascendent Gemini	Taurus Venus / Aries Sun Mercury
Virgo Mars		Pisces Moon Saturn Jupiter
Libra / Scorpio	Sagittarius	Aquarius / Capricorn

15
p. 32
16

| I This nativity is diurnal, and the ascendent is Gemini, and the Sun in this nativity is the first lord of its own triplicity, Jupiter the second, and Saturn the third, and the three of them are in a good place. This man will abound in gold and silver except that his end is evil because the lord of the triplicity of [the cardine] under the earth, from which the matter of the end and the situation of death are known, is Venus, and Venus in this nativity is cadent in the sign of calamity.

"Quarta"

Libra / Scorpio Saturn Sun Mercury	Ascendant Virgo	Leo / Cancer
Sagittarius Venus Jupiter		Gemini Moon
Capricorn Mars / Aquarius	Pisces	Taurus / Aries

This nativity is nocturnal; so I looked at the two lords of the triplic-   17
ity of the Moon, and I found the first of them to be Mercury, then
Saturn, and both of them were in a cadent. Mars indicates the loss of   18
the property of his father and its dispersal in [all] directions, and the
lords of the triplicity which are in a cadent indicate poverty and indi-
gence, and he will be beseeching all his days, but he will eat in misery.
All this is from what Mercury and Saturn indicate, but since Jupiter   19
and Venus are in cardines they indicate that he will be of noble lineage,
but that he will be brought up and will grow up in houses of slavery,
and he will curry favor with [his] brothers and nobles and will become
acquainted [with them], but he will fail because of the evil effect of the
lords of the Moon's triplicity. If you look concerning something like   20
what I told you about this [any] error will be evident to you, if God —
He is exalted! — wishes.

| **Chapter 25. On the knowledge of the excellence of fortune.**

I-25
p. 33

Know that the best of things with regard to fortune is that the lord   1
of the triplicity of the luminary be in a good place with the Moon or in
opposition to it or quartile or trine. If you find the lord of the triplicity   2
not aspecting the ascendent nor the Moon nor the shining luminary
and the lord of the sign in which the luminary is is also thus, then let
this be a bad indication for that native. If Jupiter and Venus and Mer-   3
cury are not in these places, then this is more harmful and worse,
because this indicates also that he will not long survive, especially if
Saturn or Mars is in this place. But if then there is a benefic which is   4
in its [own] house or exaltation or triplicity and is not under the
rays [of the Sun] or retrograde, and the lord of [its] triplicity aspects
the ascendent but does not aspect the Moon, then this native is middling in [his] livelihood, [and] good and evil are mixed together in
him.

It is also necessary for you to look at the lord of the ascendent and   5
the lord of midheaven and the lord of the house of property, which is
the second place from the ascendent. If you find these in their places   6
with benefics and they are not malefics, and you find them in cardines
or in what follows cardines, then predict that the native will possess
fortune, eminence, commendation, praise, and a good livelihood. But   7
if those which I mentioned are not all of them in good places nor all in
a bad place, then the native is middling in [his] livelihood. If all of   8

them are in a cadent, then look at where are the lord of the seventh
sign and the lord of the eighth sign and the lord of the eleventh sign,
which is the sign of fortune, and the lord of the fifth sign and the lord
9 of the cardine, the fourth. If you find these also leaving the cardines,
[being] in cadents, [and] not aspecting the Moon by night nor the
Sun by day, then this native will be needing nourishment for his belly,
and it will be worse for him if a malefic is in one of the cardines.

I-26　　　　| **Chapter 26. The magnitude of fortune and property.**
p. 34

1, 2　　　　Now I will show you the magnitude of fortune and property. Look
at the lord of the triplicity of the sign in which is the shining luminary.
3 If you find it in one of these four cardines in [such a way] that there
are fifteen degrees [or less] between it and the cardine, then predict
4 about him that he will be most perfect in fortune and property. If it
is in the second fifteen degrees, then predict concerning him the second
fortune, which is what is available of what I told you in the beginning,
as the nearer it is to the degree of the cardine, the higher it is for his
5 rank in eminence and fortune. If that planet which is the lord of the
triplicity of the shining [luminary] is in the third fifteen degrees, then
the owner of this nativity will not be known, but according to this he
6 will be middling in property and fortune. If you find the lord of the
triplicity after these degrees until it reaches the next cardine, then
7 the natives will be needy [and] miserable. But you should have these
degrees in [the rising-times of] the ascendents because degrees are
equal, thirty [to a sign], but the ascendents are not equal because some
8 of them are crooked and some straight. And the crooked ones are
quicker in rising, the straight ones slower in rising; and their rising-
times in every region and clime is not the same because the region of
the vicinity of the North is long and square while the vicinity of the
9 South is low [and] excessive[?]. If you find the lord of the triplicity
of the Sun by day in a bad place and the lords of the triplicity of the
Moon by night in a good place contrary to that, then there is no good
in the native if it is thus, but according to this there was almost good
and pleasure for him in property so that, if he thinks that his affair has
drawn near, it will not increase according to this, but there was a
destiny by which he is ruled in himself.

10　　　　If you find the lords of both luminaries in a bad place, then look at
the lot of fortune as on account of it there is a change in some of these

methods because it indicates the condition of the wealthy, those in the
middle, and the poor. [For him] whose birth is in the day count from   11
the Sun to the Moon and add to it the degrees of the ascendent, and in
a nocturnal nativity the opposite of this. Then look at where it is   12
located, whether its place is good or | bad, what benefics or malefics   p. 35
aspect it, which is its lord and where it is. If he who possesses reason   13
and discernment and who is not perplexed in science looks concerning
this, he will know it lucidly and clearly.

If the lord of the lot aspects the lot from a bad place, then there is   14
no good for the native; and similarly if you find its lord in a cadent
[whether] aspecting it or not aspecting it. If the lot and its lord are   15
thus in the sixth or twelfth or the malefics aspect [them] or [they are]
under the rays of the Sun, then they have no power and no efficacy.
If by day Mars is with the lord of the lot of fortune or aspects it from   16
quartile or opposition, then there is no good in it. If its lord does not   17
aspect it, but the lord of the lot is in the sign of fortune or the fifth,
then there is born because of this [one who is] happy and wealthy,
especially if it does aspect the lot. If you find the lord of the lot of   18
fortune under the rays of the Sun, then it has no power to grant good.
The best that is [possible] is if Saturn witnesses the lord of the lot of   19
fortune in aspect, and it witnesses Jupiter or the Sun by day, and by
night it witnesses Mars or Venus or the Moon or Mercury; everything
one considers will be good. The best that is [possible] is if the lord of   20
the lot of fortune is in its house or triplicity or exaltation or term. If   21
you find the lord of the lot of fortune in a cadent, and Venus and Jupiter in [what is] like this, then let this be a harmful indication in which
will be born none except people of contempt; and it is worse for this
if the Moon does not aspect the benefics. If with this the malefics are   22
in cardine[s] or in what follows a cardine, then the native will fall
upon misfortunes and he will be injured according to that. If you find   23
the lord of the lot injured, but the benefics in a good place witnessing
it and the ascendent and the Moon, and the benefics are eastern, then
he is middling with respect to property and livelihood because Jupiter,
if it is in a good place, always indicates that the native attains good
from nobles and mighty people and from well known work, and he
will acquire property for this reason, and if Venus is in a place like
this it indicates benefit because of women, and if Mercury is in this
place it indicates benefit because of commerce and science | and calcul-   p. 36

191

ation, and if Mercury and Jupiter are mixed together he will be a con-
24 fidant with kings and bands [of people]. If the lord of the lot is in a
known good place and with this the benefics aspect it in good places
without the aspect of the malefics, then this native will be one of the
kings and the free-born, greedy for righteousness, and he will be one
25 of the mighty nobles. But if the power of the planets and the lord of the
lot is as we said, but the malefics are witnessing them, then the native
will fall from his fortune.

26   He for whom the malefics are in cardines and the benefics in what
follow cardines and he whose Moon turns away from the malefics and
comes into conjunction with the benefics, these will be at the beginning of their life despised [and] in disgrace, then they will attain pro-
27 perty and fortune and joy. If you find [that] the benefics have ameliorated the ascendent and the midheaven, but you find the malefics
in the seventh without the aspect of the benefics, then the native
will be well known [and] good in [his] condition, [but] then he will
28 fall from his fortune and his property quickly. If you find the lot of
fortune in a bad place, or the malefics aspecting [it] in conjunction
with it or opposition to it or in its quartile, or its lord not aspecting it
or being western without light, or its lord being in a bad place or in
its dejection, not aspecting the Moon by night or the Sun by day,
while the benefics do not aspect it [the lord], then judge for him [the
native] calamity and misfortune in [his] condition, especially if the
lord of the triplicity of the shining luminary is in this kind of position.

29   If you find Saturn or Mars in a sign of property, especially if it is in
the sign of property which is the second from the ascendent, then it
indicates a fall from property and status unless [these] two are in
their portions [sects] (the portion of Mars is the night, the portion of
30 Saturn the day). The malefics indicate similarly if they are in the cardine of the earth, and their destructiveness is worse if one of them is in
opposition to the other without the aspect of Jupiter because this
31 indicates flight or a terrible death and a hard fall. If you find Mars in
what follows the cardine of midheaven, then know that the native
will fall from his property because this place, the eleventh, if a malefic
is in it, indicates destruction and weakness, but if a benefic is [in it], it
32 indicates the acquisition of property unexpectedly. If | you find the lot
p. 37 of fortune in the term[s] of the benefics and a good place and the
aspect of the benefics then that native will acquire property from his

own property in affluence. If you find the first lord of the triplicity of   33
the lot of fortune not aspecting the lot, but the second is aspecting [it],
then some of the native's property will be squandered and some will
remain. If both of them are not aspecting the lot, but the benefics do   34
aspect it, then he has a good livelihood from strangers together with
praise and commendation, but if a benefic and a malefic aspect it, then
his livelihood is a mixture of good and bad. If in a diurnal nativity   35
diurnal planets aspect the lot or in a nocturnal [nativity] nocturnal
planets, then this is a good testimony with regard to fortune and property, but if they are different from what I said then his livelihood is
difficult and he will attain property after delay and despair.

Chapter 27. The decline of status and disaster.   I-27

If you find Saturn with the Moon in one of the cardines, then, even   1
if he is the son of a king, it indicates his fall from fortune and property. If with this Mars aspects [them], it will be a disaster. If Jupiter   2,3
is with them in a cardine, then his property and his fortune will
remain for some time, but after that will decline, even if Jupiter is
aspecting.

I instruct you to look at the sign which is the second place from the   4
ascendent. If you find a malefic in it or in opposition or quartile to it,   5
then judge a decline in property and livelihood. If Venus is the lord   6
of that place, then predict that that is a disaster, and there will be a
fall from his reputation among women. If Mercury is its lord, then the   7
disaster which occurs will be because of a book or calculation. If Ju-   8
piter is its lord, then the disaster [will be] because of a man, a noble,
or the wrath of kings, or because of the action of the government or
his city. If this house is the house of Mars, then it will be because of   9
violent acts or ... or anger or thieves or the burning of fire or [some-
thing] like this because this is its nature. If the house is | the house   10
of Saturn, then his disaster will be from mature men and slaves or   p. 38
from one who is freed [or] from one who has no commendation or praise
or from one whose life revolves in misery and misfortune, or with
respect to a building or from a house of burial this disaster occurs. If   11
you find this place [to be] the house of the Sun, which is Leo, then the
disaster will be because of [his] fathers or his fathers' women or his
mother's husbands, or with respect to a debt or to money which he
has borrowed. If this sign is the house of the Moon, which is Cancer,   12

[and the Moon] is not in a good place, then the disaster will be because of [his] mothers or his mother's relatives, or disaster will be his [because of] his father's wives.

13   Look at the kinds of signs — tropical or fixed or possessing two bodies, or of the kinds [which are] of water [or of] air or possessing four legs or similar to humans or terrestrial — or [whether] its lord is a malefic or a benefic because it is bad if the lord of the second house is in a bad place and is a malefic, but if it is a benefic and is in a bad place, then he [the native] is middling with respect to [his] livelihood.
14 If it is a benefic and it is in a good place, but the malefics aspect [it]
15 as you found [it], then sometimes the misery will be diminished. If the lord of this place is in a bad place, it also harms his place, or [if]
16 malefics other than it [the lord] aspect [it] or are in it. So these [men] are always anxious about [their] livelihood and have little joy, [but are] filled with grief and misery and misfortune and calamity, and they seek everything in misery and suffering and little profit, so that [even] if it is the nativity of a king, his money will be spent on inferior thing[s].

17   Look also at the Moon, as, if you find, together with what I mentioned of the goodness of the second place, the Moon in a good place aspecting the second place, increasing in its number[s] and its light, in trine with the Sun, and Mars does not aspect it, then it indicates that he is well known, mighty in his leadership and work in cities and the service of kings, a confidant of them, [and] influential because of
18 this. But if what I mentioned is as I mentioned while the Moon is decreasing, then this will decrease him, and they will not present his management in a favorable light nor will they have praise for him.

19   Look which is the lord of the second, then count from it to the second place [and add it to the degree of the ascendent] as from [that]
20 place the matter of livelihood will be made clear to you. | If you look
p. 39 concerning its condition and the condition of its lord and the aspectors
21 of these two, they will show you the condition of [his] livelihood. If its lord is in a good place and the benefics witness it, then predict good in
22 him. If the lord of that place is a malefic and aspects another malefic
23 or is with it, then it indicates great misery in his livelihood. If the lord of this place is a benefic and it is favorable in a cardine in its own
24 place, then he will be wealthy [and] rich. If it is western but will rise

in seven [days], then he will be rich, but will have no fame and not
everyone will know of his wealth.

See which planet is found in the lot. If you find the lot of property   25, 26
in a good place and its lord also in [something] like this [and] eastern,
then what it indicates will last for a long time. But if the lord of the   27
lot of property is in a good place but under the rays of the Sun, then
what the lot indicates will not remain except for a little while. If you   28
find the lot in a bad place, then his condition will have no rise and no
conclusion.

If you find the planets retrograde in a nativity in which the planets   29
are strong, then he will be distressed, a coward. If it is thus in a bad   30
nativity, then his condition [tends] toward deterioration.

Also know the lot of livelihood. If you find Jupiter in a cardine or   31, 32
what follows a cardine, then your saying that he will be brought up
will become clear. If there are some malefics in his nativity, they   33
indicate hardship. If a malefic aspects it or the planets indicate his loss,   34
then they indicate misery in his nativity and that he will leave his
parents; and so also is the judgment about him. But even if he leaves   35
his parents as the planets indicate, yet he will inherit their property
because in bad nativities if Jupiter is in such a place, the injury becomes insignificant and the misfortunes dissolve; even if he does not
attain a good livelihood, yet he will achieve something because of the
position of Jupiter. Similarly if Venus is in a cardine or what follows   36
a cardine, except that its strength is not the equal of Jupiter's strength
save in the matter of women, then there will be seen for him because
of these two participation in livelihood and pleasure. If these two   37
benefics which I mentioned to you | are in strength from their place[s],   p. 40
they indicate good and beauty in cities and groups of men because
many are his acquaintances and friends, and sometimes his enemy will
turn to agreeing with him so that they will become friends with him,
especially if these two planets are in their places aspecting the Sun by
day and the Moon by night in trine, because this increases their strength
and their efficacy and their steadfastness. If you find Mars, the mur-   38
derous one, or Saturn, the destroyer, in what is near those places in
which I mentioned that Jupiter and Venus were, then they indicate
the severance of [his] upbringing, and that, even if the work of the
native is good among men, all will not be grateful to him nor will they
praise him, but one whom he did not harm in anything will treat him

as an enemy until he shall see from the generality of men grief and
39 sorrow. If he is a king, then his people and his city will be destroyed
40 for him and will fall into discord and quarrel[s] and necessity. Similarly predict in the case of middling and inferior nativities because the
sons of his paternal uncle and his kinfolk will treat him as an enemy,
41 and he also will not love anyone of them. If you find Saturn in this
place, then this native will be reflective and anxious, ugly, malicious,
42 [and] haughty to himself and to those who mingle with him. But if it
is Mars, it indicates insolence and that he is a laborer insignificant in
his thought and reflection, but Saturn or Mars is less harmful if
43 Jupiter or Venus aspects it. See, when a native is born, which [planet]
will reach the ascendent after his birth or the place of the Moon, as
from this planet the matter of fortune and his property and what its
extent is will be clear to you.

I-28   **Chapter 28. Knowledge of masculine and feminine signs, eastern
and western, and diurnal and nocturnal.**

1   Aries, Leo, and Sagittarius are masculine, eastern, [and] diurnal;
their lord by day is the Sun, by night Jupiter, and the associate of
2 these two is Saturn. Taurus, Virgo, and Capricorn are feminine,
northern, [and] nocturnal; their lord by day is Venus, by night the
Moon, and the associate of these two is Mars, while Mercury has a
3 share in Virgo. Gemini, Libra, and Aquarius are western, diurnal,
[and] masculine; their lord by day is Saturn, by night Mercury, and
4 the associate of these two is Jupiter. Cancer, Scorpio, and Pisces are
feminine, nocturnal, [and] southern; their lord by day is Venus, by
night Mars, and the associate of these two is the Moon.

p. 41 | The first book is finished. Praise to God, the grantor of fortune to
whom He wishes of His servants because of his excellence, and Who
removes misfortune from whom He wishes of His servants because
of his faith, and Who is generous, beneficent, just, [and] compassionate. May His blessing be upon His prophets whom He has chosen
and [upon] all of His messengers.

The second book of Dorotheus
from the stars on the judgments concerning nativities: p. 42
on marriage and children

In the name of God, the merciful and compassionate, to Whom I resort.

This is the second book of Dorotheus which he wrote on marriage   1
and children and the judgments of the planets. The beginning of its   2
beginning is from marriage. He said:

Look at Venus where it is and which are the first, second, and third   II-1, 1
lords of its triplicity as, if they are with Venus or in a cardine or in
trine to it [Venus], then this is a good indication because Venus is full
for the matter of marriage. If you find the lords of the triplicity of   2
Venus with it or in the cardines or what follows the cardines, rejoicing
in their light and direct in [their] motion, all of this is a good indication in the matter of marriage so that the father of the child was
happy. But if you find the lords of the triplicity of Venus in a bad   3
place or a cadent, corrupted, or they are under the rays of the Sun or
near the West, then predict differently from that about the badness of
the marriage because those who are born will be of those who will
never marry or whose marriage is with slave girls or whores or old
women who are disgraced or those young in years, or he is a leaser of
whores; we have seen someone in [a nativity] like this who leased his
wife, and he was disgraced in this. If you find the lords of the triplicity   4
of Venus in a bad place, but Venus is with a benefic planet and [they
are both] beneficial in one house, then he will marry an agreeable wife.
But when the lords of the triplicity of Venus come in between [Venus   5
and the benefic], they indicate disaster and disgrace because of women
and anxiety and grief because of them.

Venus' being with Jupiter while Venus is in a good place indicates   6
his marriage to an agreeable wife. If you find Venus cadent [and] Mars   7
and Jupiter aspecting it by day while the lords of its triplicity are in
midheaven, then they indicate that the wife will be a whore, well
known in the mouths of the majority of men, because Jupiter indi-
cates fame in the city, but this [native] will attain | disgrace from its   p. 43

8 [Venus'] badness. If you find Venus in a bad place and Jupiter and
Mars aspect [it] while the lords of its triplicity are in midheaven, then
9 the aspect of Mars indicates that she will long for marriage. If a malefic
is with Venus or overcoming it or in opposition to it, then it indicates
the badness of the marriage from men and women so that his life will
revolve in grief and misery because of women, especially if the malefic
is the Moon.

10   If you find Mercury in the house of Venus and Saturn aspects it, it
indicates the marriage of that native to slave girls or the like and ser-
11 vants and strangers, and similarly also in the nativities of females. If
Jupiter is with Venus, then predict that he will have intercourse with
12 a praiseworthy woman. Especially if Jupiter aspects the Moon, then
he will have intercourse with his mistress or his lady or the wife of one
13 of the nobles. If with this Saturn and Mars aspect, from [different]
directions, the Moon, [which is] the king of the night, then he will
have intercourse with his lady or the wife of one of the nobles, and so
14 also predict in the nativities of women. If Venus in the day is in the
ascendent or midheaven under the rays of the Sun and Mars is in a
cardine or with the lot of the wedding, then it indicates for the native
15 a wife of the lowest [class], a stranger and a pauper. If Mercury and
with it Venus aspect the lot, it indicates a wife [who is] a singer or
a dancer.

16   If you find the malefics aspecting the sign of wedding, which is the
seventh from the ascendent, and you find the lord of this place cadent
or corrupted by the aspect of the malefics or by a bad position, then
17 it indicates what I will tell you. If the lord of that place is Saturn,
then the injury is because of the fathers and mature men or because
18 of the dead. If the lord of that place is Jupiter, he will attain this because of kings or wealthy men or because of the decree of his city.
19 If it is Mercury, then this calamity and injury is because of argument
and talk, and some of them will marry a woman who has been in ser-
20 vice as a concubine, but thieves stole her away. If the lord of that
place is Mars, it indicates a marriage [that is] shameful [and] disgrace-
21 ful. If Mercury is with Mars, | then it is bad because he will kill his
p. 44
22 wife with his own hand and [her] blood will stick to him. If it is Venus,
then the bride's dowry is damaged, and she will be furious with him
like the burning of fire because of women, and the marriage will be
with this thing.

Chapter 2. Knowledge of the lot of wedding.   II-2

Look at the place (which I shall tell you) of the lot of wedding.   1
Count from the degrees of Saturn to Venus and add to it the degrees   2
of the ascendent [by day] or subtract it thirty at a time from the
ascendent [by night]; wherever it reaches, then there is the lot of
wedding. If you find any of those planets in this place or in quartile   3
to it [the lot], then this is the indicator of the wedding. Look: perhaps   4
then a malefic or a cardine of the lot is in the sixth or the twelfth so
that this happens to be in a sign full of grief [and] scanty in benefit.

Chapter 3. Knowledge of the lot [in] the nativity of a woman.   II-3

If you want to see in the nativity of a woman the lot of marriage,   1
then count from the degrees of Venus to Saturn and add to it the
degrees of the ascendent. If you find any of the planets in the lot or in   2
quartile of this place, then it is the indicator. If it is Mars, then it   3
indicates women who will marry [several] men in succession and will
play the whore with men. If the lord of the lot of wedding is in the   4
seventh sign and the lord of the lot is Saturn, then it indicates that
that man who will marry her is an old man, and if Saturn is in its
own house, then it indicates that he will be her grandfather or her
paternal uncle or her maternal uncle or one of those possessing rela-
tionships to her. If the native is a slave girl or a servant, then this   5
man who marries her will be her master. If the lord of the lot is Mars,   6
then that man will not be known and he will be one who pursues one
of the professions of Mars. If the lord of that is Jupiter, then the man   7
who will marry her is well known [and] possesses fame in the towns and   8
cities. | If Venus is the lord of the lot, then he will bring this matter   p. 45
to an end with [other] things and [with] joy from wine. If it is Mercury,   9
then [he will bring it to an end] with deceit and quarreling about this
many times, especially if Mars aspects it [Mercury].

Always if you find Venus in nativities of men or of women in a bad   10
place, then it indicates a disgraceful marriage. If Jupiter aspects Ve-   11
nus from wherever it aspects, it indicates benefit because of females,
but if a malefic aspects Venus while Jupiter is aspecting, then it diminishes the evil of the malefic. In the nativity of a woman predict   12
similarly about their benefiting from men. If you find Venus in a   13
sign possessing two bodies or possessing two figures, then the marriage

199

14 of the native will not be with [only] one [wife]. If Mars stops in the
house of Venus and Venus [in] the house of Mars, it indicates for the
native disgrace and debauchery and destruction; Mars indicates
15 similarly if it is with Venus or in opposition or quartile to it. If Venus
is with Mercury and Mars, then this indicates that he will be one who
will have no stability in marriage, but he will rejoice in this woman
16 one time, in that woman another time. If with this they are in midheaven or Venus is in midheaven while Mars and Mercury aspect [it],
17 then this native will be one of those men who befriend women. If he
is one [for] whom [the planets] aspecting Venus are eastern, then this
18 will occur publicly. If Jupiter aspects one of [those] which are there,
then it ameliorates some of this, since the aspect of Jupiter indicates
her benefit because of this and the existence of the lords of Venus'
triplicity in midheaven indicates that her debauchery will occur pub-
19 licly and in renown. If Jupiter is with Venus in a bad place, but [that
place] is a cardine or in what follows a cardine and it aspects the lords
20 of the triplicity, all this will not be corrupted. But if you find Jupiter
in a nativity like this in a bad place, then it indicates disgrace and
debauchery and a bad reputation because of this, because both of the
two benefics happen to be in a cadent and, with the cadent, [their]
21 dejection[s]. If | the first of the lords of Venus' triplicity is in a good
p. 46 place and the second in a bad place, then his condition in the matter
of women is good in the beginning of his age, and in the last it is a
bad [indication], because the first of the lords of Venus' triplicity
indicates the first years, the second indicates the middle years, and
the third indicates the end of [his] life, so that whichever of the lords
of the triplicity is in a good place, then it indicates good in its own
time.

II-4   **Chapter 4. The lot of marriage.**

1   If the lot of marriage is in opposition to Venus or in opposition to
the ascendent or in a bad place, or Venus is also in a masculine sign
and with this is eastern, then, because the feminine signs are of the
portion of the night and Venus is of the portion of the night, most
[of what was predicted for] one who was born thus will remain till
2 the end of his life except for his wife. Because the diurnal planets rejoice in the East and the nocturnal planets rejoice in the West, what
3 I told you of this is secure. If you find the lords of Venus' triplicity

aspecting neither midheaven nor Venus, then men will have no
pleasure in marriage. If with this the lords of the triplicity of the lot 4
of wedding are aspecting neither the lot of wedding nor Venus nor
midheaven, then this [native] will never marry. If the lord of Venus' 5
triplicity is at the end of signs or in the term[s] of malefics or in the
cardine under the earth or not in its own place, or the malefics aspect
it, then this native will never marry. But if the lord of Venus' triplic- 6
ity is in its own place, it indicates marriage.

If Venus is in the seventh place from the ascendent, it indicates 7
injury and misery and calamity because of women and that he will
have little stability with them, but will have intercourse with those
who have need and poverty and slave girls [and] servants [and]
strangers, but according to this he will be married because of the
place of Venus in a cardine, | but because of the place of the ascendent p. 47
opposite it [Venus] it indicates injury because of women. If Venus is 8
in a bad place without the aspect of a benefic while Saturn does
aspect it and is free of Jupiter, then it indicates that this native will
remain without marriage, but he will have intercourse with those who
are disgraced and in whom there is no good. If Venus is in [one of] its 9
own places, it indicates marriage, and the marriage will abound in
children. If Venus is in a tropical sign which is its own place in the 10
strength of places, it indicates his change from [one] wife to [another]
wife, especially if planets aspect it [the place]. If Venus is in the car- 11
dine under the earth, it indicates the death of the native's woman and
of his child, and [his] grief on this account. If the cardine under the 12
earth is a tropical sign, especially Cancer or Capricorn, then this is
bad and worse because the native will be desirous of intercourse with
disgraced women or whores in public, and debt will always come upon
him because of this. If Saturn is with Venus or Venus is in the term 13
of Saturn while Saturn aspects it [Venus], then it is bad concerning
marriage because he will marry a widow or an old woman or a woman
who is deficient in the matter of caring about him or a young girl or a
slave girl, insignificant in everything, or a woman disgraced in the
matter of livelihood; it is also similarly bad in the nativity of women
with respect to their husbands and children. But if Venus is with Mars 14
or in the term of Mars while Mars aspects it [the term] in the nativity
of a woman, then the wife will be desirous of adultery and grief on
account of [her] children will come upon her; it indicates similarly in

the nativities of men that sometimes the wives of the men are among
those who are barren because of the existence of Mars with Venus or
15 in opposition to it. If you find Jupiter and Venus under the rays of the
Sun, then these two indicate an obscure marriage because he will
16 marry widows and her whose childbearing has been cut off. If you
find the Moon in its own house or exaltation with Venus while Jupiter
aspects, then these [natives] will marry from among their own women.
17 If you find Venus and the Moon, each of them in opposition to the other
or in quartile or both of them are in one sign in a bad place, then this
indicates harm to the marriage, but if they are in a cardine they indi-
p. 48 cate [that] the marriage of the native is to his sister | or the closest [to
18 him] of his women. If you find the Moon and Venus together in the
cardine under the earth while Jupiter aspects [them], it indicates [his]
marriage to one of his relatives, but he will have children at the end
19 of his life. If you find the lord of the lot of wedding in [the place of]
the lot of wedding or the lord of the lot aspecting it or the Moon, then
these [natives] will marry from among their relatives their brother's
20 daughter or their sister's daughter. If Saturn is with Venus in the
house of one of the two in the ascendent, then he will have intercourse
with his daughters and his older sisters, but if the Moon is in quartile
21 to these two, then he will have intercourse with his maternal aunt. But
if the Moon does not aspect while Mars does aspect from quartile, then
he will marry a woman in whom he will take pleasure, but, however
that is, the loss of his property will come upon him because of the
22 woman, but if the native is female, then the woman is a Lesbian. If
Venus is in an alien house or in a tropical sign while the Moon aspects
[it] or if the Moon is with it, then the woman will be desirous of intercourse, and from her longing for this that she will give men pay, and
23 also if Saturn also aspects. If each one of the two, Venus and Mars, is
in the other's house or term, it indicates debauchery and wickedness,
and similarly if they are together or one of the two aspects the other
from quartile or opposition or they are in the East, so that this de-
24 bauchery will be in public. If it is in the West, then it will be kept quiet
and will be a secret, but it will be the most public that is [possible]
and the worst in infamy if the Sun aspects it also, because this is harm-
25 ful. If with this the lord of the sign of wedding is Mercury and Mercury
is in the sixth, western, or in a quadruped sign while the sign of wedding is a quadruped [and] injured, then a marriage is not judged for

this native while he is a youth, and if he does marry, his wife will
survive [only] a brief time because most of these [men] are worried
about their own lives without marriage. If the lord of the sign of   26
wedding with this is in a good place, then he will have intercourse with
a sick woman or a stranger who has no one, and he will have no con-
stancy among women, and trouble and injury will come upon him | p. 49
because of them. If the lord of the lot of wedding is under the rays of   27
the Sun or under the earth while the malefics aspect [it] and it aspects
its own place, then he will have intercourse with whores and slave
girls or he will have intercourse with one with whom a multitude of
men has had intercourse. But if you find the lord of the lot rejoicing in   28
its light, aspecting its own place while the benefics aspect it, and its
place is strong in a cardine or what follows a cardine, then this native
will marry a good woman with no blemish in her, virtuous, praiseworthy in this, and he will be noble in his condition and his benefit.   29
If the lord of this lot which I mentioned is Jupiter, then this benefit
and the good which he attains will be from the nobles of men and it will
be on account of women. If it is Saturn, then this benefit and the good   30
will be the inheritance of the property of [his] wife's father or her relatives, however this came to him, or the inheritance from a slave
whom he freed. If Mars is the lord of that lot, that benefit is be-   31
cause of a strange man whose work is work like the works of Mars,
or his benefit is from violent deeds. If the lord of the lot is   32
Mercury, then that benefit which was on account of women will
have as its cause calculation and words. If it is Venus, then he   33
will be praised and benefited on account of women and females.
If the lord of the lot is Mercury and it is in a bad place while be-   34
nefics aspect that place or a benefic is in it, then he will marry a
virtuous [and] good wife, but he will be anxious and unhappy because
of the position of Mercury. If the lord of this place is in a good place   35
while a malefic aspects this place or is in it, then misery and misfortune on account of women pass these [natives] by or according
to this they attain joy and profit because of them. Look at the se-   36
venth place from the lot, as, if you find its lord in the lot and the
lot's lord in the seventh, then these [natives] will keep quiet about
their marriage[s] and will have intercourse with women secretly,
then they will marry them after that and they [the women] will bear
children from them.

| Chapter 5. **Knowledge of how many wives he will marry.**

1   If you wish to know how many wives he will marry, then mark off
from midheaven to Venus; whatever number of planets is between
these two, that number of wives will he marry, but wherever you find
Saturn, then know [his] coldness and distress; wherever you find

2 Mars, [his] death unless a benefic aspects it. In the nativities of women, if you wish to know how many husband[s] she will marry, then
count from midheaven to Mars, but if Mars is in midheaven then count
from midheaven to Jupiter; whatever number of planets is between

3 these two, say this is the number [of men] whom she will marry. If you
find Venus cadent from midheaven, say [that there is] little constancy toward women in men, and say similarly in the women with
respect to their husbands if you find Mars in the seventh.

4   Remember this lot: count from Venus to the degree of the seventh
sign and add to it the degrees of the ascendent [by day] or subtract it
from the ascendent [by night] thirty at a time; wherever it reaches,

5 there is the lot of happiness and wedding. See which [planet] is its
lord and which is with it and which aspects it, as, if a malefic is in this
lot or aspects it, say that the native will marry disgraced [women] and

6 one in whom there is no good. If the lord of this lot is in a bad place
while Venus is under the rays of the Sun and the malefics aspect [it],
then most of those whose nativity is thus will never marry.

7   The time of the wedding: whenever Jupiter transits where the lot
was or in quartile from it or in opposition to it or in trine to it or
[transits] the triplicity [trine] of Venus or Venus' quartile or opposition, then the marriage will occur unless Saturn aspects from opposition or quartile, because if Saturn aspects thus, it chills it [the wed-
ding] and there will be nothing but destruction, or, if there is a mar-

8 riage, it will not last. Whenever Jupiter transits in the place in which

9 Venus was, it is suitable for the marriage. If the year ends at the sign
in which the lot was, it indicates marriage unless Saturn is as I mentioned because Saturn will chill it, but sometimes the transit of Saturn,

p. 51 if it was in the base-diagram of the nativity in | a powerful place and
ruled something of the lot, aspecting the lot, indicates marriage —
especially if Jupiter helps it with [its] aspect because Jupiter and Ve-

10 nus indicate good wives. If a multitude of women was predicted for
the native in his nativity, then, whenever Venus transits in its own

house or aspects its own house, he will marry, but [his wife] will
neither stay nor be suitable. Also if Mars aspects Venus and Venus   11
also aspects it [Mars] as I mentioned to you, it indicates a marriage of
short duration.

The man is suitable for the woman and the woman for the man if   12
the ascendent[s] of these two are the same cardine. If the two lumi-   13
naries or one of the two is in the ascendent or midheaven, then also it
is suitable. Similarly [does it happen] if you find that wherever is the   14
Venus of one of the two [marriage partners], there is the Moon of the
other, or wherever is the Moon of one of the two, there is the Venus of
the other, especially if the Moon of one of the two is in trine with the
Moon of the other. But if, wherever one luminary of one of the two   15
[marriage partners] is, in this sign there is a malefic for the other, then
it indicates injury and little agreement, but if, wherever a luminary of
one of the two is, in it there is a benefic for the other, or all the benefics of the two natives are in cardines, or the lot of both of them is in
the same sign, it indicates agreement and suitability.

Chapter 6. Knowledge of the lot of wedding by day and by night. II-6

Calculate also the lot of wedding by day and by night from the Sun   1
to where the Moon is, and add to it the degrees of Venus [by day] or
subtract it from where Venus is [by night] thirty at a time; wherever
it reaches, there it is. If Jupiter is in opposition or quartile to it, it   2
indicates marriage. If the lot of wedding happens to be in opposi-   3
tion to the ascendent or in the cardine under the earth while the malefics aspect [it], then the native will see the death of his women. If   4
you find the lord of the triplicity of Venus in the cardine of the West
or the cardine under the earth, it indicates the death of his women.

Similarly look in the nativity of a woman at the lot of wedding;   5
as I told you in the consideration about the wedding of men [it is] from
Venus, so similarly for women look from Mars. If Venus is in the car-   6
dine of the West or the cardine under the earth, it indicates for men
the death of their women and the smallness of their constancy toward
women. Similarly if you find Mars in the cardine of the West or the   7
cardine under the earth, it indicates for women the death of their
husbands.

| If you find Venus western with a malefic or in its aspect, it indi-   8
cates for the native the death of his women. If Jupiter aspects Venus   p. 52 / 9

from the tenth or eighth and you find Venus in the twelfth or sixth,
then the native will marry a good woman, but she will die, and fear
10 and weeping and anxiety will reach him because of her. But your consideration concerning the time of their [the women's] death [should
be] as I told you in the matter of the parents and brothers.

II-7   **Chapter 7. Knowledge of sodomy.**

1   Now I will make clear to you sodomy and [what is] like that of
2 what is in men and women. If Venus is in the house of Mercury and
Mercury is in a bad place, then the native will not love women, but his
3 pleasure will be in boys. If the lot of wedding is with Mercury and
Mercury is in a masculine sign which is a cardine, he will be desirous
4 of boys, [but] will not love intercourse with women. If you find Mars
in the house of Mercury and Mercury in the house of Mars, then he
will be covetous of males; the aspect of Mars to Mercury from quartile or opposition indicates the same.

5   If Venus is in one of the signs of desire, which abound in lust (they
are Aries, Capricorn, Pisces, and Taurus), and Venus is under the
[Sun's] rays with Saturn or Mars, then this indicates [something] like
what I told you of the act of scandals; [it indicates] similarly if you
find Venus in what I named for you of the signs of desire and one of
the two malefics, Saturn and Mars, is overcoming it [Venus] from
6 quartile. If Venus is in the cardine of the West in opposition and the
Moon is in the ascendent, then, if the native is female, it indicates
that she will be a Lesbian, desirous of women, and if the native is a
male, he will be desirous of males, especially if Venus is in Leo or
7 Virgo or [one of] the houses of the malefics. If the malefics aspect it
8 [Venus], then it will be worse. If Venus is under the [Sun's] rays, then
9 it will be worse and more evil. If Venus is in a house of Saturn and
Saturn in a house of Venus in the cardine of the West or the cardine
under the earth or the sixth or twelfth place, then the native will be
effeminate [and] will be one of those in whom one does [something]
p. 53 like what | one does in women. Venus also indicates thus if it is cadent
¹⁰ or in a bad place while the malefics are in a feminine sign which is a
cardine; then the native will be effeminate, weak in his joints and
11 strength, and one will do in him the act of women. And it will be worse
for him if the two luminaries are in a feminine sign or one of the two
12 luminaries is in a feminine sign which Saturn or Mars aspects. If it

[Saturn or Mars] is in Capicorn, Aquarius, Aries, Taurus, or Pisces,
and the lot of illness is with these two in a feminine sign, if the native
is a woman then she will be a Lesbian; if they are in a masculine sign,
if the native is a male, then they will not do to women as they ought
to. It will also be thus if Venus is with one of the malefics, and it will   13
be worse than this if Mercury is injured. If Jupiter aspects [something]   14
similar to this, it will relax that misfortune or keep it secret.

If you find the Moon in Pisces, Taurus, or Aquarius, while Mercury   15
is with Mars, then the woman will be notorious for adultery, especially if Venus is in the ascendent or in midheaven. If you find, in the   16
nativity of females, the two luminaries in masculine signs and Venus
in a masculine sign, in the cardines, and one of them is in opposition
or quartile to another, then this native, if it is a female, is one of those
[women] who do in women the act of men. If you find Venus ... in the   17
nativity of women while each one of the two luminaries is in trine with
its lord, then these [women] will have much intercourse with men and
a great number of men will have intercourse with them.

Up to here is the section on marriage.

Chapter 8. Exposition of the matter of children. II-8

Look at [the first and the second] lord of Jupiter's triplicity; if they   1
are both together in a good place departing from the Sun's rays, then
the two of them indicate children and benefit from them. If one of   2
them is in a good place and the other in a bad place, | then he will   p. 54
have children, but misery and lamentation and weeping will reach
him because of them. Consider with respect to the lords of the tripli-   3
city as I told you in the beginning of this my book: in which of the
times [the children will be born], and for how much of his life will joy
and happiness reach him, and in which of them [the times] will misery
and misfortune come to him. If you find the lords of Jupiter's triplici-   4
ty, both of them, in a cardine under the [Sun's] rays, then he will be
one of those who will not be blessed with children, then especially if
Jupiter [also] is cadent under the Sun's rays.

Chapter 9. Knowledge of the number of children. II-9

Calculate the number of children as I shall tell you. Look at the   1, 2
lords of Jupiter's triplicity, which of them is the stronger, and calcu-

late [its] place which is above the earth, and count from it till it reaches
the ascendent; whatever signs are between these two, according to that
3 is the number of [his] children. If Jupiter and Venus are in what is
between these, they indicate an increase in this number, and whatever
4 planets there are also besides this will increase [the number]. If
you find in what I told you of signs a sign possessing two bodies,
5 then double it. If you find in what is between these Mars or Saturn,
it indicates the death of the child, especially if Mars and Saturn
6 are in a bad place. But if these two are in a good place, then they
indicate an increase in [the number of] children, except that
this [extra] child will be expelled, especially if that sign in which
the malefic is is the cardine of the West or the cardine under the
earth.

7   If you find the lord of Jupiter's triplicity, which is the indicator of
the matter of children, in midheaven, then predict for him that he
will have four children or one, but if it is in the cardine of the West,
then predict that they will be seven or one, especially if the cardine of
8 the West is Aries. If you find the lord of Jupiter's triplicity cadent
from the cardine of midheaven or the cardine under the earth,
then count from the ascendent to it; whatever is the number of
signs between these two, that is the number of children he will
9, 10 have. The rest of the investigation is as I told you. If the lords
of Jupiter's triplicity are in signs abounding in children, then
predict that the number of children will be greater than what I
said; their number will also be made clear to you from the section on
brothers.

11 | If you find the Moon and Venus in Capricorn and Cancer or their
p. 55 triplicities, then see which of them is better in [its] position; let this
12 strong one be the indicator of children. If they are both in other than
these triplicities, then let your consideration be from the lords of
13 Jupiter's triplicity. If you find the indicator of the matter of children in
the ascendent or midheaven or in the sign of fortune, then he will be
14 blessed with children in his youth. If it is in the second from the
ascendent or in the sign of wedding or in the eighth sign or the cardine
under the earth, then [children] will be born to the native in the middle
15 and the end of his years. If you find the indicator of children [to be]
Jupiter, in a good place under the Sun's rays, then he will have
children, but they will not live.

Chapter 10. Knowledge of the lot of children.

The lot of children: count from Jupiter to Saturn and add to it the   1
degrees of the ascendent [by day] or subtract it from the ascendent
[by night], thirty at a time; wherever it happens to be, look at its
lord. Then count from the lot to its lord how many signs there are, or   2
from its lord which follows it [to the lot]; whatever there is of signs
between these two, that is the number of children. If you find a ma-   3
lefic between these two, it indicates the death of the children. If the   4
Sun or the Moon is in quartile or opposition with the lot, then the
Sun will increase the male children, the Moon the female. If you find   5
that there is no [planet] in the lot or aspecting it, then the first child
will not be benefited by it because he will be miscarried or will die
horribly. If you find the lot in a cardine or a good place, then it is a   6
good indication in the matter of children. If it happens to be in the   7
sixth or twelfth place, then neither a male nor a female will be born
to him, and he will suffer distress and grief from this; but if he should
have children, they will not stay with him so that they will part from
him in the cities. If the lot happens to be where none of the planets is   8
in quartile or opposition to it, then these [natives] have a need for
children. But if there are planets in opposition or quartile to the lot,   9
then it indicates that he will have a multitude of children. If the lot   10
happens to be in a sign of few children, then it indicates a small number of children. If Saturn is with it, then it indicates that he will be   11
sterile or will have few children or will be grieved with an intense
grief on account of [his] children.

| Jupiter and Mercury indicate children if they are in good pla-   12
ces, but deny [it] if they are in the sterile signs, which are Gemini,   p. 56
Leo, Virgo, Capricorn, the beginning of Taurus, the middle of Libra,
Aries, and Sagittarius. As for Aquarius and what is like this, it   13
abounds in children, but Scorpio abounds in children and in deaths
for them.

If you find a planet in opposition or quartile to the lot, then predict   14
that he will abound in children. It is necessary for you to consider the   15
lot, [whether] perhaps it is in a sign of few children as, if it is thus, it
indicates a small number of children. If Saturn is in the lot, then it is   16
very bad because he will be sterile or have few children, and distress,
grief, and misery in the matter of children will reach them.

II-11   **Chapter 11. Lot of transit with respect to children.**

1, 2   Remember this lot which I told you about. Count from Mars to
       Jupiter and add to it the degrees of the ascendent [by day] or sub-
       3 tract it from the ascendent [by night], thirty at a time. Wherever your
       counting ends, when Jupiter transits that lot or its opposition or
       4 aspects it from quartile, then will be born children to this native. When
       5 Venus happens to transit this lot, it indicates children. When the
       year comes to where Jupiter or Venus were, it indicates children.
       6 When Saturn also comes to that place, it also indicates children.

II-12   **Chapter 12. Knowledge of females and males.**

1   Count what of degrees is between Jupiter and the Sun and add to it
       the degrees of the ascendent; wherever it comes to, there is the lot
       2 of male children. Count from the Moon to Venus and add to it the
       degrees of the ascendent [by day] or subtract it from the ascendent
       3 [by night]; wherever it ends, there is the lot of female children. Look
       at the two lords of these two lots and their power in their places, and
       know whether the birth of males or of females is more numerous and
       better.

p. 57 $\overset{4}{}$ | If you find Saturn in opposition to Mercury, it indicates the death
       5 of the children. If you find Venus, while Saturn is in opposition to it
       [Venus], without the aspect of Jupiter, he will be sterile or will have
       6 few children. If with this Saturn aspects the Moon [which is] in the
       tropical degrees with one of the malefics, or [when] a malefic aspects
       it [the Moon] from quartile, then it indicates that children will not be
       born to [those] men.

7   If you find the two lots which I mentioned to you [having] one of
       the malefics in quartile, it indicates the loss of his [the native's]
       8 children. If you find the lot in the twelfth or the sixth while Saturn
       9 aspects, then it indicates the death of the children. If you find Jupiter
       in the cardine under the earth or in the cardine, the seventh, with a
       malefic, or [if] a malefic is in opposition or quartile to it [Jupiter],
       then it is the indicator of the death of his [the native's] children, and
       10 worse than this if Jupiter is without light. If the Sun is with Saturn
       11 in a sign, it indicates grief in the matter of having children. If Ju-
       12 piter is cadent, it indicates the loss of his parents. If Saturn injures
       Venus without the aspect of Jupiter, then it indicates grief on account
       of children, or they will have children but will not enjoy them, or no
       210

children will be born to him, but if he has children, then sorrow and weeping will reach him because of having children, especially if Saturn aspects the Moon together with its [Saturn's] aspect of Venus.

Now I will make the whole [of it] clear to you. If you find in nati-   13, 14
vities Jupiter and Mercury not injured, then judge an abundance of
children. If these two are in their illuminator [the Sun] or their fall   15
[dejection], then they do not indicate the existence of children, but if
he should have a child, then he will die and grief will reach his father.

Look from the midheaven in the matter of the nativity [and] which   16
[planet] aspects midheaven, and where its lord is, and of what sort
the sign is, and where its witness is, and which [sign] follows midheaven;
this indicates males and females. Look from the fifth, from the sign   17
which is the sign of children, and its lord — in what place it is, whether
it is a benefic or a malefic, and how great its strength is in this nativity, because if it is cadent while Jupiter and Venus do not aspect the
fifth place but the malefics do aspect this place, it indicates the fewness
of [his] children, and if he should have children, it indicates the shortness of their remaining [with him] and the briefness of their lives. But   18
if one benefic aspects that place, then you should not at all despair
for [his] children, but | he will have some. If a benefic aspects the   p. 58
fifth place and its lord is in a good place aspecting midheaven, then   19
this is an indication of the abundance of [his] children and of their
goodness.

Chapter 13. Knowledge of whether females or males are more nu-   II-13
merous.

If you wish to know if the females are more numerous than the   1
males, then look at that place which I mentioned to you and at its
lord. If it is a feminine sign and its lord in a masculine [sign], judge   2
males for him. If the place is masculine and its lord feminine or the   3
opposite of this, then judge males and females for him. If a malefic is   4
in a cardine aspecting the Moon, then this native will not cease ex-
pelling his children in his life outside of his house.

Look concerning the situation of the matter of pregnancy. Whenever   5, 6
Jupiter transits where Mars was or aspects it from opposition or quartile or trine, then she is pregnant. If the Moon is in a cardine in the   7
equatorial degrees where the night and the day are equal, then it indicates sterility for men and women.

　　Chapter 14. Aspect of trines, if one of the planets aspects another from trine.

1　　If Saturn aspects Jupiter from trine while Jupiter is in a good place, then it indicates an abundance of property and land and trees and buildings and mosques; sometimes he will be lord of a group and will agree with his father, and sometimes he will direct the affairs of his city and of landed estates, and he will benefit because of strangers and
2 will be lucky and will be honored in [all] ways. If Saturn aspects Jupiter and Mercury from trine, then he will be secretive, learned in hidden [and] secret things, or he will direct the affairs of kings and of cities, or with this he will be pious and will raise a child other than his own, and he will not be benefited by his own children, because they
3 will die or will be separated from him. If Mars aspects what I mentioned, what I mentioned of good will decrease and misery and evil
4 reputation and misfortune will increase. If Saturn aspects Mars from
p. 59 trine | without the aspect of Jupiter and Mercury, then he will be rich, a ruler of reason, strong, well known in the metropolis — he will be put up in the manner of kings, but he will see the death of his
5 older brothers. If Saturn aspects the Sun from trine in a diurnal nativity, then the matter of [his] livelihood will be good because he will be well known, a possessor of renown, praiseworthy — he will seek
6 leadership and will be lucky for his father. If both of them are in a masculine sign, then it is better; but if the nativity is nocturnal, then he will have a good livelihood, but there will be a decrease from his
7 property and his father's property. If Saturn aspects the Moon from trine, it indicates respect and great benefit from kings or those like kings, and he will be praiseworthy, especially if the Moon is increasing;
8 if the Moon is decreasing, much of what I mentioned will decrease. If Saturn aspects Venus from trine, it indicates a good livelihood in good repute [and] favor, except that calamity will come upon him on ac-
9 count of his inferiors and he will have no marriage. If Saturn aspects Mercury from trine, it indicates that he will be calm, reasonable, not vacillating in [his] thought, firm in reflexion, learned in calculation and book[s], outstanding in his livelihood.

10　　If Jupiter aspects Mars from trine, he will be a leader, a ruler for action, learned in affairs — he will have benefit and honor from the
11 chiefs. If Jupiter aspects Venus from trine, then he will be handsome

in his appearance and face and will have elevation because of women
and love. If Jupiter aspects Mercury from trine, he will be quick-witted, 12
intelligent, perfect, and it indicates that he will be better than his
relatives and his relatives will desire honor for him — praiseworthy,
he will not cease in the work of great cities and kings; some of these
[natives] are learned in the stars of heaven. If Jupiter aspects the   13
Moon from trine, it will increase the praise for the native and he will
have rank and status. Look concerning what I told you at the time of   14
the native's fortune; one of these will sometimes be a leader, a chief
for men, while another of them will be a leader in business, and another
of them for commerce, and another of them in the leadership of armies,
especially if the Moon is increasing. If Jupiter aspects the Sun from   15
trine, it indicates wealth and abundant good fortune and children and
a wedding and life in a high rank.

| If Mars aspects the Sun from trine and the nativity is nocturnal   16
and Mars is the lord of the hour, then he will be elevated in the good   p. 60
because sometimes he will be a powerful king. If Jupiter is in [the   17
other] one of the triplicity or in a cardine, then he will be a leader
mighty in nobility, but if with this the Moon is good, then he will be
valiant, governing life and death and assassination, and [it indicates]
lodgings quick to change, and a suspicious nature quick to distrust —
he will [even] distrust himself, especially if it is in a masculine sign.
If Mars aspects Venus from trine, then he will be wealthy, rich, abound- 18
ing in steadfastness, good in horse[-riding], mighty in endeavour[s],
except that he will love intercourse with women and riding forbidden
[mounts]. If Mars aspects Mercury from trine, he will be a supervisor   19
in work, learned in quarrels, power will be plentiful for him, [but] his
situation will not increase because of quarrels and books. If Mars   20
aspects the Moon from trine, if it [the Moon] is decreasing or is lord
of its triplicity in a nocturnal nativity, it indicates that he will be
good in supervising work, quickly successful in what he seeks, but if
Jupiter aspects these two, he will be a governor possessing good
fortune and leadership, one abounding in power. But in a diurnal   21
nativity when the Moon is increasing it indicates sickness in his
body.

If the Sun aspects the Moon from trine, look at the power of the   22
planets and their aspect[s], then judge according to that.

If Venus aspects the Moon from trine, then he will be handsome   23

[and] happy, [but] he will have no constancy in marriage, and he will make his appearance in debaucheries.

24   If Mercury is in trine of the Moon, it will make him quick-witted [and] learned.

Chapter 15. Quartile [aspect].

1, 2   This is aspect in quartile. If Saturn aspects Jupiter from quartile, it will diminish him in his property, and whatever he thinks about will become a curse upon him, and his works will be interrupted, and he will be a spoiler for his parents — in each of the two quartiles will he spoil and the properties of his parents will be overturned; it is worse than this if the place of these two is exchanged and Saturn is above
3 Jupiter while Jupiter is in left quartile. But if Jupiter is overpowering Saturn, then it is less for evil — his parents will not obtain nobility
p. 61 except in some of the houses, and he will be deficient in property, |
4 [having] neither wealth nor poverty. If Saturn is in quartile of Mars while Saturn is in the tenth sign, he will have little medical treatment, he will be weak in his body, unceasing in diseases because of fevers, he will be shaking, and the properties of his parents will be destroyed,
5 and he will see the death of his brothers. But if Mars is higher in the tenth place from Saturn and Saturn is lower than it in the fourth, then it will hasten [his] father to death before [his] mother, and they will not survive long, but they will spoil the properties of [their] parents
6 and will envy [their] parents and will harm their food. If Saturn aspects the Sun [and] if it [the Sun] is in its [Saturn's] quartile in the tenth sign, then he will spoil his parents' legacies, and he will be an enemy of his relatives, and the clearness of the open air will become cloudy with work, and diseases will rise up upon him, and he will worry about chains, and he will toil with respect to his livelihood, an
7 unknown in his city. But if Saturn overpowers the Sun in quartile, he will be confused or he will run away or he will hasten to death or his mother will beat him or there will be leprosy in him, which is the worst of diseases, or his belly will cool until this harms him, and he will be
8 cold in his body and his work. If Saturn is in quartile of Venus, it indicates his fall from women, [that he will be] rejected [and] devoid of
9 good, and every evil will come to him. But if Venus is overpowering it [Saturn], then he will be weary [and] difficult, but he will be blessed with a good wife who will be better than he in lineage, one who is

admirable in herself together with her agreeing with his parents. If   10
Saturn is in quartile of Mercury in the tenth sign from Mercury, it
will bring many misfortunes to these nativities and will make the
native base, listless in work, a cheater — he will love the fault that is
not his own and with this he will be afflicted, a lisper or a mute or a
deaf man. But if Mercury is overpowering Saturn, then it will not be   11
good, but the evil which I mentioned will be less. If Saturn is in quar-   12
tile of the Moon, it will harm the owner of this nativity, and if Saturn
is in the tenth place from it [the Moon], a flaw in his manner of walk-
ing and a chronic illness in his body will come upon him, and he will
not be courageous for any of his work, and he will spoil his mothers'
properties, and there might be among them some who hate their
fathers. But if the Moon is in the tenth from Saturn, the years will   13
reach him immediately, and this native will be diseased [and] will have
little property, and if it is in a feminine sign, there might be a judgment
that he will be blessed with a wife who will be his enemy, and who
will consider harming him — he will not be about to enjoy his children.

| If Jupiter is in quartile of Mars and is overpowering it, he will be   14
noble, steadfast, compassionate, and some of them will be honored for   p. 62
aid in the houses of kings [and will be] well known in the house[s] of
the kingdom, and some of them will control the work of the king, and
their status will increase high up, but they will spoil their fathers' property and be worried by the matter of children, that they will have few
children. But if Mars is overpowering Jupiter, then it will make them   15
quick in seeking their livelihoods, and he will be in this feeble-minded,
tiresome, fatigued, and slander and quarrel[s] with men will reach him
because of [his] work for the government. If Jupiter is in quartile of   16
the Sun while the Sun is in the tenth sign from Jupiter, it indicates
that his father will be noble but his property will diminish, and he will
rise up from his homeland, and the people of his city will elevate him,
and some of the more powerful of his enemies will be furious with him.
But if Jupiter is in the tenth place from the Sun, this native will be   17
noble and his father [will have] great good and connections with kings
and many benefits together with honor, and he will lord it over many
men. If Jupiter is in quartile of Venus to the right of it [Venus], it   18
indicates that this native will be loving to people and he will profit
because of women, [will be] good at calculating for [his] livelihood,
approaching near to God (be He exalted!), forceful in [his] oaths. But   19

if Jupiter is in quartile of Mercury, overpowering it, it indicates that
the native will be a scribe, a learned man, a calculator, [and] he will
20 live on a side different from his relatives in a good condition. But if
Mercury is in right quartile of Jupiter, then it indicates that this native will not be rich, but he will be great in generosity, but if in some
of the houses in which he stays good reaches him, he will not be
21 charitable in his work and will not be thankful to people. If the Moon
is in quartile of Jupiter in a diurnal or a nocturnal nativity, it indicates that the native and [his] mother will be good in [their] livelihood,
superior in [their] nobility and [their] retinue, loving among their
kinsfolk, [and] the native will have fame [and be] well known among
the mighty of the people, a rich man, and they will praise him, and
22 better than praise. But if the Moon is in the tenth place from Jupiter,
then it indicates that he will be good in great matters, praiseworthy,
generous to the chiefs, but there will be a clear fate in him, a diminishment and an idleness from work.

23   If Mars is in left quartile of the Sun, then it will be harmful in the
matter of his father and of himself, [he will] abound in calamity, misfortune in his property will reach him until everything that he possesses disappears, and he will be frightened, perplexed, obsessed with
delusions, and his vision will grow dark and his sight will be in error;
p. 63 in | a diurnal nativity the misfortune will be worse except that some-
24 times he will die from this and perish. But if Mars is in the tenth
place from the Sun, then it indicates that this [native] will relax at the
beginning of his life, but disease will increase at the end of his life,
and ruin will descend upon him, and calamity will be continuous.
25 If Mars is in the tenth place from Venus, then it is bad in nativities
because it produces misfortune and disaster and diseases because of
women; and if it is thus and the sign is tropical, then he will be
effeminate [and] he will perform this vicious act, and if marriage is
judged for him, then he will marry slave girls and disgraced women or
he will be debauched by whores, and if the nativity is of females then
she will be a whore, one of the women who have intercourse with men
26 wickedly. But if Venus is in the tenth sign from Mars, then those
things reach him which we mentioned before, but he will keep this
27 quiet for shame and will repent in the end. If Mars is overpowering
Mercury, he will do things shocking among people, and it will imbue
the native with reasons for misery from every place and it will harm

216

him in quarrels and work and everything that he concerns himself
with, and slander will come to him from his relatives and the place of
his secret; the misfortune is worse than this at a diurnal nativity,
while at a nocturnal nativity it is less. If Mercury is overpowering   28
Mars, [and] the incitor to war is in left quartile of Mercury, it indicates that this native will be inferior, feeble, illegally seizing the properties of the people — he will not have power over any of their goods
without taking it and he will think of a thought because they will
argue with him lest he be malicious — and he will be exasperated with
his relatives, [and] his own eagerness is for the future, or he will be
spiteful, greedy for properties, and most of his effort will be in the
pursuit of wealth. If Mars aspects the Moon from right quartile, then   29
it indicates that his mother will be a widow, and he will decrease in
his livelihood and his property, and his mother will perish or one of
his brothers will die horribly, and [his] grief [will be] great, and some
of them will be afflicted with madness, and they will flee to a house of
worship, or it will afflict him with the destruction of [his] vision and
[with] dismay, especially if Mars is in a term of Saturn or the Moon
in a term of Mercury or a term of Mars as sometimes the power of the
terms changes nativities. But if Mars is in left quartile of the Moon   30
and the Moon overpowers it [Mars], then it indicates the small standing of his mother and scarcity in her livelihood, and for the native a
spoiling of [his] property and misfortune.

If the Sun is in quartile of the Moon or [they are in] the cardines   31
while the benefics aspect these two, it indicates for the native an
abundance of properties and nobility and happiness, but if the malefics
aspect they will be in alarm about their livelihood[s] and | their   p. 64
live[s]. If the Moon is approaching Jupiter and [Jupiter] aspects it   32
[the Moon] while the malefics [also] aspect it, it indicates approximately what I mentioned for him as it indicates that the native will be
noble, but will arrive at trouble, and some for whom he intends evil
will envy him; but if Jupiter does not aspect it [the Moon] while the
malefics do aspect, the danger will be more suitable that misfortune
and misery will reach them.

If Mercury is in quartile of Venus [and] one of them overpowers his   33
companion, then it indicates that the native will be learned in a mar-
vellous [and] beautiful craft, [and] he will be known among people
because of taking pains at this, and their sayings about him will

34 abound, and the mother of women will regret [his existence]. If the
Moon is in quartile of Venus and the Moon overpowers Venus, then
it indicates that he will be wealthy, and it indicates in the nativities
35 of men [that there will be] censure on account of women. But if the
Moon is in left quartile of Venus and Venus is to its [the Moon's]
right, then it will increase his good, and he will be good in [his] condition and livelihood and complexion, he will be handsome [and]
clean, and he will be charming in [his] speech, but he will have no
constancy in [his] union with women; and it indicates that his mother
will be clean [and] well supplied and his wife beautiful, but she will not
be virtuous [and] will not love her husband.

36   If Mercury is in quartile of the Moon in the tenth place, then it
indicates that this native will be good in [his] opinion, good in [his]
words, a reasonable man, but he will worry about the affairs of his
city; if the malefics overpower Mercury in [its] quartile of it [the
Moon], then he will be caught in a contract and a book, and will be
37 thrown in prison and chains. But if Mercury is in the tenth from the
Moon, then it indicates that this native will be insignificant, cold,
[and] shameless, without having any satisfaction in anything or any
trust in [his] heart or [his] speech.

II-16   **Chapter 16. On the planets' aspect from opposition.**

1   If Saturn aspects Jupiter from opposition, there will be no good in
2 his condition or his work, and he will grieve for his children. If Saturn
is in the ascendent and Jupiter in the West, then in the beginning of
3 his years he will be miserable but in their end happy. If Saturn aspects
Mars from opposition, it indicates for the native misery and misfortune in [his] livelihood and grief and disease and harm and a decrease
in his life and a paucity of children and an abundance of enemies and
distress and a struggle concerning what is between him and his relatives and a quick death for his father and misery on top of misery.
4
p. 65 If these two planets are in | a wet place, then this native will be
miserable in streams and the sea or near this, and diseases from
5 dampness will reach him so that he will be harmed in his body. If it
is in a quadruped sign, then injury and biting will reach him from
6 lions or he will be poisoned at the end of his life. If these two are in
quartile, it indicates approximately this or whatever of falling may

come to the native until he sees that he is dying, and it is worse for
him if the two malefics are injured by the Moon without the aspect
of Jupiter. If they are both, together with this, in cardines, then this   7
is an indication of death in separation from his relatives and his
country, and some of them will tumble from the good or fall into the
hands of the people. But if they are both in what follows the cardines,   8
one of them in opposition to the other, it indicates the end of hope and
destruction, especially if it is in a feminine sign. If they both are in   9
cadents, then there will be less for the evil of these two, but according
to this the native will fall and [this] will sadden him, but if the Sun
aspects it dissipates this injury. If Saturn aspects the Sun from oppo-   10
sition without the aspect of Jupiter, it indicates trouble for his father
in [his] livelihood and chronic illness, and the spoiling of his father's
property — if his father dies he will quickly spoil his property — and
his death will be a bad death, and the native will fall upon evil,
especially if it is in a feminine sign. If Saturn aspects Venus from   11
opposition, he will be excessive in fornication, a disgraced man, and
he will not marry; if he does marry, he will marry a disgraced song-
stress or a stranger or one in whom there is a chronic illness or a servant or one in whom there is sickness, and joy will not reach [him] in
the acts of Venus. If Saturn aspects Mercury from opposition, it indi-   12
cates a stammer of the tongue and few words, or he will be a lisper,
especially if Mercury is in a sign which has no voice (they are Cancer,
Scorpio, and Pisces) and is under the Sun's rays and with this aspects
the Moon. If Mars aspects it, it diminishes from these evils but in-   13
creases [his] trouble; but he will be perfect in intellect [and] sedate,
but no gain will reach him from his intellect and his reason except
that he will be learned, stuffed with intelligence, and because of
this he will be good in rank because, even if he is younger than
they, his older [brothers] will die and he will be their leader, and
his father will die before his mother. If Saturn aspects the Moon   14
from opposition, it indicates the spoiling of his mother's property
and pain and hidden illness and grief and irritation. If a benefic   15
does not aspect it, it indicates a blemish in his mother's body and
badness of condition in the matter of livelihood. If it is in a quad-   16
ruped sign, it indicates injury from lions. If it is in one of the signs   17
which | resembles a human, this evil will reach him. If the sign is   p. 66
                                                                        18
wet, then [the injury] is from water and streams and diseases. If the   19

benefics do not make it ineffectual, it indicates chronic illness in his body and darkness in [his] two eyes, and some of them will live exiled from their city.

20　[.....] If Jupiter aspects the Moon from opposition while the Moon is western [and] increasing in number, then he will be celebrated with respect to [his] livelihood, a famous man, and he will be one of those who relies on himself and will not obey another, especially if the Moon
21 is less in degrees than Jupiter. If the Moon is greater in degrees, then it is harmful because [there will be] a decrease in [his] livelihood [and] afflictions and agony will come to him.

22　If Mars aspects the Sun from opposition in a diurnal nativity, it indicates a horrible death for the native's father or a decrease in his sight, and the native will fall from a lofty place and afflictions will come to him; in a nocturnal nativity his work will be slight and his
23 property will be dissipated. If Mars aspects Venus from opposition, it indicates that he will be one of those in whom there is no constancy with respect to [his] thinking, and it will harm his father and his mar-
24 riage. If it is in a tropical sign, it indicates quarreling and misfortune
25 because of women. If Mars aspects Mercury from opposition, then he will have little shame [but will be] a master of lies and books or bewitchment and injury, and his livelihood will be from this, and he will have little property, but his wife will be good, and he will not cease being surety and giving guarantees for it, but he will run away from the discharge of [his] trust, and he will submit it to the judges and to argument, and fear will come to him and dread of [his] superiors, and he will depart for places in a land other than his own, especially if
26 Mercury is in Saturn's term or in its own term and house. If Mars aspects the Moon from opposition, it is bad because his life [will be] short, and as long as he stays alive [it will be] in misery and calamity, and some of them will die before they marry and some of them will die a terrible death, and he will be discontent and his limbs will be cut off or tied up.

27　If Venus aspects the Moon from opposition, there will be no good in [his] marriage and no children (even if there were, they would die), and he will be disgraced and beaten because of women.

28　If Mercury aspects the Moon from opposition, it indicates quarrels and affliction from groups of people and great slander, and he will be a coward in speaking.

220

| **Chapter 17. Aspect of the planets from sextile.**

II-17
p. 67

The aspect of sextile: judge it in this about as the aspect of trine except that it is weaker.

Chapter 18. If Saturn is with one of the seven.

II-18

If Saturn is with Jupiter, he will abound in landed estates [and will be] the steward for kings and nobles, entrusted with properties other than his own, and he will be noble if Mars does not aspect it. If Saturn is with Mars, it indicates good in [his] character, but there will be no good in regard to his property, and reason will keep him waiting, and he will marry, and his body will be weakened, and [his] bile and black bile will be aroused against him, and his father will die before his mother, and he will spoil his father's property, and he will turn to his brothers who were born before him because they will die or their disease[s] will be severe, and grief will come [upon him] and dependence, misery and blemish. If Jupiter aspects, it will make easy and dissipate this misery [and he will] bear it. If Saturn is with the Sun, he will spoil his father's property and his end will come to misery, and worse than this in a nocturnal nativity, [if Saturn] is eastern or western, with regard to his father and his brothers and his own peculiarity. If the Sun is less in degrees, then it is more terrible and worse because a horrible death will come to his father and like this, as I told you, of what the native will suffer, and he will fall from his good fortune, and disease from dampness and weakness will befall him, and he will love building[s] and sometimes will acquire wealth from them so that his living is from them, but still he will be miserable. If it is in the house of the Sun or in the house of Saturn, it indicates that his father will be noble and will not be discomforted, but the native will be hostile to his father, and what is like this as I mentioned. If Saturn is with Venus, he will marry a blemished woman for whom he will not be suitable, or he will have intercourse with a barren woman or one in whom there is a chronic illness, and he will be blemished and will be despised because of this, and he will have few children, and the one for whom children are judged will have few male [children]; he will have no constancy toward women [and] will have no comfort, but it will chill him; and according to that practice predict in the nativities of women. If Saturn is with Mercury, he will be a lisper, cumbersome with [his] tongue, slight in [his] work, but a calm man, a smart fellow

1

2

3

4

5

6

7

8

9 [and] profound. If Saturn is with | the Moon, then it will spoil the
p. 68 good of his mother and her work, and she will be emaciated, [but it
will be] strong in decrease for his mother's property, weak in [his]
10 body and in his mother's similarly. If the Moon is increasing and the
nativity diurnal while the benefics aspect, then it will remove the
11 evils. If the nativity is nocturnal and the Moon is increasing or decreasing in the aspect of Jupiter and Venus, then it indicates an increase in everything.

II-19   **Chapter 19. If Jupiter is with one of the seven.**

1   If Jupiter is with Mars, it indicates leadership and property and
honor in metropolises and cities, and he will be one of the judges for
2 communities, abounding in work. If they are both in the house of one
of them, then he will be powerful, steadfast, celebrated in arms, and
3 the like. If Jupiter is with the Sun under its [the Sun's] rays, it indi-
4 cates a decrease of everything. If it [Jupiter] is eastern, it indicates
good fortune and property and gain and luck to his parents and joy in
5 [his] children. If Jupiter is with Venus, he will be one of those who will
be brought up in honor and wealth, he will love the generality of
people, [he will be] merciful, good in [his] intention, good in [his]
appearance, pleasant in the eyes of chiefs and nobles, desirous of good
and of fame; property and leadership will come to him because of
women and houses of worship, and [he will be] good in [his] marriage
6 and children. If a malefic is between these two, then he will be beloved and received wherever he may be; thus [also] in the nativities of
7 women. If Jupiter is with Venus in a strong place and the Moon and
Mars aspect these two, then a disgusting and shameful affair involving
8 one of his relatives will be added. If Jupiter is with Mercury, he will be
an expert in law, victorious in words, and perfect in reasoning and
intellect, learned, the raiser up for the great among the people, and
some of them will be secretaries for the more powerful grandees or
9 kings. If Jupiter is with the Moon, it indicates an increase in property,
10 dignity, and good fortune. If Jupiter is powerful [and] eastern, there
11 will be good for the native from his fathers. If the Moon is less in
degrees and Jupiter is not bright, then this will decrease the good
fortune of the native.

12   If Mars is with the Sun, it indicates the swiftness of his father's
13 death. It is worse and more terrible if it is in a cardine or what follows

a cardine — it indicates pain for the native and aches, and he will be
envious, squandering | his father's property, and iron or fire will fall   p. 69
on him; he will be mixed up in his opinion[s and] will have no constancy in them. If Mars is with Venus, it indicates quarreling and   14
disaster and injury because of women. If the sign is tropical, then he   15
will have intercourse with a bad woman, and however it may be
quarreling will come to him because of women, and he will be excessive
in sexual intercourse; predict similarly in the nativities of women that
they will be disgraced in sexual intercourse. If Mars is with Mercury,   16
then he will be a liar except that he will be reasonable, intelligent,
learned, desirous of culture, [and] he will love arguments. If Jupiter   17
aspects it, [he will have] praise for that. If it is Venus, then [it will be]   18
like this and he will be strong in love for his children. If Saturn aspects,   19
then there is no good in it because he comes to hatred and defects. If   20
Mercury and Mars are thus under the [Sun's] rays in a cardine and they
aspect Venus, then he will be misleading in his intention and thought,
[and] the leaders of thieves will be opposed to him, [and] he will act
perfidiously in pleasure. If Jupiter aspects, the evil will desist from   21
him. If Saturn aspects, then it will punish this [native]. If Mars is   22, 23
with the Moon, then it indicates the shortness of his survival and a
terrible death and a chronic illness, and some of his flesh will be cut
with iron, and it indicates misery for his mother. If they both are in a   24
cardine, then he will be relaxed in his work [and] refractory, and in
addition to this it indicates injury.

If the Sun is with Venus, western in nocturnal nativities and eastern   25
in diurnal nativities, then he will be praiseworthy [and] welcome. If   26
Mercury is with the Sun, eastern or western, then he will be gentle, a
scribe, [and] he will have status for his culture and reasoning, and he
will be a chief and will benefit others.

If Venus is with Mercury, he will be lazy in [his] jobs, desirous of   27
joy and pleasure, abounding in women, adorned with culture and
words, loquacious in poetry because he will compose pleasing [and]
beautiful words, but he will be disconcerted because of intercourse
with women so that his pleasure and his desire will be in slave girls. If   28
both are in the ascendent, then it is better and more secure for their
strength, or profit and nobility will come to him from women if Jupiter
aspects it. If Venus is with the Moon, he will be great in [his] appear-   29
ance, good in [his] children, joyful, fortunate, but he will have no

constancy in [his] marriage [and will be] desirous with respect to women other than his own, and the wives of some of them will do similarly in having intercourse with other than them.

30   If Mercury is with the Moon, then he will be praiseworthy in [his] reason and understanding, perfect except that he will be a liar [and]
31 will not be constant with respect to an affair. If a benefic aspects these two, this evil will diminish and it indicates for his mother good
p. 70 except | that she will be disgraced by men. If the Moon is greater in
32 degrees than Mercury, then it will be good because, if the Moon's degrees abound, it accomplishes the strength of the planets which it is leaving because the Moon is nearer the earth than the planets [are].

II-20   **Chapter 20. Knowledge of the places of the planets.**

Look with this at the places of the planets and their portions, and know this as says the honored [and] praiseworthy by three natures, Hermes, the King of Egypt.

II-21   **Chapter 21. Arrival of the Moon in the places.**

1   If the Moon is in the ascendent or midheaven good in its light, then, if the malefics aspect it it decreases his [the native's] good and liveli-
2 hood, but if the benefics aspect it they increase his good. If the Moon is in its house or its term or its exaltation by night, in the cardines or what follow the cardines, then it will be good because he will be well known, abounding in friends and acquaintances, [and] staying a long
3 time, he with his mother. If a malefic is with it or aspects it, it will cut off [his] hope, and if he is master of something he will not take pleasure
4 in it. If a benefic aspects it without a malefic, then he will be powerful,
5 a chief [and] a commander. If a benefic and a malefic aspect it, then he will be miserable [but] will attain some nobility and status, or his
6 brothers will die a terrible death. If the Moon is in the West, which is the sign of marriage, it indicates sudden death for his mother, and for the native a decline in his livelihood and character from his position
7 and grief for his children and his women. If the Moon is in the cardine of the earth and malefics aspect it, then it indicates an intense dis-ease in a hidden place, and argument[s] and grief for [his] children,
8 and women will be roused up against him. If a benefic aspects it, it indicates that he will benefit from an evil job.

Chapter 22. Arrival of the Sun in the places.

If the Sun is in the ascendent or midheaven in its own house or a 1
male sign, then it will be good. If the benefics aspect it from the tenth 2
place, he will be praiseworthy, a leader over groups in nobility; and it
indicates similarly if it is in midheaven except that he will have few
brothers. If the Sun is in the house of marriage, it indicates hidden 3
misery for his parents and his brothers. If Mercury is with it, then he 4
will abound in property, | especially if Mercury is western. If the Sun p. 71
is in other than its place and the malefics aspect (especially if it is 5
Mars from opposition or quartile), then it indicates terror because of
fire or a terrible death or evil rising up in him or a [bad] name or
yelling or murder arises, and some of them will be food for lions; if
the Moon is injured, then it will be worse, but if the benefics aspect
they will diminish the misery. If the Sun is in the cardine under the 6
earth, it indicates a fall and a decrease in the property of his fathers,
but if the lord of its house or its exaltation overpowers it, it will
ameliorate this evil.

Chapter 23. Arrival of Saturn in the places.

If, when the nativity is diurnal, Saturn is in the ascendent in its own 1
house or in one of its places, then he will have no harm because he
will be a lord of landed estates and buildings and he will lead in this.
Consider the measure of the condition of the nativity, and predict 2
about him according to this except that he will be weak in body,
conspicuous in diseases, [and] he will not attain complete nobility, but
he will be mediocre, he will not profit in the matter of marriage, and
he will leave his parents. If Saturn is in the house of its enemies, then 3
it will be more injurious because his reputation will become bad and
his children will be few; in a nocturnal nativity it will be worse because he will have difficulty in affairs, [will be] tormented by diseases,
ugly in [actual] appearance and [in] rumor, secretive, injurious in
nature and [to] most of the things which are near [him, and children]
will not be born to them nor will they love their relatives. If Saturn is 4
in the ascendent while Jupiter is in the sign of marriage, these two
indicate the death of the brothers who were before him and the native
will fall in the hand[s] of his enemies. If Saturn is in the ascendent 5
while Mars opposes it in the West, then it indicates abundant evil and
a bad death for the native and [his] parents. But if Saturn is in the 6

ascendent while Venus [is] in the West, it indicates the death of his
7 women. If Saturn is in the ascendent while Mercury is in the West,
8 it indicates for his parents sudden death. If Saturn is in midheaven, it
mars his livelihood for the native for thirty years and his good fortune,
especially [in] nocturnal nativities when the sign is fixed because this
evil will be fixed, but if it is in a sign possessing two bodies he will
9 emerge from this but [his] good fortune will be slight. If Saturn is in
p.72 mid|heaven with Mars, it indicates a bad end for the native unless
10 one of the benefics is in the western sign. If Saturn is in the cardine
under the earth, it indicates the death of [his] children and brothers
or their paucity, and he will be heavy in [his] body, diseased, and injury will come to him from the sea or [from] water or from the coldness of his limbs, and his death will be a terrible death, but also he will
11 see what he loves in his enemies. If Mercury is with Saturn, then it
will be worse in the matter of his children and his slaves and his servants, and his good fortune and his property will be spoiled.

II-24　　**Chapter 24. Arrival of Jupiter in the places.**

1　　　If Jupiter is in the ascendent, he will possess a good marriage and
children and brothers and reputation, especially in a diurnal nativity;
2 in a nocturnal nativity there will be less of this. If Jupiter is in a feminine sign, then his mother will be better than his father, but if it is in
a masculine sign then his father will be better than his mother; if it
is in a sign possessing two bodies, then the native will raise up his
3 parents. If Jupiter is in the ascendent while Saturn is in the West,
then he will destroy his brothers who were born before him and will
harm his father, and he will see what he loves in his enemies together
with praise and commendation, and he will be in the houses of worship
4 and the houses of kings entrusted with a throng of people. If Mars from
this [ascendent] is in the tenth, which is midheaven, or in what follows
5 it, it diminishes that which I mentioned or spoils it at its end. If Jupiter is in the ascendent while Mars is in the West, then the native will
be better than his enemies and superior to them, but if Venus witnesses
Jupiter then it will be better, and if the Moon is with this then it will
6 be higher and better. If Jupiter is in midheaven, then he will be far out
in his fame, noble, having good fortune and children, especially in a
7 diurnal nativity. If Mars is with this in a good place and its own por-

tion, then he will be one of the chiefs and lords of armies, well known
[and] praiseworthy. If Venus aspects, it will increase his good fortune
because of women, and he will be praiseworthy [and] famous. If
Mercury aspects from a good place, it will increase [his] learning and
reason and intelligence. If Jupiter is in | the cardine of the West, it
indicates that in [his] old age his condition and his status will be
better, and his end will be good; it is better than this if Jupiter is in
his house or his exaltation, but he will be troubled and miserable in
his youth and he will see the death of his women and his brothers,
especially if a malefic aspects it or is with it, but he will have work
and medical treatment in the houses of kings and of chiefs, and he will
be a lord of property and goods from what he attains of power, and his
reputation will grow, and, if he dies, he will leave behind a good name
and a pleasing reputation. If the West is a tropical sign, then he will
rise up and escape from his neighborhood and rob kings and spoil the
property of his fathers, especially if a malefic aspects it (we have seen
[people] like this who were lords and leaders, [but] then were expelled
from their properties [and were] empty), and one of them will be con-
soled with a woman servant or a foreign woman or one who is worse in
[her] lineage than is he. If Jupiter aspects Venus and Mercury and
Mars while the Moon is with it, it indicates debauchery and misfortune and misery. If Jupiter is in the West and Venus aspects it while
both of them aspect the Moon, then he will be learned, a fortune-teller,
[and] will predict things before they happen. If Jupiter is under the
earth, it indicates [success] from an act of secrecy, and the native will
rise, and his control over his property and his goods will improve, and
the condition of his parents will be better, but [there will be] no good
in his marriage, or he will marry at the end of his life and [children]
will be born to him at the end of his years or their middle, and he will
fall in the middle of his years from his good fortune, [but] then he will
get up and his affairs will prosper.

Chapter 25. Arrival of Mars in the places.

II-25

If Mars is in the ascendent when the nativity is diurnal, it indicates
misery and pain and a decrease in his good, and he will be malicious in
character, have few children, be filled up forcibly, [and] he will love
debauchery and do this in other than charity and the like; it indicates

similarly in the nativities of women, and it is worse than this if Saturn aspects, but better than it if Jupiter aspects because it strengthens

2 him [the native] and he will be welcome. But if Mars is in the ascendent while [one] luminary is in the West and the other in the cardine under the earth, and Jupiter is cadent, then his parents will die suddenly a terrible death, and the native will be taken, but will not remain long in prison, and chronic illness will be in him, and this will be

3 as if he had no upbringing and good. If in nocturnal nativities Mars is in the ascendent and a feminine sign while Jupiter aspects, then it indicates intelligence and prosperity in [his] works and courage and

p. 74 daring, and besides this he will not escape from any | of the misery.

4 If Mars is in the house of property, it indicates the ruination of his property, but if a benefic aspects, then it will spoil some and leave

5 some behind. If Mars is in midheaven in diurnal nativities or in what follows midheaven, then it indicates a fall and a terrible flight from

6 his land. If this sign is tropical or possesses two bodies, then he will return to his city, especially if a benefic aspects it, but if a malefic aspects, he will spoil his father's property, especially if the Sun

7 aspects. The calamity is less in nocturnal births, especially if Jupiter aspects because Jupiter diminishes the indolence and evil and in-

8 creases the reason [and] intelligence. If Mars is with the Moon in midheaven or under the earth, he will destroy property and goods, but if a malefic aspects, the native will repair what he had destroyed.

9 If Mars is in opposition to the ascendent, then it is bad because he [the native] will die or run away from his city or fall in misery, and it is worse than this if it is in other than its portion and not in its place as misfortune and fire and disobedience will come to him from an evil

10, 11 act. Know which this is of the kinds of signs in which Mars is. If Jupiter aspects, it will make it easy for him, and misfortune will come to

12 some of them until they look at death, [but] then they will escape. If Mars is in the West and aspects the Sun or the Moon, it indicates his

13 separation from his parents and his deflection from a livelihood. If Mars is in the West while the Moon is increasing [and] aspecting it, then it will be bad because sometimes death and a terrible harm will come to him, and this will come to some of them in individuals or

14 things, and with this misery he will be taken in blood. If Jupiter does not present itself, it will increase that which I mentioned very much, but in nocturnal nativities less.

Chapter 26. Arrival of Venus in the places.

If Venus is in the ascendant or in what follows the ascendant,   1
eastern [and] rejoicing in its light, he will be praiseworthy, handsome,
a master of women, well known among kings and lords of men, well
known in metropolises and cities, and some of them will have intercourse with the women of the rich, but they will not profit or excel
by means of this, and some of them will occupy houses of worship
[and will be] pure (we have seen something like this), great, one whom
praise will lift up and his head will be crowned, and he will be good in
[his] character [and] will love wealth, especially if the Moon aspects.   2
If with this Mars and Mercury aspect, he will be delighted with joy, | p. 75
openly rich in this. If with this Saturn aspects, he will have inter-   3
course with a mature woman who is not praiseworthy and is not fa-
mous for goodness. Predict like this in nativities of women. If Venus   4, 5
is in the ascendant which is a sign possessing two bodies, then the
native will be named with [the names of] two fathers or two mothers
or with two names. If, while Mercury [is] in the ascendant or mid-   6
heaven or the cardine under the earth, Venus is eastern, then it indicates nobility and honor and praise in groups of people, and this will
be because of insight and knowledge. If the sign is feminine, then it   7
is better, and if it is tropical, then it is good. If Venus is in the ascend-   8
ent or midheaven or aspects the Moon, then it indicates his marriage
to one of his relatives. If Venus and Mercury are in the ascendant while   9
Mars is in the West, then it indicates the ruination of his father's
property and the expenditure of what was acquired because of nobles
and the quest for knowledge and approaching houses of worship
because he will seek glory and high rank, but will fall in quarrel[s]
because of an evil affair or on account of a woman, and he will be
seized because of blood or poison, a shameless fellow, and emptiness
and fear will reach him from this, but this evil will fade away by his
donating property — afterwards he will be in charge of death. If   10
Jupiter aspects, it will diminish the evil, but if Jupiter does not aspect,
misery will reach him and flight and a fall from his property; in the
nativities of women they will have intercourse with the nobles and
some of them will get remuneration and profit. If Venus is in the   11
ascendant while Saturn is in the West, it indicates that his wife will
give him poison to drink so that he will die by means of it. If Venus is   12
in the ascendant while Saturn is in the tenth, he will be satisfied,

wealthy, he will believe in God and will be a mightier noble than his
fathers were, and he will travel to many cities and countries, but he
will return to his city and will fall into contracts because of women,
and children will be born to him unless a malefic aspects (these
children were explained in the chapter which I mentioned to you);

13 predict similarly in the nativities of women. If Venus is in the ascendent which [is] a feminine sign, then it indicates that his mother is of

14 nobler lineage than his father and she will live long. If Venus is in
midheaven or under the earth or in the sign of good fortune, rejoicing,
he will be praiseworthy [and] welcome, but if a malefic aspects it

15 [Venus], it diminishes its [Venus'] power. In nativities of women if
Venus is in midheaven which [is] a masculine sign, then she will be a
harlot, especially if Mars or Mercury aspects because she will be a
Lesbian [and] will perform the act of men; it is worse if the Moon

16 aspects it [Venus] from a masculine sign. In nativities of men if Venus
is in midheaven which [is] a feminine sign, he will not be satisfied and
the character of a woman will be in him, [he will be] weak; if Saturn
aspects, it will enfeeble him and make it difficult for him in the acts of

17 Venus. | If Venus is in the West, it indicates that he will have a good
p. 76
end except that he will have no good in marriage, especially if there is

18 none between these two [?] without the aspect of Jupiter. But if Venus
is in this place in nativities of women, then [it indicates] what is better
than this because she will be one of those who do not perform

19 the act of Venus in an unnatural way. But if the Moon is with it
[Venus] in the West in nativities of men, then he will be effeminate
and will marry a whore whom many men have had intercourse

20 with. If Venus is [in the cardine] under the earth which [is] a masculine sign while the nativity [is] diurnal, it indicates disgrace because
of women, and if Saturn or Mars aspects he will see the death of his
women; if the sign is tropical, then it will not happen once but many
times.

II-27   **Chapter 27. Arrival of Mercury in the places.**

1   If Mercury is in the ascendent, he will be bent over in everything
and for everyone, and he will have many children, be reasonable,

2 well known to everyone, desirous of instruction and words. If Mercury
is in midheaven or in what follows the cardine of midheaven or in

what follows the ascendent and [in] a tropical sign, he will be well
known, praiseworthy among tribes and praiseworthy people. If the 3
sign possesses two bodies, then he will be a trainer, a teacher or the
leader of others' children. If it is in a feminine sign, he will attain 4
nobility because of women. However you find Mercury in midheaven 5
or the ascendent, then he will be wealthy or a scribe or possess [his]
livelihood from calculation. If Venus is with it [Mercury], then he 6
will be intuitive or an artisan for words, and he will be praised among
most men. If Mercury is [in midheaven] while Jupiter is with it, then 7
he will speak in revelation and be mighty and overpower many men
and be a chief in the houses of worship or the houses of kings or in
metropolises or in cities, especially if it is in a tropical sign. But if it 8
is beneath the Sun's rays, he will be silent for secrets, will not be about
to reveal anything of what is tricky within himself. If Mercury is in the 9
West, then there is no good in his brothers or his children, and quarrels
and slander will be stirred up against him, especially if it is a sign
possessing two bodies or tropical or Mars aspects it; it indicates similarly also if it is under the earth. If Mercury is under the earth, 10
rejoicing in its light, with | the benefics or the malefics, he will be good p. 77
in [his] intention[s], intelligent, a disclaimer and a secretive [fellow],
but if the malefics aspect, with this he will be a magician or a thief,
vicious, filled with falsehoods.

Chapter 28. Arrival of Saturn in another's house. II-28

If Saturn is in the house of Jupiter, it indicates a good condition 1
and honor, and he will raise the children of others, and he will be a
steward, and he will love his wife and will be one of those who love
nobles together with a goodness of livelihood; it indicates similarly
if it is in Jupiter's term. If Saturn is in Mars' house, he will be difficult 2
in his own and in other's work. If Saturn is in Venus' house, then there 3
is no good in the matter of marriage because he will marry a young
girl or an old woman or a whore, or grief and misery will come to him
because of women, and some of them will come to fornication in order
to acquire its fee. If Saturn is in Mercury's house, he will be secretive 4
and will love silence except that he will be reasonable, learned in the
secrets of books, and injury will come to him for this reason, and his
tongue will not be distinct or clear.

II-29   **Chapter 29. Arrival of Jupiter in another's house.**

1   If Jupiter is in Saturn's house, he will be wealthy and for this no
praise or honor for him will be known, and his secret affair[s] will not
be looked into, but he will live in easy circumstances [and] will not be
according to the extent of his condition, and with this he will be
charming in forgiveness and will not stretch out his neck to power and
praise, and will not consider it, but tribulations will come to him in
2 time. If Jupiter is in Mars' house, he will be one of the chiefs, a leader
or a calculator for the stars, but if it is in a cardine aspecting the Moon
and the Sun while these two are in cardines, then he will attain praise,
but if both of the luminaries are in a masculine sign, then he will be
a chief of the armies on land and on the sea, put in charge of death and
3 life. If Jupiter is in Venus' house, he will be an overseer in the houses
of kings and their works and his livelihood will be from nobles, and
we have seen some of them abounding in secret intercourse with
a noble woman so that because of her he attains wealth and goods, and
she is his backer; some of them control the properties of women and
4 their works. | If Jupiter is in Mercury's house, he will be one of those
p. 78
who stand up in probity in cities or [he will be] a calculator for
everything, [and] he will stand healthy in [his] reasoning, and he will
be praised for this, and [men] will resort to him.

II-30   **Chapter 30. Arrival of Mars in another's house.**

1   If Mars is in Saturn's house, he will be pleasant, courageous, agile
in what he improves, but he will squander his father's property and
2 kill his younger brothers. If Mars is in Jupiter's house or its term, he
will be friendly to kings, beloved among them; if Jupiter is aspecting
Mars which is in its house, then he will be one of the nobles and com-
manders of armies, a leader of soldiers and forces, and he will be ruling
3 in cities, one who has ascended in nobility. If Mars is in Venus' house
or its term, then he will be a master of fornication, he will love the
women of others, and he will harm his relatives, and he will rejoice in
an evil sexual intercourse, and most of them [will be men] who murder their wives with their own hand and consider how the death of
4 their women may occur. If Mars is in Mercury's house or term, then he
will be reasonable, desirous of marriage, clear in [his] thinking, intelligent, but he will collect property illegally and will be poor and an
ascetic in his work.

Chapter 31. Arrival of Venus in another's house.

If Venus is in Saturn's house or its term, he will be sterile or will
have intercourse with his brothers' wives or women; if he is a slave,
he will be set free and will have intercourse with his mistress. If Venus
is in Jupiter's house or its term, he will have power and property from
[his] wife or the work of [his] wife, and some of them will be stewards
for women and will amass wealth on this account, and he will rejoice
and will be in a house of worship and will love his wife with a powerful
love. If Venus is in Mars' house or its term, then he [will be] one of
those in whom greed and evil quarrels are stirred up and injury, and
this misery will reach him from women, and he will have intercourse
with a woman not his own, [but one who is] subservient or disgraced
or a serving girl, and women will not be not constant with him but it
will confuse him. If Venus is in Mercury's house or its portion, then
sometimes he will rejoice in women and sometimes he will work for
women, and an argument will come to him because of this, and some
of them will be some of the masters of a craft and of painting and
artisans of magnificent things, and they will sell perfume.

1

2

3

4

| Chapter 32. Arrival of Mercury in another's house.

If Mercury is in Saturn's house or its term, he will be dumb or
lisping or deaf, silent, [and] he will inform no one of what is in himself,
[he will be] contemplative, inquiring about all the affairs of men so
that he will be enthusiastic about this, and some of them will know the
secrets of the book which [belong] to the people of religions, and some
of them will be learned in the stars, and some of them will drive away
birds [be augurs]. If Mercury is in Jupiter's house or term, he will
possess dignity, [be] an orator, or control the affairs of kings or nobles,
or instruct the people in words and arguments and judgments, and
he will always be about the business of metropolises or kings. If Mercury is in Mars' term or its house, then he will be a fool, insignificant,
a liar with no shame, and he will not believe in God or in good work[s
and] he will love adultery, and some of them will act with perfidy, and
some of them will keep company with magicians or confer with them
or investigate their affair[s] in regard to measures, and they will re-
fuse to receive religion, and the people will treat them as enemies who
have no fidelity and no good reputation. If Mercury is in Venus'
house or its term, he will be welcome, pleasant, rejoicing, [and] he

1

2

3

4

will do all his work [and] will hurry it up and will press on with it, and some of them will be learned or intuitive or wealthy or will make dye[s], and some of them will be learned in backgammon and the like; if Mercury is in a cardine free of the [Sun's] rays, then he will be intuitive, intelligent, acquisitive of property, needing everyone.

II-33　　**Chapter 33. On the arrival of the planets, one of them in the house of another.**

1　　　If Saturn is in the Moon's house, then he will destroy his mother's property and rob it in her lifetime, and his mother will be sick, and her limbs will complain of the cold and the black bile and the harsh
2　pain until she shall make a vow for herself to a house of worship. If Saturn stays in the Sun's house, his father will be praiseworthy [and] will increase in his livelihood, but besides this his father will complain of dampness or will die a terrible death.

3　　　If Mars is in the Moon's house, he will be sharp in his reasoning, a seeker for work and property except that his work and his livelihood will weaken and he will be chronically ill or will die a terrible death, and he will have a short life or little property, [but] will abound in
4　disease; it is worse for one who is born in the daytime. If Mars is in
p. 80　the Sun's house, | he will spoil his father's property and rob it, and he will be one of those who do difficult and unpleasant work in fire or
5　iron, and his livelihood will be from this. If Mars and Saturn are both in a house of the Sun or the Moon, they indicate the shortness of [his] life or the terribleness of [his] death.

6　　　If the Moon is in Saturn's house or its term, he will be in difficulties
7　or thwarted from work, dull in work and body, disgraced. If the Moon is in Mars' house or its term, then he will be daring, steadfast, a usurper of the property of others, and he will have no regard for truth and justice, but most of them will be masters of arms and murder, chief-
8　tains. But look at the planets' portions and the benefics' aspect be-
9　cause the benefics dissolve evil. If the Sun is in Mars' house or its term, he will be afflicted with a difficult disease, but he will be good in [his] livelihood, strong in [his] work, [but] insignificant and in difficulties in it.

10　　　If the Sun and the Moon are in Jupiter's house or its term and they are thus together, then he will be honest in [his] properties, but will have intercourse with his brothers' women, and some of them will
234

have intercourse with their mothers; it indicates similarly in nativities
of women because she will have intercourse with her mother's husband or her sisters' or one closer to her.

If the Moon is in Venus' house or its term, then he will be handsome   11
of face, pleasing, handsome in [his] eyes, agreeable, enjoyable [?] for
everyone, especially if the sign is one of a human figure as then he will
be a debaucher, wealthy in this, and scandal will reach him on this
account, and together with this he will he good in [his] condition and
livelihood. If the Sun is in Venus' house or its terms, then he will be a   12
soothsayer, truthful in [his] visions, a man of discernment, learned in
things, a calculator for the stars, but he will be moist in [his] body,
abounding in anger.

If the Moon is in Mercury's house or its term, he will be reasonable,   13
a scribe, [and] profits will come to him from [his] works except that
he will love [both] females and males and will have few children. If the   14
Sun is in Mercury's house or its term, he will be steadfast, insignificant,
silent for a secret, a confidant except that he will be afflicted with
disease and wetness. This which I have told you of the houses and the   15
terms, if the house and the term agree, then it is more secure and more
correct in judgments, if God [so] wishes.

The second book ends. Glory to God, the lord of the two worlds.

| **The third book of Dorotheus which he wrote with respect to the haylij**   p. 81
and the kadhkhudah, which are the governor
and the indicator of the time of the years of life.

In the name of God, the compassionate, the merciful. [Here] begins
the third book of Dorotheus which he wrote with respect to the haylaj
and the kadhkhudah, which are the governor and the indicator of the
time of the years of life.

At the beginning of this he says: consider Saturn, Jupiter, and Mars.   III-1, 1
If you find them eastern or in one of [their] stations, [then they are   2
used], but, if they are under the Sun's rays in the degree of the Sun,
then this is not counted, [or if it is] western. If you find them seven   3
days before the nativity or seven days after it in the positions which I
named for you in the term of [one of] these three, then it will be gover-

4 nor of the nativity. A planet is eastern if it is behind the Sun and west-
5 ern if it is between its [the Sun's] hands. If there are fifteen degrees
between Saturn and the Sun, and similarly ••• degrees between Jupiter and the Sun, and eighteen degrees between Mars and the Sun,
and ••• degrees between Venus and the Sun, and nineteen degrees
between Mercury and the Sun — whenever you find them behind the
Sun by these degrees, then say concerning them [that they have] the
6 power of being eastern. If one of them is under the Sun's rays, then it
will be one which will not be seen.

7   See also on the third day from the nativity in the term of which planet the Moon is because, if this planet is a benefic and its lord is in a
good place aspecting the Moon from a good place from trine while the
Moon is in a cardine or what follows a cardine, then say that all of the
8 nativity's condition is good. But if the lord of the Moon's term is a
malefic and it is in a cardine while the lot of fortune is in opposition
to the Moon, then say [that there is] no doubt that the nativity is bad.
9 If the lord of the term is a benefic or a malefic and is in a good place
aspecting the Moon, then it will be mediocre.

10   Look at the conjunction of the Moon and both halves of its course
and [its] opposition, which is [its] fullness, because if the Moon is in
p. 82 one of these situations, then the lord | of the Moon's term rules the
11 nativity. If you do not find the lord of the Moon's term in a cardine or
in what follows a cardine, then consider the lord of the ascendent's
term because the degree of the ascendent becomes the governor in it
12 [the nativity]. If it is as I mentioned, then look at the lord of the
[ascendent's] house, which [planet] it is, as, if it is eastern in a good
13 place, then it will be governor. If you find the lord of the [ascendent's]
house under the [Sun's] rays, then see which is its lord and see whether
that place in which it is is masculine or feminine.

14   If the lord of the Sun's term is in a good place, then it will be the
15 protector of the haylaj. If the Sun is in the seventh or eighth sign,
which sign is masculine, then the lord of the Sun's term will be ruling in it, but if the Sun is in a feminine sign, then it will not be thus
because the Sun has been feminized twice — once [by] the sign in
which it is and the other time by its position among the twelve [pla-
16 ces]. If you find the Sun in this position in a nativity, then consider the
17 Moon. If the Moon is above the earth and in midheaven or what
follows midheaven and [it is] a feminine sign, then the lord of the

236

Moon's term will be the ruler unless it is under the Sun's rays. If you   18
also find the Moon in the cardine of the West or what follows [that]
cardine in whatever sign it is, then the Moon will be the haylaj and
the lord of its term will be the ruler in the governorship of the other;
similarly [is it done] in a nocturnal nativity. If you find the Moon   19
cadent and the Sun in a nocturnal nativity [in the cardine] under the
earth or [in] the fifth place, then, if the lord of the Sun's term is free
of [its] rays, it will be the ruler in the nativity. If the lord of the Moon's   20
term is under the [Sun's] rays, then you must also at night look at
the Sun as, if it is in the fifth or fourth, then it will take over the
governorship of this. But if the Sun and the Moon are both cadent or   21
weakened and in their light and it happens that the two luminaries
have no power, or [if] one of the two luminaries is weak, then look at
the degree of the ascendent. If you find the lord of this ascendent   22
under the [Sun's] rays or cadent, then say [that there is] ruination
in this nativity and that he [the native] will have no upbringing. But   23
if together with this a benefic is in the ascendent in what is between
it and fifteen degrees, then mix this planet with the haylaj. If the   24
haylaj is the Moon and the Moon is in Cancer while the lord of its term
is in quartile or trine to it, then say that | [the native] will be brought   p.83
up; [it is] this [also] if you find the Sun [as haylaj] in its own house,
but if it is in what is like it among the houses, then look at the
lord of its [the Sun's] term or house. Calculate if the Sun is in the   25
first degrees of Aries and the lord of its [the Sun's] term or house
aspects it as this becomes the indicator. If Mars and Jupiter are   26
in cardines or some of those that follow cardines or in the places
which I mentioned above or in their houses or in their terms or in
their exaltations or in their triplicities or in their portions, then it
will be good as [those] planets will rule in the nativity which are in
their house[s] or term[s] or image[s] [decans] or exaltation[s] or tri-
pliciti[es].

Now I will explain to you the length of life and the number of   27
years as I attempt [to compute it], because sometimes you will want
to consider it in a horoscopic diagram as I will show you. The native   28
was born in the ninety-sixth year of the years of Darinus [Diocletian]
in the month Mihr on the second day in one and a half equinoctial
hours of daylight. I wanted to know the places of the haylaj among   29
which he was born because they are five places, and none of the pla-

nets was in them except in the ascendent in which the Sun was; and it is the best of the places.

Aries Taurus Saturn 4; 34 Mars 24; 55	Ascendent Pisces 18 Mercury 19; 55 Sun 6; 50 Venus 26; 50	Aquarius Capricorn
Gemini		Sagittarius
Cancer Leo	Moon 19; 7 Virgo 18	Scorpio Libra Lot of Fortune Jupiter 20; 10

30   But I calculated for this nativity from the degrees of the ascendent, and its degrees progress in the clime in which the native was born,
31 which is the fourth clime. Saturn is in Taurus four degrees and thirty minutes, so it is casting rays from sextile to five degrees of Pisces. Because the ascendent is in eighteen degrees count from the ascendent
32
p. 84 to the rays | of Saturn, and it does not come down to it. Then Mars in
33 Taurus twenty-four degrees and fifty minutes casts rays to twenty-five degrees of Pisces.

34   I wanted to know in how many years the ascendent would conjoin
35 with the rays of Mars. I took the eighteen degrees of the ascendent and I found in the [tables for] my clime and the twelve parts [signs] [that] placed under it [was] three hundred and fifty-two [time]
36 degrees and thirty seconds; I wrote this down separately. Then I took the twenty-four degrees and fifty minutes where Mars cast its rays to Pisces and I found the rising-times under this [to be] three hundred and fifty-six [time] degrees and forty-eight minutes; so I subtracted the three hundred and fifty-two [degrees] and thirty [minutes] which belong to the ascendent, and there were left four [time]

degrees and eighteen minutes. I said that the degrees of the ascendent   37
would conjoin with the sextile rays of Mars in four years and a fifth
and a tenth of a year. Because Venus [is] in this term, it dissolves the   38
fear and misery that Mars indicates and he will not die, but this misery will pass by him because whenever the rays of the benefics are
found with the rays of the malefics, then the benefic dissolves whatever the malefic indicates; but if the malefic and its term cast rays
without the benefics, then it will not be long before he dies.

Then, when the degrees of the ascendent depart from Aries, they   39
will descend to the [first] term of Taurus, which [is] the place in
which Saturn is. I computed this thus in the [table for the] clime in   40
which I was, and I found the rising-times under thirty degrees of
Aries [to be] nineteen [time] degrees and twelve minutes. I wanted to   41
subtract from these the [rising-]times which [were] under the degrees
of the ascendent. Because they were greater than the nineteen [de-   42
grees] and twelve [minutes] which [are] in Aries and I was not able to
subtract it, I added to it [19; 12] a complete rotation, which is three
hundred and sixty degrees, and I subtracted from it [379; 12] the
three hundred and fifty-two [degrees] and thirty [minutes] which
[were] under the degrees of the ascendent; there remained twenty-
six [degrees] and forty-two [minutes]. I said [that] the degree of the   43
ascendent will depart from Aries in twenty-six years and a half and a
fifth of a year. This makes clear that the conjunction of the degree of   44
the ascendent with a malefic indicates a great misery unless there are
some of the benefics which cast their rays to this term because sometimes misery and death will come to him before the conjunction of the
degree with a malefic. This [was] in twenty-six years and a half and   45
a fifth of a year.

| But I wanted to know when would be its conjunction with the   46
degree of Saturn. I took the four degrees and thirty minutes in which   p. 85
Saturn [was] and I found in the [table for the] clime and the twelve   47
parts [signs] [that] the rising-times [are] twenty-two [degrees] and
twenty-one [minutes]. Because [this was] less than what I wanted to   48
subtract from it, I added to it [22; 21] a rotation, and it became three
hundred and eighty-two [degrees] and twenty-one [minutes], and I
subtracted from it [that] which was placed under the degree of the
ascendent, which was three hundred and fifty-two [degrees] and
thirty [minutes]; there remained twenty-nine [degrees] and fifty-one

49 [minutes]. I said that in twenty-nine years and a half and a quarter
and a tenth of a year the degree of the ascendent would conjoin with
50 Saturn. Because the Sun cast its rays from sextile to the first term of
Taurus where Saturn was staying, the heat of the Sun will drive away
the maleficence of Saturn, and the harsh misery will pass him by, and
he will not die.

51   In twenty-two degrees of Taurus the degree of the ascendent will
52 arrive at where Mars [was]. I took twenty-two degrees of Taurus and
entered with them in the [table for the] clime and the twelve parts
[signs], and I found [that] the rising-times [were] thirty-five [degrees]
53 and twenty-four [minutes]. Because [it was] small [and] I could not
subtract from it what I wanted to, I added to it [35; 24] a rotation,
and it became three hundred and ninety-five [degrees] and twenty-
four [minutes], and I subtracted from it the three hundred and fifty-
two [degrees] and thirty [minutes] which belong to the ascendent;
54 there remained forty-two [degrees] and fifty-four [minutes]. I said
that it will arrive at the term in which Mars is in forty-two years and
a half and a third and two-thirds of a tenth of a year.

55   The degree of the ascendent to the degree of Mars: I calculated it
56 thus. I entered with the twenty-four [degrees] and fifty [minutes]
which pertained to Mars in Taurus in the [table for the] clime in which
I was and its parts [signs], and I found [that] the rising-times [were]
thirty-seven [degrees] and forty-three [minutes], and because of its
smallness I added to it [37; 43] a rotation, and it became three hundred and ninety-seven [degrees] and forty-three [minutes], and I
subtracted from it the three hundred and fifty-two [degrees] and
thirty [minutes] which belong to the ascendent; there remained
forty-five years and a sixth and half a tenth of a year [in which] the
57 ascendent would conjoin with Mars. Because Venus also cast its rays
on this place from sextile, it will dissolve the maleficance of Mars, and
he will not die because of Venus' aspect, and whatever of [its] rays it
cast to this place, by means of them this misery will pass [him] by.
58 Then the rays [of the malefics] will not reach it [the ascendent] until
it comes to Cancer, so that the degrees of Taurus and Gemini pass it
by because none of the malefics will aspect [it] till it reaches the degrees
of Cancer.

59 | Then the degrees of the ascendent will enter the beginning of Can-
p. 86
60, 61 cer and Saturn will aspect it. I computed thus. I entered with thirty

degrees of Gemini in [the table for] my clime and its parts [signs] and I found [that] the rising[-time was] seventy-one [degrees] and twenty-five [minutes], and because [it was] small I added a rotation and I subtracted [from the sum] those three hundred and fifty-two [degrees] and thirty [minutes]; there remained seventy-eight [degrees] and forty-five [minutes]. I said that the degrees of the ascendent will   62
enter the first term of Cancer where are the sextile rays of Saturn in seventy-eight years and a half and a fourth of a year.

Then I calculated its conjunction with the degree of Saturn. I took   63, 64
the four degrees and thirty minutes in which Saturn was and I entered with them in the [table of] rising-times of Cancer, and they were seventy-six [degrees] [and twenty minutes], and I added a rotation and subtracted from it three hundred and fifty-two [degrees] and thirty [minutes]; there remained eighty-three years and a half and a third of a year. Because the Sun aspected from trine and cast [its]   65
rays to this term in which are the rays of Saturn, it will dissolve the misfortune this time, [but] he will die then when the rays of Mars reach it [the ascendent].

Also it is not useful to look at the course of these degrees and their   66
term, but to look at the course of the degrees of the Moon because the conjunction of the Moon's degree with the malefics indicates misery, especially if with this the benefics do not aspect as, if they do aspect, they dissolve misery and death. It is necessary for you to look at the   67
transit of the planets and the revolution of years; in these sometimes it makes him miserable and spoils [his] life, but we do not find this peculiarity in everyone [of the books]. I sought for this in a long period   68
of years and I suffered every misery so that I might write it down. Look at the casting of rays in latitude also because sometimes a planet   69
is aspecting from opposition, and if you calculate it in latitude and you find one (planet) in the south, the other in the north, then this is not in opposition and also does not cast [its] rays, which according to this indicates misery. Also if you find both the Sun and   70
the Moon in the sixth or the eighth or the twelfth and the malefics aspect [them], then they indicate death when their degrees conjoin with the malefics. But if they are in a bad place but are not in-   71
jured, and you find the malefics casting [their] rays close to their degrees, then the misery which would be will pass by, and he will not die in it.

| **Chapter 2. The haylaj.**

1   The haylaj is the indicator and the kadhkhudah is the governor of
2 the matter of life. The haylaj by day is the Sun and by night the
Moon, then the degrees of the term of the ascendent, then the lot of
3 fortune. Whosoever's nativity takes place from conjunction to fullness [of the Moon, for him] it [the kadhkhudah?] is the degree of the
conjunction, and whosoever's nativity takes place in what is between
fullness and conjunction, the degree in which the fullness is; [each
period] is fifteen days in a month, and its nighttime is more powerful
4 than that [daytime]. By day the Sun and by night the Moon, and the
5 better of these two is what is in a cardine, especially the ascendent. It
is necessary that the lord of the term aspect the haylaj, or the lord of
its house, or the lord of its exaltation, or the lord of its triplicity, or
6 the lord of its image [decan]. If it is in this situation, it is the haylaj,
but if there does not witness it the lord of the term or one of those
which I mentioned — the lord of its house or its triplicity or its exaltation or its image (the first of these is the lord of the term, then the
lord of the triplicity) — then it will not be good that you make it the hay-
7 laj. See which [planet] casts [its] rays once you have found the haylaj,
casts [its] rays to it from both quartiles and both trines and both
8 sextiles or is present with it or in opposition. In a diurnal nativity if
the Sun is in the ascendent in the degrees above the earth and one of
those [planets] which I mentioned aspects it, then it will have the
9 power to be the haylaj. Similarly [is it] if you find it in midheaven or in
10 the eleventh sign, which is the sign of good fortune. Similarly look in
11 nocturnal nativities from the Moon. But if in diurnal nativities you
find the Sun cadent, injured, but the Moon in those places, it has the
12 power for the Moon to be ruling in it. Similarly in a nocturnal nativity,
if you find the Moon cadent and the Sun in the ascendent, then speak
13 about the Sun [as haylaj]. Look at the lot of fortune in the same way.

14   Look at the place in which is the conjunction of the Sun and the
15 Moon or the fullness [of the Moon]. Once you have found the haylaj,
16 look at the lord of the term of the Sun and of the Moon. If you find
them cadent, not aspecting the haylaj, then this haylaj is no good.
17 If you find a malefic casting its rays to the degree of the haylaj, it
will harm him [the native] and injury will come to him in the period
18 during which this malefic is governor of the prorogation or ray. If the
Sun is in opposition to Mars from the ascendent, consider that this is

an indicator of the squandering of his father's property, and striking
and grief from the nobles of men, and ruination will harm him and a
pain in his leg, and this will come to him in the period during which
Mars is the governor of the ray.

Because the nativity was diurnal, I looked in search of the haylaj   19
at the Sun, and I found the Sun cadent. I also looked at the Moon, and   20
I found it cadent. I found the lot of fortune and the fullness [of the   21
Moon] also in cadent[s]. There was nothing obvious from which the   22
haylaj might be found except the ascendent. The lord of the term of   23
the ascendent, Mars, was above the earth and near the East and the
four parts which have been mentioned and [in] the place of good
fortune aspecting the ascendent and casting [its] rays to that term in
which the ascendent is, from above it, because it casts to the house
and term together; if that casting were to the house only, it would not
have this power. There is left of the term one degree that belongs to   24
Mars.

p. 88

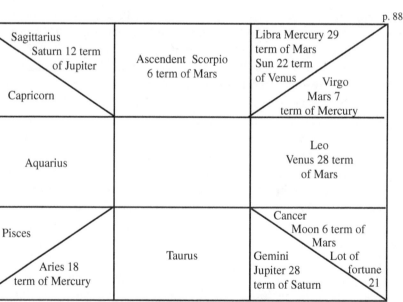

So Mars takes over the governorship of the prorogation and ray.   25
Until this degree in its prorogation and its ray ends without the ray   26
of any [other], Mars indicates in this year injury from fire and disease.
Even though Mars is in a good place, it is necessary that it indicate   27
like this. This misfortune is worse for him [the native] because the   28

29 Moon aspects it [Mars]. If it were not that the Sun stands between its
   ray and the ascendent and breaks the power of Mars, it would be
30 worse. Then the prorogation of the ascendent comes to the term of
31 Venus till the eleventh degree. Because Mars has left and Venus has
32 entered it is necessary to mix the power of these two together. Because of this the native will be blessed with love from his parents
   because both of these [planets] are in a good place, and moreover
33 pain will reach him. Then till the nineteenth degree is the prorogation
   of Mercury, and in this period he will increase [his] learning and cul-
34 ture and the like. Then the prorogation at puberty reaches Jupiter,
p.89 and it will indicate praise on account of [his] culture and good | from
   [his] eloquence and the manifestation of [his] ways which are pleasing
35 to people. Even though Jupiter is retrograde in motion and does not
   aspect the Moon and the ascendent, this will not decrease it because,
   whenever the planets are thus, their power is weakened and its gift
36 is muddied. If Jupiter were in a better place than this, it would in-
37 crease the good. Then the prorogation comes to Saturn while Venus
   casts [its] rays to the twenty-seventh degree of Scorpio from quartile,
38 so that Saturn and Venus govern this prorogation together. Saturn
   indicates his slowness in work and disease and distance from his land
   and grief and obstruction and difficulty, and this is worse because
39 Mars is elevated over Saturn. If it were not that Jupiter aspects Sa-
40 turn it would be worse. Because of the place of Saturn his mother will
   die in this period, but he will acquire goods because Saturn indicates
   these, and he will marry a wife with a dowry, and [a child] will be
   born to him who will live a short while and die in the third year; his
   enjoyment of women and children will be from Venus, but his lament
41 and the death of his child will be from Saturn. Then the prorogation
   arrives at Sagittarius, the first term, which is the house of Jupiter
42 and its term. Because Jupiter makes this place its house and its term,
   it governs the prorogation alone without any [other] of the planets
43 [and] it increases its power. It indicates for the native leadership and
44 honor among groups of men, and his elevation among them. Because
   Saturn is in the twelfth degree, it indicates the last day of his life, and
   he will live after the twelfth degree forty-eight nights because Saturn
   is in the beginning of the degree [at 12; 8°].

45   If you want to know how each planet increases the nativity and
   how it diminishes it, then look at the transit of the planets and which

aspects the haylaj from right or left, and [look] at the term of the
ascendent and at the lord of the ascendent's term and the planets
which are in it. Consider well the rays, whether of benefics or of   46
malefics or mixed, because if the rays are of malefics without benefics' then it is bad. See which [planet] casts [its] rays in aspect or in   47
being with it [the haylaj?], and in how many degrees of rising-times in
the clime in which you are it will arrive at the prorogation. Consider   48
that planet which casts [its] rays to the planet which aspects it [the
haylaj?] or [is] with it and the lord of the prorogation; then mix them
together in proportion to their maleficence and their beneficence and
their power in the places and the planets' aspect of them and their
portions and their terms and their houses, and judge in accordance
with how you find them.

The third book of the books of Dorotheus is finished. Praise to
God — He alone deserves praise and merits it.

| The fourth book of Dorotheus on the transfer of years.   p. 90

In the name of God, the compassionate, the merciful, to Whom I
have recourse. The fourth book of the books of Dorotheus, relating to
the transfer of years.

When a native is born, the lord of the year is the lord of the house   IV-1, 1
[ascendent] in which the native was born. Thus count from the   2
ascendent a year for each sign until you reach the year which you
desire; the lord of that house is the lord of the year. Look at the lord   3
of this sign, whether it is a benefic or a malefic, and in the base-
nativity how its position was and in which foundation it was. From   4
the base-nativity is known what is concerning him [the native] at
the beginning of the year, and the beginning of the year is always
when the Sun enters the beginning of the minute in which it was on
the day of the native's nativity. If the lord of the sign is western,   5
misfortune will reach the native. If the planet also is under the Sun's   6
light [in opposition or inferior conjunction] and is retrograde, then
[something] similar to this [will happen]. If the planet is under the   7
Sun's rays and is increasing in counting and not decreasing, then it
will be better for him and it will be good. Similarly the ancient wise   8

men of the people of Babylon and Egypt said: If the Sun or the Moon
is aspecting this sign from the triplicity of this sign in which it is —
they said: if it is thus, then make sure that the planet, which is the
9 lord of the year, is in its own house so that it will not cause harm. If
it is in the house of its enemy, then it will be worse for its evil because
he [the native] will be sick, and injury and loss with respect to his
property will reach him, unless God wishes [otherwise].

10   If it is thus and it is Mars which governs the year, then his reasoning
and his thought will diminish, and his reasoning will drain off to the
right and left and various places, and some blood and iron and nose-
bleed will reach him, or [a defect] in [his] reasoning and his logic, and
sometimes the disease and injury will be difficult, or he will go on a
journey in which [there will be] no good and no profit, and he will be
11 in exile from his city. If Saturn is as I mentioned above the earth,
then it is bad with respect to [his] property and disease will reach him
in his body from cold, and pleurisy and injury, and his property will
diminish, and sometimes a sting will happen to him and also evil will
reach him from work in his hand[s], and frustration in everything,
12 and worry and grief and disease will reach him from his work. If it
is Jupiter, then he will have little greed for property, and his property will diminish without it being robbed and without his being pleased
p. 91 by it, | but so that he will be pleased or will have kindness from the
13 town of his fathers or from [his] children. If Venus is thus, then injury
14 will reach him from women, and quarrels and an ugly blemish. If
Mercury is governing the year and is under the Sun's light, then
injury will reach him from commerce or from an associate or from a
book and computation or from slaves, and his hope will be cut off
except for what God wills, and he will be told what he should not make,
and sometimes property and the good will be offered to him, but he
will not receive it.

15   Valens also said: Look at the planet which is the lord of that year;
if it is seen on the day on which the Sun enters the minute in which it
was on the day of the native's birth, then see at that hour in which
this degree rises what [is] the ascendent, which [is] the sign which
16 rises from the East. Look at where the Moon is and in which sign it is,
then know to how many [degrees] it is from that degree in which it
was on the day of the native's birth; then make that sign the ascendent of the year.

If the lord of this sign is Mars, the lord of the year, [and it is]   17
eastern, then the work which is in it he will quickly make a success of,
and the man will increase in [his] reasoning. If Saturn is lord of the   18
year and is eastern in its own light, then the native will be an owner
of land and crops and plants and everything new, and he will dig
canals and rivers. If it is Jupiter and it is in its own light, appearing   19
from under the rays [of the Sun and] eastern, then he will have a good
reputation among the nobles, and every work in his hand will be completed, and he will be exalted above the nobles, and if children are
judged for him, then they will inherit their fathers' property. If Venus   20
is the lord of the year [and is] eastern, then joy and marriage and good
will reach him on account of women. If it is Mercury [and it is] eastern   21
in a good place, then he will accumulate property and attain good
from wisdom and opinion and science and a good reputation, with the
help of God.

Now I will make clear to you [what happens] if the year reaches   22
where the planets were in the nativity. If the year reaches the sign   23
in which Saturn was and Saturn is in it or aspects it from trine or
quartile or the seventh, then the native will have a bad reputation,
and there will reach him folly and injury and hostility from men and
[his] city, and some of them the government will be angry at and
treat as an enemy. If the year reaches the cardine [under] the earth   24
or the cardine of the West and Saturn is in it or aspects it as I men-
tioned above, | then injury and hostility from men will reach him, and   p. 92
the evil will debilitate him; if this is [the situation] and Mars aspects
it also, then the evil will be worse, some cutting with iron will reach
him or strangulation or burning in fire or sweat and fever, if this is
necessary for him. If Jupiter aspects these malefics, then the disease   25
will be minimized. If the year reaches where Mars was and Mars is as   26
I told you in the case of Saturn, then some evil similar to what I said
above this will reach him. If the year reaches the place of Jupiter and   27
Jupiter is in it or aspects it as I mentioned above, then, if children
are necessary for him, then he will have a son-in-law as well and his
property will increase. If the year reaches the place of Mars and Mars   28
and Saturn aspect this sign, then calamity and grief will reach the
native in this year and he will be afraid of kings and their anger. If   29
the year reaches the place of a malefic which is in it or [if] another
malefic is in it, then he [the native] will not work at anything, but

will run away and will be discovered in a crime [leading] to exile and
30 haste [in departing]. If the year reaches where Venus was, then it is
not maleficent, but is beneficent, admirable, so that if he has attained
[the age of] marriage, he will marry and will have children, if [Venus]
31 is good in its position in the base[-nativity]. If the year reaches where
Mercury was and Mercury is good, then he will attain good, and
32 [children] will be born to him. If Saturn aspects it, then he will be
ashamed of his children and will grieve on account of [his] slaves, and
murder and grief will reach him.

33   If it reaches at the turning of the years the place in which the Moon
was and Saturn is aspecting it, then disease will reach this native and
34 his body will waste away. If Mercury is aspecting Saturn, then it will
be worse for him, his work will increase, and murder and sorrow and
35 disasters from the dead will reach him. If it reaches the ascendent at
the turning of the years and Jupiter and Venus aspect it, then good
and honor and joy and children will reach the native, and he will
36 marry a wife. If Saturn and Mars are aspecting, then his property and
37 his good will diminish, and he will grieve for his relatives. If at the
turning of the years it reaches the sign which was the fourth or the
seventh and Saturn is in it or aspects it from the fourth or the seventh,
then this is a difficult indication, and a severe pain or grief for [his]
38 property will reach him. If Mars is with it [Saturn], then it is worse,
blood and disasters from fire will reach him, and hot diseases will
reach him, and he will fall from a distant place, and he will not attain
39 good, or he will be like the form of a madman. If at the turning of the
years it reaches [what was] the tenth sign at the hour [in which] he
was born [and] ... is in it or aspects it, then every evil and misfortune
will reach this native and no good will reach him [save] from God.

40 | Look at that sign which it reaches at the turning of the years and
p. 93
41 the seventh sign from it, which of the seven [planets] aspects it. If
Saturn and Mars or one of the two is in the seventh, then there will
42 be no good in it. If Jupiter and Venus also are in it, then it will be
43 good [and] elevated. Similarly [in the case of] the months also, if the
malefics aspect them or are in them, then there is no good in it also.
44 If the benefics aspect them, then it diminishes from the evil of the
45 malefics. If the benefics are not aspecting, then the malefic will
destroy the mother of that native in that month.

46   Now I will make the matter of months clear to you so that you will

248

know them. If you want to know this, then mark off from the sign and   47
degree and minute in which the Moon was at the hour of the native's
birth, then subtract it from the ascendent; wherever the number is
used up, know which of the seven is the lord of that sign which you
have reached, and this planet will be the lord of the month at the
hour of the native's birth. If the lord of the month is in a good place,   48
rejoices in it, and is strong in its light, and was thus in the base-nativity, then it is good. If it was in a good place in the base-nativity but   49
is in a bad place when you look, then the matter of this native is
middling between this [and that]. If it was in a place without good in   50
the base-nativity and is in a place without good when you look, then
the maleficence is strong, there is no good in it; it will be worse for
this [native] if it is not visible in the East and is under the Sun's
light. If the Moon is the lord of the month, look at the Moon on what   51
side [of the ecliptic] it is. If it is ascending and increasing in counting,   52
then it is good, but if it is descending and decreasing in counting, then
its condition is middling between this [and that], but if it is in a decrease in light and is increasing in counting, then there is no good in
it, and it is worst for this [native] if it is increasing in light and decreasing in counting. Together with this look also at the planets; if   53
the Sun is lord of the month, then it is good if it is increasing with
regard to the length of daylight, but it is worse for this [native] if it
is decreasing from the length of daylight. It is necessary together with   54
this that you look at the witnesses of the planets.

If you want to know the ruler of the days, see where the Sun and   55
Moon are at the time for which you wish to know this, then count from
the Sun to the Moon, then cast it from that which was the ascendent |
at the hour of the native's birth. Wherever that number is used up,   p. 94
see which of the planets [is] the lord of that sign as it is the ruler of the   56
days. [With regard to] the days, it is also necessary for you to convert   57
all the years into days from the first day of the native's birth till the
day which you wish; you make each year three hundred and sixty-
five days and a fourth of a day, then subtract successive sevens, and
give each planet of the seven seven and begin from the planet which
was in the ascendent, then to the first which follows [it]. First you   58
subtract the number from forty-nine days so that what is left over is
less than forty-nine days, then give seven to the lord of the sign of life
[the ascendent], then seven to [the planet] which follows it until your

59 number of days is used up. Wherever the number of days is used up,
60 know which is that planet and in which sign the Moon is. If the Moon
   is in that sign which the days reached and a malefic was in that sign
   in the nativity, then disease and evil will reach them [the natives].
61 Similarly if the place is bad [and] if a malefic aspects it at that time
   or this is the sign in which Saturn or Mars was in the base-nativity
   and this sign is the house of [one of] the malefics but benefics aspect
62 it in transit, then his case will be middling. If this is reverse, then re-
63 verse it. Look at the Moon, which of the benefics and malefics aspects
64 it. If the planet which aspects the Moon is a benefic at the beginning
   of fifteen degrees [within its sign], then this day will be hard for the
   native, but on that night he will find rest and recovery in the morn-
   ing.

65, 66   Now I will make clear to you a section on chronic illness. Look at
   the sixth sign from [the sign of] life and know [whose] house it is of
   the seven, and look at the base of this sign — whether it is one of the
   human signs or one of the quadrupeds or the wild animal signs; then
   look at the lord of the sign and know what its base and nature are.
67 If the two [sign and lord] are bad together and their base is of moisture,
   then disasters will reach this native from pain due to moisture and
68 cold and pain in his joints, and a long-lasting pain will seize him. If the
   sign is the house of Mars, then a cutting with iron will reach him, and
   he will be burned in a fire, or dogs or lions will bite him, and some of
   them will be transfixed by a spear, and many disasters will reach him.
69 These are the disasters if this planet is shining [and] luminous, but
   if this is covered up under the Sun's light then pain or torment will
70 reach him, and his belly will be split, and he will die from this. It is
71 necessary that you know the place of that sign and its nature. If that
p. 95 sign is the house of Jupiter, then this | native [will be] one who loves
72 wine, these disasters will seize him, and his liver will swell. If this sign
   is the house of Venus, then the disasters will be from the love of women, their malady will seize him like the form of a madman, his reason
   and his [sense of] shame will depart in the search for women; it will
73 be worse for this [native] if Venus is in a masculine sign. If this sign
   is the house of Mercury, then the reputation of this native will be
   spoiled and his words, and he will not be about to speak except in
   misery, and his hearing will decrease, and wretchedness in his throat
74 will seize him. If this sign is the house of the Sun or the house of the

Moon or the house of Mars, then a chronic illness in his eyes will
reach him, and a pain in his heart will reach him from the Sun, and a
pain in his spleen will reach him from the Moon.

There were men among the ancient scientists who calculated by day 75
from Saturn to Mars and by night from Mars to Saturn, then they
cast their number from the ascendent; wherever their counting
reached or the number was used up, they saw what was the lord of that
sign, then they said to what limb of the body this sign belonged, then
they predicted that the chronic illness [would be] in such and such a
limb of the body according to what was named for that sign. Aries is 76
the head, Taurus the neck, Gemini the two shoulders, Cancer the two
hands and the chest, Leo the two sides and the heart, Virgo the belly
and the tube of the back [spine], Libra the bladder which is between
the two hips, Scorpio the male [organ] and the two testicles and the
buttocks, Sagittarius the two thighs together, Capricorn the two
knees, Aquarius the two shanks, [and] Pisces the two feet.

There were also some of the ancient scientists who looked at the 77
body of men from the Moon. They said: If the malefics are aspecting 78
the Moon from quartile or from the seventh — and they were looking
at life from the ascendent and Venus and Mercury (and the malefics
aspect them) and the nature of the place in which they are, if this sign
is one of the quadruped signs or one of the human signs or one of the
watery signs — and they were looking at this sign, to which of the
limbs of the body it belongs, so that they might say that the chronic
illness is in this limb of the body of men.

If you want to know whether this chronic illness will be on the right 79
side or on the left side, look from the tenth sign to the sign of life.
If any of the seven is in it, then the right side will be named, [but] if 80
there is none of the seven in it, then the left side will be named.

Look at the cardine, the fourth from the ascendent, and the lord 81
of its triplicity by day and the lord | of its triplicity by night, which p. 96
planet it is. Death is known from the first lord of its triplicity, chronic 82
illness from the second. Look at this planet and the lot of chronic 83
illness which I mentioned to you, [that] from Mars to Saturn. We 84
take this and we desire that you know it and tell it to whoever asks
you the true way of science.

The ancient scientists among the people of Babylon and Egypt, all 85
of them, said: if the Moon and the lot are in the eleventh from the

251

ascendent and Mars is in the second, then the body of this native will
86 be broken and his joints will waste away, all of them. If Saturn is in
the place of Mars, then this native will fall from a high, elevated
place; if this sign is one of the moist signs, then these disasters will be
87 from water, or some of the animals of the sea will devour him. If
the malefics are rising after the Sun and the Moon or the malefics
are with the Sun and the Moon or the malefics are greater in degrees
[within a sign] than the Sun and the Moon, ... , and it will be worse
for this [native] if it is Mars because nothing will cover up the evil of
88 Mars except God alone, the truth of the world. If Mars is in the second sign from the Sun's sign or from the Moon's sign, then disasters
will reach the native in his eye or his vision will depart, and it will be
worse for this if the Sun and the Moon are in the [sign of] life and the
89 malefics are setting after the Sun and the Moon. This will happen also
if the Sun and the Moon are in the West and you find the malefics in
the cardines, and it will be worse for this [native] if the fullness of the
90 Moon is like the Sun. As for the Moon, if the Sun is like this, then there
will be no good in it, but if Jupiter is aspecting the Sun, then it indi-
91 cates that this native will see a little with his eyes. If Saturn and Mars
are rising after the Sun and the Moon, and the Sun and the Moon are
in the seventh, then judge for this that chronic illness in his eyes will
92 reach this native. If the Moon is aspecting Mars from the seventh and
the Moon is full of light or Mars is rising after the Moon, then a chronic
93 illness in his eyes will reach this native. If Mars is with the Sun in the
seventh from the ascendent, which is the house of marriage, and Mars
94 is seen by Jupiter, then the state of the native will be thus. If Mars
is with the Sun in the [sign of] life, then a chronic illness in his eyes
95 will reach him. If the Sun and the Moon are in one of those places which
96 I mentioned, then the state of the native will be thus. If the Sun rises
after it [the Moon] or if the Sun is rising at the Moon's rising and Mars
is between the two of them, then the state of this native will also be
97 thus. If the Moon is with Saturn in Sagittarius, then a chronic illness in
98 his eyes will reach this native. | If also the Moon is in Sagittarius, but
p. 97 Saturn is aspecting it from the fourth or from the seventh, his state
will also be thus.

99   What is said in this is according to the calculation of the indication
100 of the base[-nativity], not of the transfer; so know this. If the year of
the nativity is transferred while the Moon is blockaded between the

two malefics, the native will dread this, but discomfort will not get
hold of him by the decree of God, and he will escape from the aggregate of ailments and misfortunes. I said that this is in the calcu-   101
lation of the indication of the base[-nativity]; know this if God wills.
If the malefics are aspecting the Sun and the Moon from the fourth or   102
the seventh, then a chronic illness in his eyes will reach him.

See if the nativity is by day while the Sun is bad, as then the   103
chronic illness will reach him in these —his right side and his right eye
and his right hand. If the nativity is by night while the Moon is in a   104
place that the malefics spoil, then the chronic illness will reach him in
these — the left side and the left eye and the left hand. If the Moon is   105
with the malefics because of which occurs the chronic illness or [if]
it is aspecting them from the fourth, then this native will not escape
from the chronic illness, neither because of the remedy of physicians
nor by asking God for health, so that he will die in his chronic illness.
Look at the twelfth portion [dodecatemorion] of the Sun and Moon.   106
If the malefics aspect it, then a chronic illness in his body will reach   107
this native.

The ancients among scientists wrote the judgment: If the Moon is   108
in [certain] signs and degrees and the malefics are aspecting it from the
fourth or the seventh, or the malefics are with the Moon, then this
native, will be blue in [his] eye, and there will be darkness in his eye or
his eye will be spoiled. The mane of the lion in Leo eighteen degrees,   109
the stinger of the scorpion in twenty-three degrees of Scorpio, the
face of the scorpion and its eyes in eight degrees and nine degrees and
ten degrees of Scorpio, the point of the arrow in three degrees of
Sagittarius, the Pleiades in six degrees up to the ninth degree of
Taurus, ... the ninth degree of Cancer. If the Moon is in one of these   110
places and the malefics are aspecting them while [the Moon] is
decreasing in light, then this native [will have] darkness in his eye. If   111
the Moon is full of light, then a chronic illness in his eye will reach this
native, but his eye will not be blinded.

If Mars is in the sign of life or in the seventh sign and the Moon is   112
aspecting Mars from the seventh (it is worse for this [native] if the
Moon is | decreasing in light), then this native will have little life and   p. 98
madness will seize him. If the Moon is in Taurus or a sign cut off at the   113
base while Mars [is] in a part [dodecatemorion?] of the house of life
aspecting it from the seventh, then one of the limbs of this native will

be cut off by iron so that that limb will be wretched because of it.
114 It will be thus also if Mars is within five signs from the [sign of] life
and the Moon is aspecting it from the seventh.

115　If Jupiter is in the seventh and the Moon is with Mars in the house
of life, then madness will seize this native and he will have no reason,
116 and he will not be aware of what he is doing. If Saturn is in the house
of life or in the tenth while the Moon is in the seventh, then also his
117 case will be thus; it will be worse for him if the Moon is with Mars. If
they are thus in that position and the benefics are rising after them,
then the benefics are spoiled in this [and] injured; that time is the
118 first day of the month when the new moon appears. If the Sun and
the Moon are in the same sign and Mars is between them while Saturn
is aspecting them and rising after them, then this native will not have
119 reason. If this is in the eighth sign, it will be worse for him. If the
120 benefics are aspecting them or rising after them, then he will escape
121 from this misfortune. If the Moon and Jupiter are in the house of life
and Mars is aspecting them from the seventh, then this native will
not have reason.

122　If the Moon is under the Sun's light or is decreasing in light and is
leaving the malefics while these malefics are in the cardines, then this
native will have no strength and no power, and he will be emaciated
[and] sick; it will be worse for this [native] if the other malefics are
123 aspecting the Moon. If the Moon is leaving Saturn, then a pain in the
belly will seize him, and his belly will defecate, and a pain of coldness
will seize him, and his pain will last a long time, and a pain in the
spleen will seize some of them, and he will ask for a drink, and his belly
124 will be split open, and a cough will seize him. If the Moon is leaving
Mars, then a pain of the blood will seize him in [his] belly but the medi-
125 cine of doctors will help him. If this native is a girl, then all of these
diseases will seize her and together with all these diseases other
diseases will reach her because her belly will swell up and her child
will not live, but her child will be cut off in her belly but she will
126 keep the black bile. If the Moon is leaving the benefics [and] then
conjoining with the malefics within the thirty degrees of the sign in
which it is, then this native will be healthy for half his life, then after
this he will swell up and diseases will seize him from which he will
not escape.

p. 99
127　| If Saturn and Mars are in the second sign and are aspecting the

Moon while Jupiter is not aspecting the Moon, then every misery will
reach this native in his body. If Saturn is aspecting Mercury, then he   128
will be dumb, one who has lost [his] reason, and he will not be able
to speak, or he will be stammering, not speaking except with difficulty. If Saturn and Venus are in the tenth and the Moon is in the   129
tenth and Mars is aspecting them, then this native will not be able to
have intercourse with women and will be a vicious man. If the native   130
is a girl, then she will not marry and will have no children. If Mars and   131
Saturn are aspecting Venus and the Moon, then the male [organ] of
this native and his testicles will be cut off with iron. If this native is   132
a girl, then she will be barren [and] will not give birth; it will be worse
for this [native] if the two [malefics] are in the sixth and twelfth
sign from the [sign of] life. If Jupiter is aspecting these two, then he   133
will be one who does the work of God in worship, a prayer-leader in a
mosque or the like, and his livelihood will be from this. If Jupiter is   134
in the place of Venus or Mercury is in [one of] the houses of these two
or Mercury is with Jupiter (it is worse for this [native] if the two are
in a sign possessing two bodies and the malefics are aspecting them),
then this native will be effeminate, and this, that the native will be
named Mercury or with the name of the Moon. If the Moon is in thirty   135
degrees of the sign in which it is and Saturn is aspecting the Moon from
the fourth, then this native will be a midget, the shortest of all men.
If Saturn and Mars are in the same sign and the Moon is between   136
them, then this native will be a leper, and scabies and itching will
seize him. If the Moon is in Aries or in Taurus and Saturn and Mars   137
are with it, then leprosy and erysipelas will seize him, and his body
will swell up.

Look with your intellect and your heart at that planet, if [the   138
illness] is from it and it is on the side of the East, then that chronic
illness will be at the beginning of his life. If it is in the South, then   139
that chronic illness will be in the middle of his life. If it is in the   140
North, then that chronic illness will be in his old age. Look at that   141
planet, whether it is seen in the East or in the West. If it is seen in the   142
East, then it is worse; if it is seen in the West, it is more ideal and it
will be good if he is treated in his youth.

Now I will make clear to you the matter of death. Many men of the   143
                                                                                 144
learned have spoken regarding death; some of them look at the base
of the eighth sign from the [sign of] life so that they may see what is

the base of this sign and its nature and know whether it is one of the
p. 100 watery signs | or one of the dry signs or one of the human signs or one
145 of the quadruped signs or one of the wild animal signs. They look at
the lord of the eighth sign, what it is and which of the seven aspects
146 the eighth sign. If the lord of the eighth sign is Saturn and Saturn is
in the place of the West, then they asserted a judgment for him that
147 this native will die in other than his own land. If Saturn is in a moist
place, they said that this native will die in the water or the belly of a
148 sea monster or a fish. If the sign in which Saturn is is one of the earthy
149 signs, then the native will die at the peak of a mountain. If the Sun is
with Saturn, they said that this native will fall from a high place and
150 will die. If the lord of the eighth sign is Mars, then thieves will fall
upon this native and kill [him] or [his] enemies will kill him in a fight
or he will burn in a fire or an animal from among the earthy animals
151 will bite him or lions will devour him. If the Sun is with Mars, then
this will reach him from the anger of kings or the anger of a great man
so that he will be killed or crucified on a post, or his middle will be cut
with a sword, or a lion and a tiger will slay him, or animals or hogs
152 will vie [with him]. If the lord of this eighth sign is not in its place,
153 then he will die in exile from his land. If the lord of the eighth sign is
in its place, then this native will die because of women or by means
154 of poison and drinking a drug. If Mercury is the lord of the eighth
155 sign, then he will die from the anger of kings. If the malefics are
aspecting from the eighth and the lord of the eighth is corrupted with
no good in it and the lord of the eighth is not in its own place, then this
156 native will die on a journey. If the lord of the eighth is in its own place,
then this native will die in his own land and in his place and among his
157 people. If this eighth place and its lord are benefic [and] are corrupted, then the death of this native will also be thus, but his death will
be better for him.

158   Also there were some of those learned in the stars who counted
from the Moon to the eighth, then cast it out from Saturn; wherever
it reached, they looked at that sign, which it was and which [planet]
was the lord of that sign, [and] then they judged good or evil for him.
159 Some of them looked at that planet which reached to the degree of the
seventh, and not in the casting [of rays], but they saw which of the
two would be more quickly cadent in the West so that from that one
160 they might judge death for him, if God wills. Some of them calculate

the seventh sign and the lord of its triplicity [and] then judge death
for him. If Mars stands in the seventh and Mars is the lord of the
seventh, then the neck of this native | will be struck by a sword. If
Mars is under the Sun's light, then this pain will strike this native in
another limb of his body. If the Moon is standing in the seventh, then
this native will die by fire. If the seventh and its lord are malefic and
the lord of the seventh is aspecting the house of life and the Moon is
aspecting the house of life, then this native will kill himself with his
own hand.

161
p. 101
162

163
164

    If Mars is in the tenth but not in the cardines while the Moon is in
a cardine, the seventh, and the malefics aspect the Moon, then enemies and thieves will kill this native. If the malefics are rising after
the seventh sign or are aspecting it from the seventh (it will be worse
for this [native] if the malefics are in cardines), then this native will
die a difficult death.

165

166

    There were some of the learned in stars who looked at the cardine,
the fourth, and at the lords of its triplicity as I wrote for you above
this. The first of the lords of the triplicity indicates death and the
second indicates chronic illness. When the two are together in a place
in which [there is] no good, then judge for him with your intellect at
the native's birth that he will die a difficult death. If the first lord of
the triplicity is in the fourth or in the seventh, then this native will
die and not one of men will appear to him, and they will not know
how he died, and they said that this man will be named as a messenger.
If that [planet] from which is the chronic illness is in the seventh, then
this native will be chronically ill [and] miserable; if it is aspecting the
house of life, it will be worse for him. If the lord of the seventh sign
is a malefic and is under the Sun's light, then this native will die from
[his] slaves or from a matter which no one knows. If this planet is seen
in the East, then this native will die publicly, but if it is retrograde,
then this native will die from a drug in which [there is] no good, and
his suffering will be prolonged.

167

168
169

170

171

172

173

    Look at the nature of the sign as, if it is one of the human signs, then
he will die because of men, and if it is one of the watery signs, then he
will die because of water, and if it is one of the quadruped signs, then
he will die because of quadrupeds or lions will eat him. If the malefics
are with the Moon or the other malefics are aspecting the Moon from
the seventh, then he will die from surgery. If the Moon is in a new sign

174

175

176

when it shines from the Sun and... is aspecting the Sun from the fourth
or the seventh but not aspecting the Moon, then this native will kill
177 himself. If the Sun is eclipsed in the seventh sign or the Moon is pass-
p. 102 ing from a degree which aspects | the degree in which the Sun is,
then this native will die in fire or in water, and many people will die
with him.

178   Look at the nature of this sign, and if the lord of the seventh is in
a place in which [there is] no good or is in the tenth while the malefics
are with the Moon, then this native will fall from a high place and will
179 die from it. If the lord of the lot of the seventh is with the lot of luck
and the malefics are determinative, then he will die because of his
180 friends. If Venus is in the seventh house and the Moon is in a house
strange to it and the malefics are with it, then the death of this native
will be because of a woman who has had many husbands, [but] then they
181 died. If Jupiter is like Venus, then he will die because of [his] children
or from his good name and good reputation which they will be en-
182 vious of. If Mars is like Venus, then [he will die] because of his broth-
183 ers. If it is the Sun, then he will die because of his mother and his
184 ancestors. If the Moon is like Venus, then he will die because of his
mother and his father's wife.

185   Now I will also make clear to you the transfer of some of the seven
186 to the places of the others. As each planet of the seven reaches the
place which it aspected from the seventh on the day on which that
187 native was born, then it is difficult in its maleficence. If it reaches
that place which it had reached on the day of the native's birth, it
188 also is malefic. It is worse for this [native] and more difficult in its
maleficence if Mars is reaching the place in which Jupiter or the Sun
was by day, or [if] Saturn is reaching the place in which the Moon was
189 by night. It is worse for this [native] if a malefic is in it as disasters
190 will reach this native in his body and quarrels with his father. If
Saturn or Mars is in the triplicity of that sign in which it was on the
day of the native's birth, then it will be more perfect than that if
191 they are both in the fourth or the seventh. If the malefics are in right
quartile, then [there will be] no good in it, but if the benefics are, then
192 it will be good [and] his face will be clear. If the benefics are in their
193 triplicities, then this native will attain good. If the malefics are in
their triplicities, then it will harm this native because the lord of the
triplicity [being] Mars by day and Saturn by night is the worst of

what might be; it is worse for this [native] if the two in the base-
nativity were in a place in which [there is] no good. If the native passes   194
thirty years, then it will diminish from the disasters of Saturn, or
around [that] year. If Saturn and Mars are rising after cardines, then   195
also quarrels and misery will reach this native. If in the base-nativ-   196
ity Saturn and Mars were in their places in which [there is] no good,
so [if] at the turning of the years the benefics also are in a place in
which [there is] no good, then it will diminish from that good which
belonged to this native in that year.

| If the Moon reaches its own place in the turning of the years, then   p. 103
this native will be cheerful and will rejoice. If the Moon is with Venus   197
198
and Jupiter, then this native will rejoice and will be cheerful. If the   199
Moon reaches the Sun's place in the turning of the years, then it will
be good in what belongs to the native after his day [?]. If the Moon   200
reaches Mars' place, unless the benefics are aspecting the Moon, then
disasters will immediately reach this native. If the Moon reaches Mars'   201
place or the Sun's place while the Sun or Mars is in the place [in
which it was] on the day of the native's birth, then the blood will be
expelled from this native's body. If the Moon reaches Venus' place   202
and the malefics are not with the Moon, then in that year this native's
property will be wasted in fornication, and he will disgrace himself,
and he will be greedy, [and] people will know about him. If Saturn   203
is with the Moon, then cold will seize this native in this year. If Saturn   204
reaches the place in which it was in the turning of the years, then good
will reach this native. If the Moon reaches Mercury's place in the turn-   205
ing of the years, then this native will do some work in accordance
with the nature of Mercury. If the Moon reaches the house of life, then   206
the life of this native will be spoiled. If the Moon reaches the cardine,   207
the tenth, then the work of this native in this year will be publicly in
accordance with the aspect of the benefics or the malefics. If it   208
reaches the cardine, the seventh, then the native will prosper and
triumph over his enemies and obtain his income. If the Moon reaches   209
the cardine, the fourth, in the turning of the years, [it will be] concerning a secret matter which he will conceal and keep quiet about,
but if this native talks himself into [making] a will, then it will be
good.

If Saturn and Mars reach Jupiter's place in the turning of the years,   210
then these two spoil the goodness of Jupiter. If Saturn and Mars reach   211

the place of Venus and Mercury in the turning of the years, then these
212 two diminish from their good. If Saturn reaches Mars' place in the
turning of the years, then it will spoil the native's heart and it will
spoil him, and he himself will be wicked.

213   If Mars reaches Saturn's place in the turning of the years, then it
will ameliorate the soul of the native and make it firm and render
214 [him] victorious over his enemies. If Mars reaches Venus' or Jupiter's
place in the turning of the years, then it will take away all the native's
215 good in that year. If Mars is under the Sun's light, then fever and a
hot temperature and a hot pain will seize this native in this year, and
it will destroy his reason; if the father of the native is alive, then
grief will reach this native because of his father and his state with
216 regard to work and the authority of kings will be spoiled. If Mars
p. 104 reaches the Moon's place in | the turning of the years, then a pain
will reach this native in his body, then afterwards he will use his
intellect and be victorious over his enemies [with] trouble and difficulty.

217   If Jupiter reaches Saturn's place in the turning of the years, then
it will remove the corruption of Saturn in that year, and he will attain
218 property and good. If Jupiter reaches Mars' place in the turning of
the years, then good will increase with regard to the native's properties and he will be victorious over his enemies in that year; it will
219 also be thus if Mars reaches Saturn's place. If [Jupiter] reaches ...

220   If Venus reaches Jupiter's place in the turning of the years, then
[he will have] no good in the case of women, [and] grief and quarrels
221 will reach the native in this year. If Venus reaches Mars' place in the
turning of the years, then the native will leave him in anger and will
222 not look at anyone. If Venus reaches Mercury's place in the turning of
223 the years, then it will increase the native's work. If Venus reaches the
Moon's place in the turning of the years, then he will be good in [his]
work, but a bad reputation in the matter of women will be spread
224 against him. If Venus reaches the Sun's place, then it will spoil the
life of that native and disasters will reach him because of women.

225   If Mercury reaches the benefics' place[s], then it will be good; if it
226 reaches the malefics' place[s], then [there will be] no good in it. If
neither the benefics nor the malefics aspect it, then this native will
not be good in his work, but he will remove grief and hardship from
227 himself. If Mercury reaches Jupiter's place, then he will be good in all
260

work; it will be better for this [native] if this native desires entry to
[the palaces of] kings. If Mercury reaches Mars' place, then this na-   228
tive's heart will be strong in every falsehood. If Mars reaches Mer-   229
cury's place in the turning of the years, then this native will worry and
will persuade himself of what has no good in it, and he will treat his
friends as enemies, and his opinion of them will be low, and their
slaves will scorn some of them, and disaster will reach him in his property. If Mercury reaches Venus' place, then his work will be good and   230
he will attain good. If Mercury reaches the Moon's place, then the   231
body of this native will be cured and the pain in his joints will depart.
If the Sun and the Moon are in the malefics' places, then [there will   232
be] no good in it. If the malefics are in the cardines, then [there   233
will be] no good in it.

Now I will make clear to you the matter of the cardines. Look con-   234
cerning these four cardines: the appraisal of the native is known from   235
the ascendent which is the first cardine, the matter of children and of
work is known from the tenth, the matter of women and of marriage
is known from the cardine, the seventh, the matter of old age and of
the end of life is known from the cardine, the fourth, and the matter
of body and of property is known from the prorogation of the degrees
and [their] varieties. Look at the cardines because the ascendent gives   236
the matter of youth, from that place at which the Sun rises from the
water, and the darkness in their eyes is raised up | for the people of   p. 105
the world, and sheds light on the eyes of the messengers who sent them
forth to creation. After youth look at the cardine, the tenth, and its   237
gift [lasts] until the body of this native becomes warm and hair grows
on his pubic area and he loves sexual intercourse. From the cardine,   238
the seventh, will be the gift of old age, and it will diminish the strength
of this native for sexual intercourse [so that] the native will be insignificant in this, and the Sun sets and darkens [their] eyes. From the   239
cardine, the fourth, is known the gift of death. If the planets are lu-   240
minous in these four cardines, then this native will attain good; if
they are darkened, then [there will be] no good in it.

The fourth book of Dorotheus on the revolution of the years of the
nativity is completed by the praise and grace of God.

The fifth book, about interrogations, follows it.

V 1

The fifth book of Dorotheus, on interrogations.

In the name of God, the compassionate, the merciful; where is my success save in almighty God?

V-1
1, 2
This is the book of Dorotheus, King of Egypt. There are five books; he wrote four of them on nativities in which he mentioned every good and evil, and misery or happiness that men may attain from the beginning of their situation till its end, and he wrote one of them about the matter of commencements, and it is this book, which is called the fifth book, in which he mentioned the condition of every action which is begun, whether its limit is determined or it is not determined where the beginning of this action or its middle or its end will end up and

3 what of good or evil will happen in it. He says in his book that he is following the tracks of the learned men who practised from among the learned of Babylon and Egypt since they were the first who looked concerning the science of the stars and their calculation and the revolution of the sphere and the motions of the seven stars and the rising-times of the twelve signs so that he might extract this from their books, then give this to himself as an example in his following [them].

4 He says that, wherever he looked concerning what they dealt with and arranged of the science of the stars, he followed the best of their science and acquired it and explained it and collected it and extracted it from their books as he made it an example for himself in his following their tracks, and he made it this book like a bee when it follows the most delicious of fruits, and the best of it is made into honey; then he began to write for this book a comprehensive introduction in which he mentions the power of the seven and the twelve, and their soundness and their corruption.

5 He said: look concerning the commencing of each matter you desire at the straight in rising from among the signs and the crooked, and the tropical and the twin from among them, and at the position of the star which is in the ascendent in the commencement of each action,

6 [to see whether] its end will be good or bad. It is necessary if you commence [something] to know what is the nature of the signs straight

7 in rising and crooked. I shall make clear to you [those] of them that

8 are straight and crooked. The straight among them are Cancer, Leo, Virgo, Libra, Scorpio, and Sagittarius because each one of these six

262

rises in two hours and a part of an hour of the equinoctial hours, which
are the hours [of the nychthemeron] in which the night and the day
are equal; the length of each of these hours is fifteen [equatorial]
degrees. The crooked among them are Capricorn, Aquarius, Pisces,   9
Aries, Taurus, and Gemini, because each one of these six rises in less
than two hours of the equinoctial hours.

| Chapter 2. Judgment according to the crooked and the straight.   p. 107 V-2

Look concerning each commencement there is to the sign which is   1
rising at that hour, whether it is one of the straight in rising or one of
the crooked. If it is one of the straight in rising, then this action will be 2
difficult [and] slow, in which there will be misery and misfortune and
trouble. Then look at the positions of the seven in the places because if   3
one commences an action while the ascendent is one of the crooked
signs and any one of the benefics is in it or any of them aspects the
ascendent, it will remove the burden and help bring this action to a
successful conclusion, if God wills. If the ascendent is one of the signs   4
straight in rising and there happens to be in it any one of the malefics
or they aspect it, slowness occurs in this action and trouble and pain.
If you find the benefics and the malefics together in the ascendent or   5
they aspect the ascendent, then know that this action will be middling with a mixture of good and evil in it.

Chapter 3. Judgment according to the tropical [signs].   V-3

If you find the ascendent to be a tropical sign, then it indicates the
breaking off of the end of this action before it is finished, and it indicates that he will commence this action a second time.

Chapter 4. Judgment according to the twin [signs].   V-4

If you find the ascendent to be a twin sign, then it indicates that   1
that action which he commences at that hour will not be finished until an action other than this occurs in it, and it [the second action]
will be finished before the first action is finished; it happens thus in
every action in which the ascendent is a twin sign.

Look at the diurnal and nocturnal signs; I will make clear to you   2
the diurnal among them and the nocturnal. The diurnal among them: 3
Aries and its triplicity, Leo and Sagittarius, are diurnal, and Gemini

4 and its triplicity, Libra and Aquarius, are diurnal. The nocturnal:
Taurus and its triplicity, Virgo and Capricorn, are nocturnal, and
Cancer and its triplicity, Scorpio and Pisces, are nocturnal.

5   If one commences an action by day, then the strongest of what is
[possible] is if the ascendent is diurnal and the Moon is in a diurnal
sign, and [if] it is by night [if] the ascendent is a nocturnal sign and the
Moon is in a nocturnal sign because this is what is best in calculation,
especially in that [one] who desires a journey or desires to board a
p. 108 ship as this commencement | will be easy, fortunate, convenient, if
God — be He exalted! — wishes.

V-5   **Chapter 5. The corruption of the Moon.**

1   Then he mentioned the condition of the Moon and its corruption in
which a commencement is not to be made in an action or anything
when you find this until the condition of the Moon and its lord is
2 ameliorated. I will make clear to you its corruption if it is eclipsed,
and worse than this if its eclipse is in the sign in which the Moon was
at the birth of this native or its eclipse is in trine of the sign in which
3 the Moon was when this native was born. If the Moon is under the
Sun's rays [and] its light is destroyed and it is not seen, then it is corrupted but it is beneficial for one who desires theft or treachery or
something which is kept secret against him, and for every hidden or
secret action which its master does not wish to be made public.

4   If it is an action which its master wishes to keep secret, commence it
when the Moon is immersed under the Sun's rays as there is good for
him, and it will be more concealed if he commences it at the withdrawal of the Moon from the Sun and [its] appearance from under the
5 rays. If the Moon is in the dodecatemoria of Mars or Saturn and if the
Moon is in the middle of the equator descending towards the South and
if the Moon is in opposition to the Sun, then it is bad and it indicates
the accession of quarrels and that the younger of the two will be the
6 winning antagonist. If the Moon is with a malefic or aspecting it and
if there is withdrawal of the Moon from the Sun in longitude and latitude and if the Moon is in its least motion, that is if it is decreasing in
its counting and its motion in a day and a night is less than twelve
7 degrees, then this motion of it is like the motion of Saturn. If it is
thus, then in the action which he commences at that hour will occur
8 difficulty and slowness. If the Moon in its motion is in the path which

the learned call "the burned path" (the burned path is the middle of
the equator, which is Libra and Scorpio) and if the Moon is in the last
degrees of a sign, then it is according to this in the term of Saturn or
Mars, and none of the terms which are at the end of the signs are
harder than the terms of these two. If the Moon is cadent toward the 9
ninth from the cardine [which is] the house of government [the tenth]
and it happens to be in a double place, then the action which he
commences at that hour will be nullified and will not remain in one
condition, and a transformation and disturbance will occur in it.

| Understand when you think about what I wrote for you of the 10
p. 109
corruption of the Moon and do not commence anything in it as the
matter will stop for which it is not fated that it linger on till the condition of the Moon is ameliorated. Let Jupiter or Venus be in the 11
ascendent or in the house of government [the tenth]. Look concerning 12
the condition of [these] stars and their positions as, if they happen to
be under the [Sun's] rays or are retrograde in their motion or happen
to be in a bad place that is double, which is when it is cadent from a
cardine, then they will not have much power. If any of the malefics is 13
with them in one degree, or they aspect it from trine or quartile or
sextile or are with it in one sign, then it indicates that this action will
have no strength. If the planets are in the signs which the learned 14
call "the dark", then they will have no power, nor will their rays if
they are thus.

Look concerning the totality of every commencement in the manner 15
of Valens the Philosopher; then take into consideration his words as
he was making a brilliant [and] learned investigation concerning
[these] matters. He said: Look concerning the commencement of 16
each action at the Sun and the Moon and the lord[s] of the two signs
in which the two luminaries are, and together with this look at the
ascendent and midheaven. Commence the commencement and action 17
when the Moon is in the ascendent or midheaven or another of the
cardines; and [if] the lord of the Moon's sign happens to be in a double
place or cadent, withdrawing from a cardine, then the beginning of
this action will be good but its end bad [and] from this calamity will
befall him and whatever he doesn't desire. The Moon is the indicator 18
of the base of every action and the lord of the sign in which the Moon
is is the indicator of its end. If you find the lord of the Moon in a good 19
place while the Moon is in a bad place, then the commencement of

that action is bad but its end is good [and] he will benefit by it, if God
20 — be He exalted! — wishes. If you find the lord of the Moon in a strong
place and the Moon in a double place, then it indicates that the beginning of this action will be difficult [and] slow, with no good in it,
21 but [its] end will be good [and] it will come to him as he wishes. If the
Moon and its lord happen to be in a strong place, then it indicates
that the beginning of that action and its end will happen according to
22 what he desires. If the Moon and its lord happen to be in a double
place, then the beginning of this action will be bad and its end worse
23 than the beginning. If the lord of the Moon happens to be in [one of]
the signs which follow the cadents, which are difficult, then it indicates that that action which he commences will have a delay in its
beginning and slowness in its end.

24, 25 	Look at which of the stars the Moon is flowing [from]. If you find
it flowing from the benefics, then it is good for every action which he
commences except for one who wishes to flee from the government or
p. 110 from his land and a fugitive from | his master as the condition of
these is the best of what is [possible] if the flowing of the Moon at
that hour is from the malefics, and nothing more suitable is fated for
26 them. Together with this look at the lord of the navamsa and at [the
planet] which the Moon conjoins with as the consideration concerning
the commencement of a matter in this way and its end is not correct
until you look concerning its commencement at the lord of the lot of
fortune and [concerning] its end at [the planet] with which the Moon
27 conjoins. This section is described in the chapter in which he mentions
the matter of flight and theft.

28 	He said: Look at the Moon and the lord of the house in which it is
and the star with which the Moon conjoins and how you find the
position of the Moon and of the star with which it conjoins and the
power of these two in the cardines as these two are the indicators of
29 this. If the Moon is with two malefics in one sign and the Moon is
immersed between the two in this sign while the benefics aspect it
from quartile, then the misfortune and misery in which men suffer
30 at that hour they will escape from and get rid of. If the Moon happens
to be positioned [where] the lords of its triplicity are benefics, and
none of the malefics is in opposition to the Moon, and benefics and
malefics aspect it from quartile, then it indicates that they will escape
from what happens in it, but they will fall in a second misfortune be-

fore they get rid of their first misfortune, [and] then they will escape
if God — be He exalted! — wishes. If you find the Moon in trine of   31
the benefics while the malefics aspect it from quartile, then it indicates the like.

Look concerning the commencement of every matter at the ascen-   32
dent and the Moon. The Moon is the strongest of what is [possible] if   33
it is above the earth, especially if this is at night; the ascendent is the
strongest of what is [possible] if the Moon is under the earth by day.
This is what he says in the introduction of his book, then he writes   34
for each action which people commence a chapter commensurate with
it in which [are recorded] the power of the seven and the twelve and
on which day and hour the master of that action because of the seven
and the twelve must commence each action.

Chapter 6. One who wishes to build a building.   V-6

It is best to lay the foundations of a building if you build it when the   1
Moon is increasing in computation and in light and is in the middle of
the zone which is the equator, ascending toward the North while
Jupiter or Venus is with the Moon or aspects the Moon from a strong
place. If Saturn is with the Moon or aspects it from a strong place,   2
there occurs in this work difficulty and dissension and slowness or | p. 111
trouble and misery. If Mars is with the Moon or aspects it from a   3
strong place, then a conflagration or injury from fire will reach that
building.

Chapter 7. If you wish to demolish a building.   V-7

It is necessary that you begin this when the Moon is leaving its   1
elevation, descending towards [its] low point. It is necessary concern-   2
ing this situation also to look at the strength of the benefics and
malefics as the benefics indicate ease and success while the malefics
indicate slowness and difficulty and misery.

Chapter 8.   V-8

If you want to hire something or let out for rent some cultivated   1
land or trees or vineyards or houses or anything like that, then the
ascendent indicates the condition [in] which you will hire these things
or take them for rent, and the seventh sign indicates the owner of
these things, and the tenth sign indicates the rent and the price, and

the house of fathers [the fourth] indicates the outcome of this action.
2 If you find any of the malefics in the ascendent, then he who desires
to hire these things or take them for rent will withdraw from that and
3 take none of them. If he does hire them or enters in one of them, then
whatever he enters he will deceive him [the owner], desiring that sin
4 and debauchery occur in it. If you find any of the malefics in the seventh place or aspecting the seventh place, then the owner of these
things will withdraw from that and will not let out any of them for
5 rent or a price. If he does do it, there will occur debauchery or pro-
6 stitution and deception in it. If you find malefics in the tenth sign or
aspecting it, this matter will not be proper, but there will be a pile of
7 coins in the rent. If you find malefics in the fourth place or aspecting it,
then, even if this matter is proper, its outcome will be bad [and] from
8 this there will occur in it misery and what is not desired. The flowing
away of the Moon and its conjunction indicate these things [also].

V-9   **Chapter 9. Buying and selling.**

1   If you want to sell something or to buy it, then look at the position
of the Moon as the star with which the Moon conjoins indicates the
buyer and the price, and the star from which the Moon flows indicates
p. 112 the seller, and [the Moon] indicates | the commodity which you sell or
2 buy. So look at the Moon and at the star from which the Moon flows
3 or with which it conjoins. If you find the malefics with the Moon or
with the star from which the Moon flows or [with which] it conjoins,
or [if] the malefics aspect it, then it indicates that misfortune or
misery occurs in the matter which is attributed to the Moon or to that
4 star from which the Moon flows or with which it conjoins. If the benefics happen to be in one of these positions, then joy and happiness
and success in [his] desire occur to the master of that action which is
attributed to this star or to the Moon, if God wishes.

5   I will make clear to you this subject also from the four cardines,
6 and I will explain it to you. The ascendent indicates him who buys,
the seventh him who sells, and the tenth indicates the price, and the
house of the fathers [the fourth] indicates the commodity which is
7 sold or bought. Look in these places according to what I wrote for you
in the matter of the Moon in the first section as whenever the benefics
and malefics happen to be [in it] or aspect it, there will occur loss or
gain in the matter which is attributed to this cardine.

Chapter 10. The buying of land.

If you desire to buy land, then look at the condition of this land from 1
the house of the fathers [the fourth], and from the house of the government, which is the tenth, at what is in this land of trees, and from
the seventh at what is in this land of grass or herbs or plants, and
from the ascendent [at] the cultivation of this land. If the house of the 2
fathers [the fourth] is one of the watery signs, then it indicates that
this land is near a river or on the sea or in a place abounding in water;
if it is a twin sign, then it indicates that this land is not in one direction, but
from it the condition.... Look with regard to the rest of these 3
cardines according to what I wrote for you of the strength of the malefics and benefics.

Chapter 11. The buying of slaves.

If you want to buy a slave, then, if the Moon is in Aries, it indicates 1
that this slave will be a runaway and will not get used to [his] station
and will be incompatible with his master. If the Moon is in Taurus, 2
then the slave which is bought will be a worker, patient, strong, ob-
edient, sticking to the work of a slave | with his whole self, a humble p. 113
man. He will also be thus if the Moon is in the last degrees of Gemini. 3
If the Moon is in Cancer when you buy a slave, then he will be weak, 4
lazy, unreliable, [and] putrid [?]. If the Moon is in Leo, then the 5
slave which is bought will be a master, trained for [his] craft, educated,
good in the goodness of his upbringing, except that he will be wrath-
ful, abounding in food, and he will be frivolous and a pain in [his]
belly and stomach will not cease happening to him because of this,
and he will be an embezzler of things. If the Moon is in Virgo, then 6
the slave which is bought will be uncommon, a custodian, a worker,
a sincere adviser to his master. If the Moon is in Libra, then the slave 7
which is bought will be dedicated to his work, knowledgeable in the
work, a legist with respect to religion and quarrels. If the Moon is in 8
Scorpio, then the slave which is bought will be a thief [and] a runaway.
If it is in Sagittarius, then, as for the slave which is bought, the basis 9
for buying him will not be good, but he will be a master in whom
[there is] vanity and admiration for himself. If the Moon is in Capri- 10
corn, then the slave which is bought will be a liar and will not cease
himself changing over from [one] situation to [another] situation, and
there will be some of them who will make a habit of running away. If 11

the Moon is in Aquarius; then the slave which is bought will be a lover of work, a good man, and this is because Aquarius is in the figure of a

12 man. If the Moon is in Pisces, then the slave which is bought will be a slanderer and will conceal in himself disloyalty to his master and ca-

13 lumny to him. If the ascendent at the buying of the slaves is one of the signs in which I wrote of the location of the Moon, then it will indicate

14 like this. This is what the ascendent or the Moon indicates when neither benefics nor malefics aspect the Moon or the ascendent or are

15 with them in a sign. Look concerning the condition of the seven and their power as they are far stronger than the signs.

V-12   **Chapter 12. The buying of animals.**

1   If you want to buy an animal, then look; and if the animal is tamed
2 and used, then buy it at the hour in which the ascendent is Aries. If
3 it is obedient, if the Moon is in Aries also, then it is better. If the
4 ascendent is Taurus and the Moon is in it, then it is good. If the animal is not tamed and not used, then buy it at an hour when the ascendent is in the last degree[s] of Leo while the Moon is in it, or in the last degrees of Sagittarius while the Moon is in it.

V-13
p. 114   **| Chapter 13. If you want to free a slave.**

1   Look before everything at the condition of the Moon and its lo-
2 cation in the places which I made clear to you. If you find it free of the misfortunes which I wrote of in the beginning of my book, then it
3 will be good. Then look also at the conjunction of the Moon and its flowing away as, if you free [a slave] at an hour when the Moon is flowing from the benefics and conjoining with the malefics, then the slavery in which this slave is is better for the slave than the freeing
4 which happens to him. If it is different from what I mentioned, then be concerned differently from this; if you find the Moon flowing from the malefics and conjoining with the benefics, then it will be good for that slave as they will escape from evil and misfortune and will meet with good and joy.

5, 6   Look concerning this matter from the four cardines also. The ascen- dent indicates the master of the slave, the seventh indicates the slave who is freed, the house of the government [the tenth] indicates the reason for which the slave is freed, and the house of the fathers [the
7 fourth] indicates the outcome of the matter. Look, and if the Moon is

in the seventh place with the malefics, then it indicates that this slave, even if he has escaped from slavery, will return into it. See from the rest of the cardines the condition of what is attributed to each one of them according to what I wrote for you, if God—be He exalted!— wishes.

8

Chapter 14. If you want to ask from a ruler or from a man for a request or a gift or other than this.

V-14

Ask for this when the Moon is in the ascendent or in quartile to the ascendent or in trine to it while the Moon is increasing in computation and in light or the lord of the ascendent is direct in [its] motion [and] not retrograde and is with the Moon in one sign and the Moon conjoins it. It will be better if the Moon is in its house or aspecting its house while Mercury is with Jupiter. If you ask for a request when Mercury is with Saturn or it aspects it from a strong place, then he will neither grant nor confer that request. If you ask for the request when Mercury is with Venus and his desire is in front of women and is something pleasing him and he is amused by it, then he will grant [it] in this. If the request and desire are in front of kings and nobles of men and leaders, then you will be disappointed if you ask for this at an hour when Jupiter is retrograde or at an hour when Saturn aspects Jupiter. If the request is in front of traders or in front of scientists and people of culture | and masters of calculation, then ask for this at an hour in which Mercury is strong. If the request is in front of a man having years or a man with no children or a man caught in a crime or in front of slaves, then ask for this in an hour in which Saturn is strong.

1

2
3

4

5

6

p. 115

7

Chapter 15. If you want to write to a man or you want to teach a man a science or writing.

V-15

Let this be when Mercury is with the Moon and none of the malefics is with it or aspecting it while Mercury is eastern and is not under the [Sun's] rays or retrograde in [its] motion and the Moon also is free from the misfortunes which I wrote of [and] untroubled.

Chapter 16. Marriage and matrimony.

V-16

Look at the condition of the man from the Sun and the ascendent and the Moon's departure from it, and at the condition of the woman

1

from Venus and the seventh sign and the place with which the Moon is conjoined, and [from] the house of the government [the tenth] to whatever of agreement or irritation or good or evil will occur between the man and the woman, and from the house of the fathers [the fourth at] the outcome of this matter and what is handed over to

2 them of a dowry or other than that. If, when they begin this, you find the Sun injured and Venus with Jupiter or Jupiter aspecting it [Venus], then it indicates that this marriage will not be useful for the man, or a misfortune will reach him, but the woman will attain joy

3 and happiness and benefit. If Venus is with Mars or with Saturn or the two [malefics] aspect Venus, then it indicates that misery and misfortune and shame will come to the woman, and the two [spouses] do not delay that there should be separation and estrangement be-

4 tween them. If you look concerning the matter of a marriage and you find the Moon injured, then evil and misfortune occur to these two

5 together, the man and the woman, from this marriage. If Mercury is with the benefics or they aspect it, then it indicates that a child will

6 soon be born to these two. If the Moon or Venus is in a tropical sign, then the marriage will have no good in it as it indicates that this woman is a whore, a harlot who will secretly frequent the beds of

7 men. If the Moon is in a tropical sign, then this marriage will not be good for the man or for the woman as there will be no agreement between these two and [their] association will not last long.

8　　　I will make clear to you the condition of the Moon in the twelve
9 signs. If the marriage takes place when the Moon is in Aries, then the
10 marriage will have no good in it. If | it is in Taurus in its [Taurus']
p. 116 beginning or at its end, then the marriage will have no good in it as it indicates that the woman will be disloyal to her husband; if the Moon
11 is in the middle of Taurus, then it will be good for the marriage. If the Moon is in Gemini in the first half, then it will not be good, but [if]
12 it is in the other half it will be good. Avoid marriage when the Moon
13 is in Cancer. If the Moon is in Leo, then it will be good for the marriage except that each one of the man and the woman will not maintain the property of his companion, that he will spoil and waste it, and the two of them will bring down the level of the property of
14 others. If the Moon is in Virgo, then marriage to a widowed woman
15 will have good in it, but as for a virgin it will not be good. If the Moon is in Libra, then the marriage will not have good in it, but

courtship and requesting will be good in it. If the Moon is in Scorpio   16
in the first degrees, then it will be good, but it will not be good at
the end of the sign as the association of these two will not last long. If   17
the Moon is in Sagittarius, then it indicates many kinds [of things],
and it will be good for some of the things, but it is better if they post-
pone this marriage and do not begin it. If the Moon is in Capricorn in   18
its beginning, then the marriage will have no good in it, but it will be
good in its [Capricorn's] middle and at its end. If the Moon is in Aqua-   19
rius, then the marriage will have no good in it. If the Moon is in   20
Pisces; then the woman will be spoiled [deflowered] and will not
cease wronging her husband, but it will be good in the rest of
things.

Look concerning the matter of marriage at the condition of Venus   21
as there is no good in a marriage when Venus is with the malefics in it
or the malefics aspect it [Venus], and Venus and the Moon together
are more powerful. The marriage will be good if Jupiter is overcoming   22
Venus, which happens when Venus is in quartile of Jupiter from its
left and Venus is in the tenth sign from the Moon so that Jupiter according to this is in opposition to the Moon, as it indicates that these
two [spouses] will be properly blessed with children in this marriage,
and it will be good in the rest of things also. If the Moon and Jupiter   23
and Venus are some of them aspecting the others from trine, then it
will be good for the marriage, but it will be better than that if they are
in triplicities or in signs which abound in children and progeny. If   24
Venus is in trine of the malefics, then in the marriage which occurs
according to this he [the husband] will be blessed with children, but
he will be blessed with this child when in the revolution of years the
benefics arrive at the place of the malefics in the base[-nativity] or
aspect it.

| It is necessary with regard to a marriage that you look at the   25
nativities of the man and the woman as, if in the nativities of the two   p. 117
of them together one of the benefics is in the house of government [the
tenth] of both, then the two of them will obtain a child in the year in
which they come together. If the house of the government of both of   26
them is a sign abounding in children, then the woman will conceive on
the first day in which she and her husband come together, if God—be
He exalted—wishes!. Because agreement and love are necessary in a   27
marriage, it is necessary that you look concerning this subject [at]

₂₈ what indicates love and agreement. If in the nativities of the man and
the woman you find a benefic in the same place, then it indicates the
₂₉ love of each one of the two for his companion. It is thus if, in the nativities of two men or of two women, a star from among the benefics
is in the same sign as it indicates that there will be brotherhood and
love and agreement between the two.

₃₀   Look concerning the subject of hostility and hatred between the
man and the woman and which of the two will be master of his companion and will subjugate him until he is obedient to his companion.
₃₁ Look concerning this at the nativity of one of them and at the sign
₃₂ which happens to be in the house of his misery [the sixth]. Then look
at the nativity of the second, and if you find the Moon happening to
be in the sign which was the house of misery for the first [native],
then it indicates that he whose Moon happens to be in the house
of misery of his companion will subjugate his companion and to-
wer over him until his companion becomes obedient, [and] it is
like the obedience of a slave to his master.

₃₃   The marriage is best if its commencement is at an hour in which the
ascendent is one of the signs of which I wrote that, if the Moon is in
them, it is good for the marriage, while none of the malefics is in the
₃₄ ascendent or aspects it. If this marriage is at an hour when Venus is
in a masculine sign and Jupiter is in a feminine sign, then it indicates
that this marriage will be better for the man than it will be for the
₃₅ woman. If it is different from this, predict also differently from this;
namely, if Venus is in a feminine sign and Jupiter is in a masculine
sign, then this marriage will bo better for the woman than it will be
₃₆ for the man. This is the strongest of what is [possible] if the Moon is
₃₇ increasing in light and in computation. If at the marriage any of the
malefics is with the Moon or in the ascendent, then the two [spouses]
will not agree on any matter and they will not be reconciled, and
₃₈ estrangement and discord will come between them. If in the nativity
of the woman the Moon is in a sign which is facing the Moon of her
companion, then there will come between the two of them estrangement and discord, and they will not be reconciled nor agree on any
matter, and this [happens] if the Moon of one of the two is in the sign
₃₉ Aries while the Moon of the other is in Libra. As it is opposition, it in-
₄₀ dicates hostility. If the Moon in the nativities of both together is
above the earth, it indicates that the two of them will come together

after the separation, and there will be peace and love between them so
that they will be reconciled.

| **Chapter 17. The courtship of a woman, and what occurs between a** V-17
wife and her husband when she quarrels and scolds and departs from p. 118
her house publicly.

If you want to know, if she returns to him, whether he will profit   1
from her or will see joy and happiness or other than this in her, then
look at the hour in which you are asked about this at the position of
the Sun and of Venus. If you find the Sun above the earth in the   2
house of government [the tenth] or in the house of good fortune [the
eleventh] while Venus is retrograde in its motion [and] western, then
it indicates that this woman will return to the house of her husband
and will not cease being obedient to her husband from the day she
returns [and] she will not contradict [him], but the husband will be
blessed with profit and good and joy from her. If the Sun is in the   3
position which I mentioned while Venus is cadent from the cardines
in a double place, then it is necessary that he be diligent in seeking the
woman whom he courts as profit and joy will come to him from her.
If the Sun and Venus are together in a strong place, then it indicates   4
like this. If you find Venus direct in motion, then it indicates that the   5
woman who departs from her house will subjugate her husband so
that for this reason estrangement and separation will come between
the two of them, and it indicates that the man will repent after the
separation, and it will be thus in the case of the woman who is courted.
If at the woman's departure from her house Venus is above the earth   6
in the house of government [the tenth] or the house of good fortune
[the eleventh] while the Sun is below the earth or in a double place
which is a cadent, then predict similarly about the weakness of the
man and the strength of the woman.

If the woman's departure from her house and her discord occur   7
when the Moon is in opposition to the Sun, it indicates that this woman will not be devoted to her husband except after pain and suffering. If at the woman's departure from her house it is [a time] when   8
the Moon turns from opposition and approaches it [the Sun], then it
indicates that the woman will soon return to her husband and her
house in other than pain and without affliction.

9   If when the woman departs from her house Venus is retrograde in
motion or direct [in motion] in the West, then her return to her house
will be quick, [and] she will be cheerful but will repent for what there
10 was of her departure and will experience great shame from this. If at
this time you find Venus departing from the [Sun's] rays and it is
western, then it indicates like this concerning her return because she
will not cease repenting until she returns.

11   Look every time concerning the matter of marriage at the sign in
12 which the Moon is. If the two [Moon and sign] are injured, then there
will be shouting and discord and hostility and separation between the
p. 119 man and the woman, | and the two [of them] will not settle upon
anything and will not be reconciled; thus it indicates the subject of
13 friendship and love. Look concerning both of these things at the power
14 of the benefics. If they happen to be in a strong [and] good position,
the conflict and estrangement and evil will disappear and there will
be peace and agreement and good between them, if God—be He
exalted!—wishes.

V-18   **Chapter 18. A pregnant woman, if her child will die in her belly.**

1   If you wish to extract it from her belly, then it is necessary to
treat this in the diminishment of the Moon from light and when the
Moon is descending from the zone towards the South while Mars and
2 Venus aspect from quartile or trine the ascendent and the Moon. This
is best if the ascendent and the Moon are in an effeminate sign and the
ascendent and the Moon are in signs straight in rising.

V-19   **Chapter 19. Partnership.**

1   If you want to form a partnership with someone in an activity or in
property or in anything for which there is a need of a partnership of
a man, then let this be when the Moon is in [one of] the signs of which I
mentioned that marriage in it is good, and the Moon is free [and]
2 devoid of the misfortunes which I mentioned. Then look, and if the
ascendent and the Moon are in Aries, then a partnership will not be
good in it because it will not last and there will soon occur estrange-
3 ment and separation between the two. If the ascendent and the Moon
are in Taurus, then a partnership will not be desirable with a powerful
man [but] will be dangerous, and if it is with lowly people also, discord
will occur between the two and there will be no good in the outcome

of this matter. If the ascendent and the Moon are in Gemini, then the   4
partnership will be good and they both will profit from this and there
will be agreement and the preservation of trust between them. If the   5
ascendent and the Moon are in Cancer, there will occur betrayal and
anxiety in these two, and each one of them will slander his companion.
If they are in Leo, there will be profit and good reputation between   6
them. If they are in Virgo, then there will be a good profit in it and   7
wise men will praise them, and they will have affection among the
people and will attain much profit in [their] trading, and surplus
and joy will occur to them from it. If they are in Libra, then there will   8
be no good in this partnership. If they are in Scorpio, quarreling and   9
discord will occur to the two of them, and each one of them will conceal
in himself disloyalty to his companion and slander for him. If they are   10
in Sagittarius, then | it will be good except that each one of them will   p. 120
be overbearing towards his companion and will be arrogant to him.
If they are in Capricorn, happiness and joy will occur to them both. If   11, 12
they are in Aquarius, misfortune and injury will occur to them both.
If they are in Pisces, then it will be superior, elevated, good. The   13, 14
ascendent and the Moon indicate these qualities which I mentioned if
neither benefics nor malefics are with them and they do not aspect
the ascendent and the Moon.

If Saturn aspects the ascendent or the Moon or is with the two of   15
them, then they will not agree on advice, and whatever of love is
between them will cool down, and they will discontinue in whatever
years are between them, and there will be shouting and discord between them, and misery and separation and upheaval and slowness in
work will occur to them both. If Mars aspects the ascendent or the   16
Moon from a strong place or is with them both, then there occurs to
them according to what I wrote of quarreling and fighting and discord. If Jupiter aspects the ascendent or the Moon from trine or is   17
with them both, then profit and good reputation and prestige will
occur to them from their partnership, and to the lowlier of the two in
the matter debris will occur in this partnership, but as for the more
amply provided of the two with a share and the mightier of the two
in importance, he will gain two thirds from this profit at the end
because the people of good luck and who possess importance are
worthier of preferment over others. Every time that the benefics   18
aspect the ascendent or the Moon from trine or the benefics are with

277

the ascendent or with the Moon, then this partnership will be good
19 [and] he will profit from it. If they aspect from quartile or from
opposition or from sextile, then it will be good, but this profit and
good will be less than when they aspect from trine.

V-20　　**Chapter 20. Debt and the payment for it.**

1　　If you contract a debt or pay it, consider the condition of the claim-
ant to whom the debt [is due] from the ascendent and the condition
of the borrower who seeks the debt from the seventh, and the condi-
2 tion of the borrower also from the Moon and Mercury. If the Moon is
with the benefics or they aspect it while one of the malefics injures
3 it, he will pay this debt, but he will also revert in this debt. If Mercury is with Saturn, there will be confusion and deception and trickery
4 in the payment of this debt. If Mercury is with Mars or [Mars] aspects
it from a strong place, he will revert in this debt and there will occur
in what is between the two of them for this debt fighting and shouting
5 and quarreling. If the Moon is under the Sun's rays, then look at
what I wrote for you in which the consideration is from the condition
of the Moon and its position, and make your consideration of this from
the Sun and its position and its liberation from the malefics.

6
p. 121　　If the Moon is in the burned place, that is if the Moon is in | the
middle of the zone which is the equator, taking the direction of the
qibla towards the South, or [if] the Moon is in the first degrees of Leo
or Gemini or Capricorn, or [if] those degrees of which I wrote are the
ascendent, then it will not be good if you decide anything according to
7 this. If you wish, then borrow when the Moon is in Leo or in Pisces or
in Aquarius or in Scorpio or in Sagittarius while the Moon is decreasing
in light and Jupiter and Venus and Mercury are aspecting the ascend-
8 ent or the Moon. If they are aspecting together the ascendent and the
Moon, it will be more powerful.

V-21　　**Chapter 21. The journey.**

1　　If you want or someone wants a journey or the departure from his
land to another land, then look for the traveller from the ascendent,
and [for] the land which he desires from the seventh, and for the action
and for the necessity which he seeks in that journey from the house of
government [the tenth], and for the outcome of that matter from the
2 house of the fathers [the fourth]. Let his departure be when the Moon

is increasing in computation and Mercury is not under the Sun's rays
and not with the malefics, and the location of the Moon is neither in
the twelfth place nor in the sixth place from the ascendent, and the
lord of the ascendent and the lord of the Moon are not cadent under
the [Sun's] rays. If the Moon is in the sixth place or the twelfth from   3
the ascendent, then it indicates that misfortune and pain and misery
will happen to him on this journey. If the Moon is increasing in compu-   4
tation, then it indicates that he will come to the place which he
desires in comfort.

If the benefics are in the ascendent, then it indicates goodness with   5
respect to the condition of that journey of his. If the benefics are in   6
the seventh house, then it indicates his profit from his departure to
that land which he desires. If the Moon and Saturn and Mars are   7
together in the ascendent, or [the Moon and] one of them, or in the
seventh house, then it indicates that a severe pain and an oppressive
disease and damage and shouting and fighting will happen to him on
his journey and [in] the land which he comes to. If the lord of the   8
ascendent or the lord of the Moon is in [its] station, then it indicates
that his absence will be long and there will occur slowness and difficulty in his affair. If any of the benefics is in opposition to the Moon   9
or [in] quartile to it or it [the Moon] conjoins with any of them, then
the commencement of this journey will be good. If any of the malefics   10
is in quartile of the Moon or in opposition to it, then the commencement of this journey [will be] bad.

| Chapter 22. Departure from a journey.

p. 122
V-22

If you want to know his return to his land and his home and his   1
house, whether it will be deliberate or difficulty and slowness and
length of time will occur in it, then look at the opposition to the Sun
and its quartile. If Jupiter or Venus is in any of these places, then he   2
will soon return from this journey of his safely. If any of the malefics   3
is in these places, then his departure will be delayed and will be slow,
and his departure will take place when the malefics leave their location in which the malefics were and the Moon comes to be in opposition to the place in which the Moon was or in quartile to that place,
or his departure from that place of his will take place when the Sun
returns to the place in which it was at the beginning of the journey or
the Sun comes to be in opposition to the place in which it was at the

beginning of the journey while the Sun is free [and] nothing injures it.
4 If he commenced the journey when the Moon was in quartile of the
malefics or [in] opposition to them while the benefics did not aspect it
or the Moon conjoined with some one of the malefics, or some one of
them was in quartile of the Moon, then it indicates his departure from
that journey of his to his land and his home [will be] in difficulty and
5 pain and misery, or because of illness he will not depart. If the
malefics are not aspecting the Moon from opposition or quartile while
the benefics aspect the Sun and the Moon except that the Moon
conjoins with any one of the malefics, then it indicates that misfortune
and a hideous, difficult matter and pain will happen to him because
of this conjunction, but despite this if the benefics aspect the Sun and
6 the Moon, then he will return to his land and his home. If the malefics
are in the sign which is on the right of the Moon and [in that] on its
left, then the Moon in accordance with this will be squeezed between
the malefics, and it indicates that a difficult, hideous pain will reach
him in his journey, and it will be worse for these calamities if Jupiter
is not aspecting the Moon; but if it is aspecting it, then it will diminish
this misfortune and [these] calamities.

7　　　If you want to know the condition of his departure from this journey of his, whether it will be soon [and] deliberate or slow [and] re-
mote, then it is necessary to consider concerning this if he has arrived
8 at the land which he desires. You should look at the sign in which the
lord of the ascendent and of the second house, which is the house of
9 property, happens to be at that hour. If the lord of the second sign is
retrograde in its motion, then it indicates that his departure from this
journey of his will be soon [and] quick, [but] bad [and] he will profit
in nothing from his journey and will satisfy none of his needs but will
10 be rid of them. If the lord of this sign is in [its] station, then it indicates
11 his departure in slowness and a lengthy lingering. If | the lord of this
p. 123 sign is in [its] station, [then] departs from its station and is direct in
its motion, then his departure will be middling, but with the satisfaction of [his] need and leisure from the business on which he was
12 travelling. If the lord of this sign is in the ascendent or in the house
of government [the tenth], then it indicates that he will see in this
13 journey of his health and security from misfortunes. If the lord of
this sign is in the house of the fathers [the fourth], then it indicates
that there will be the fear of death for him in this journey of his.

If the Moon is with Saturn at the hour in which the man reaches his 14
land and his place which he desired, then it will be a sign indicating
slowness and injury in property, and he will stay behind in that
absence of his because of illness and he will persist in it. If the Moon 15
at that hour is with Mercury and Mars is in opposition to them both,
then it indicates that there will reach him in this journey of his beating
and breaking and injury and the rest of misfortunes. If Mercury and 16
Saturn aspect the Moon from opposition, then it indicates that there
will happen to him in this journey of his slowness and estrangement,
and he will conceal [his] perfidy and stealing and evil, but he will be
suspected and seized on account of this and imprisoned, and his
wealth will be destroyed. If Mars is in Sagittarius with the Moon or 17
aspects the Moon from Sagittarius, then it indicates that there will
happen to him on this journey of his and [during] his absence beating
and breaking and injury.

Look at the nature of the sign in which the Moon is injured. If it 18, 19
is one of the signs which are of the nature of beasts and the malefics
which injure the Moon are also in signs which are of the nature of
beasts, then this misfortune will reach him from animals or lions. If 20
they are of the nature of men, then this injury will be from men.

If the commencement of the journey takes place when Mercury 21
is with the Moon and Jupiter aspects them both from trine or from
quartile, then it indicates that his business on this journey will be
easy, favorable, [and] beneficial, [and] the departure will be quick in
ease and well-being.

Chapter 23. Buying a ship or building it. V-23

If you want to buy a ship or to build it, then it is necessary to 1
commence this when Jupiter or Venus is in the cardine, the house of
the fathers [the fourth], and they both aspect the ascendent and the
Moon also. This is best if they both are in the house of the fathers [the 2
fourth] in a sign whose nature is moist, one of the watery signs, or a
sign whose nature is the nature of the animals of the sea, or one of the
houses of Jupiter and Venus. This is best if the ascendent is Taurus 3
when the Moon is in it, or Gemini or Cancer or Virgo | or Sagittarius p. 124
or Capricorn at the end of its degrees when the Moon is in it; the
beginning of Capricorn is earthy and its end watery. If the ascendent 4
is Pisces and the Moon is in it, then also it will be good; the best of

what I said of these signs is Taurus, then Pisces, then Gemini, then the
end of Capricorn.

V-24   **Chapter 24. Commencing to build a ship.**

1   This is the best of what is [possible] at every time when the Sun is in
trine of the benefics while the Moon is increasing in light and in computation and increasing in its latitude and its longitude and is in the
2 term[s] of the benefics. Beware of commencing this at the hour when
the Moon and the ascendent are injured from Mars as, if it is thus, it
indicates that the outcome of this work will be bad [and] harmful
3 because of fire or anger or oppression. If the commencement takes
place at an hour when the Moon is in Aquarius and the Sun and
Mars are opposite to the Moon or in quartile [to it] or are with the
Moon in the same sign, then it indicates that misfortune will reach
this ship from water and what is contained in it for the life of its
people and their livelihood, and burning will reach it, and a severe
misfortune and great fear will happen to its people, and all of them
will be cast in the sea [and there will be] a desire for the turning of
4 men from death. If the Moon is not in Aquarius but is in a watery sign
while Mars and the Sun are in the situation which we mentioned of
quartile or opposition, then it indicates the immersion of the ship and
its people and what is in it and their loss and their falling to the bot-
5 tom of the sea. If the Moon is not in [one of] the watery signs but is
in a dry sign while the Sun and Mars aspect according to the situation
of which I wrote, then it indicates that misfortune and breaking will
reach this ship from the coast of the sea or from a stone or a mountain
that is in the sea, and the planks of the ship will be separated on the
[different] areas of the sea, and whatever of thing[s] is in it will be
6 lost. If the Moon is not in a dry sign, then it indicates that misfortune
will reach this ship on the sea from pirates and those who will cut
[it] off on the sea and kill its people so that they will be drowned for
this reason and what is in it will be lost.

V-25   **Chapter 25. Commencing to row the ship in the water.**

1   If the benefics and malefics are not aspecting the Moon while the
Moon is in the first ten degrees of Aries and above the earth, then it
indicates that this ship will leave on its trip and make a good [and]
2 safe departure. If the Moon is in Taurus, then waves will befall it on

the way; if | the malefics aspect the Moon when it is in Taurus, then   p. 125
it indicates its [the ship's] loss in these waves. If the Moon is in Ge-   3
mini [in] eight degrees of it, then it indicates that what is in this ship
will reach [its destination] and there will be profit in it, but lingering
and slowness will occur in its return and its departure. If the Moon is   4
in Cancer, then it indicates that the waves will not reach it and that
it will be safe and its people will profit from it. If the Moon is in Leo,   5
then it indicates that misfortune will reach whoever of men [is] in the
ship; if the Moon is injured, misfortune increases upon misfortune for
them. If the Moon is in Virgo, then it indicates that his departure will   6
not be deliberate [and] soon. If the Moon is in Libra, from its begin-   7
ning to ten degrees, then there will be good in a journey neither by
land nor by sea because it is bad; if it has passed ten degrees of it
[Libra], then it will not be bad for the journey either on sea or on land.
If the Moon is in Scorpio, then it will be safe from the sea and its   8
misfortunes, but its people will get some fright because some of them
will be detained. If the Moon is in Sagittarius, then calamities and   9
misfortune from the waves will reach it. If the Moon is in Capricorn   10
[and] has passed nine degrees of it, then it will be good, but also it
indicates that some fear that some of themselves will be detained will
reach the people of the ship. If the Moon is in Aquarius, then discord   11
and slowness and lingering on their return will happen to them, but
its outcome will be good. If the Moon is in Pisces, it indicates that   12
misfortune and calamities will reach them. All this [is what] the Moon   13
indicates when neither the benefics nor the malefics aspect it.

I shall make clear to you something different from this. Look, and   14, 15
if the Moon is under the earth while the benefics or the malefics aspect
it, then it is bad. If the Moon is under the earth with Saturn while   16
Saturn is in its station and is with the Moon in the same sign at that
hour when the commencement of rowing the boat in the water takes
place, then it indicates that great pains and a great [and] severe misfortune will happen to them and a hideous fear will befall them and
strong waves until the water will enter the ship and the people of that
ship for whom death and loss was judged in dampness or water will
be lost in those waves while the Moon is under the earth. If the Moon   17
is above the earth while Saturn is in its station and aspecting the
Moon from trine, then it indicates that the people of this ship will
throw much of what goods [they have] on this ship into the water in

the hope of saving them[selves] and they will be saved from this after
18 pain and severe misery while the Moon is under the earth. If the Moon
is above the earth while Saturn is not in its station but aspects the
Moon from trine, then it indicates a hideous matter as if they were at
p. 126 the edge of a razor, but together with this | fear they will be better in
[their] condition, and no harm will reach them except for a little when
19 Saturn is in its station. If Saturn is in this way with Mercury, the
fear will increase the misery and hideousness; but if the benefics
aspect Saturn, then this misfortune will be easier and more comfortable, especially if the benefics aspect from the right side of Saturn
20 and [from] a strong place [aspect] Saturn. As I wrote concerning the
location of Saturn in these situations, the condition [will be] similar if
Saturn is in the ascendent even if it does not aspect the Moon.

21   If Saturn is in the sign in which it was at the nativity of that man,
and this happens to be the sign which is the ascendent, or [if] Saturn
is in trine of that sign in which Saturn was at the nativity or in quartile
of it or in opposition to it, then it will be more hideous and worse in
22 [his] condition. If Mars is in the place in which I wrote that Saturn was
and Mars is under the earth while the Moon is above the earth with
Mars striking it, then it will be the most for this matter and the worst
in [his] condition, but the fear and misfortune will not be from water
and waves as I wrote concerning the situation of Saturn, but it will
be on account of shouting and arguing and every discord, from which
there will occur enmity between the people of this ship and whatever
23 enemies there are on the sea. It also indicates that difficult surgical
operations and a breaking of their joints will reach them, and their
24 blood will flow, and the like. This violence and hideousness will
25 increase if Mercury is with Mars. If Saturn and Mars and Mercury
aspect the Moon together from the same place or from separate places
while the Moon is above the earth, then they will have neither escape
26 nor deliverance from this misfortune whose condition is hideous. It
27 indicates [what is] like this if Mars is mixed with Mercury. If Mars or
Saturn, one of the two, aspects the Sun, and the other the Moon, then
it indicates that a difficult [and] hideous fear will reach them, and
the hideousness will increase for them if their [Mars' and Saturn's]
aspect is from opposition.

28   If the Sun and the Moon are not injured while the Moon is above the
earth and Jupiter aspects the Moon from quartile, then it will be good

concerning the commencement of rowing the boat in the water and
the sea as it indicates that their actions will be favorable, easy, good,
and they will not be cut off from whatever of good they hope for and
arrange in it, but they will obtain it, if God wishes. If it is favorable   29
when Jupiter aspects the Moon, if Venus is with Jupiter or Venus
aspects the Moon from other than that sign, this situation increases
the good greatly. Whichever star of the benefics or of the malefics   30
Mercury is with, it increases [its] power in the portion of good or evil
which God judges for it. If the Moon is above the earth and Venus   31
alone aspects the Moon, it indicates that these waves and the misfortune will not reach them in their faces, and they will be blessed
with profit and good in it, but it is not like the aspect of Jupiter and
Venus together because Venus alone | is weak. If the Moon and Venus   p. 127
are together in the same sign under the earth and Venus is under the   32
[Sun's] rays, then it indicates that these waves will not befall them in
their face[s], and this ship will reach its destination which they desire
without misfortune. If Jupiter and Venus together aspect the Sun and   33
the Moon while the Moon is with Mercury, then it indicates that the
commencement at that hour of rowing the ship in the water or in the
sea is like the best of what is [possible] of commencement[s], but the
commencement is better than that.

If the malefics are in the ascendent and the benefics are with the   34
Moon, or they happen to be the opposite of this (that is, if the malefics
happen to be with the Moon and the benefics in the ascendent), then
misfortune will reach this ship from the sea, but its people will escape
from that fear, if God wishes and judges it. Even if the Moon is without   35
the aspect of the benefics in a cardine and it is in one of the signs which
we named in the introduction to this book, [saying] that [it will be
good] if the Moon is in them, it will be good, if God wishes. If the   36
Moon and the ascendent are free from the benefics and the malefics
[and] none of the malefics and the benefics aspects these two, then
let this commencement of rowing the boat in the water and the sea be
when the ascendent and the Moon are in one of the signs which I re-
ported and approved for commencing this matter.

If you wish to aim [your] face on the ship and wish to consider   37
concerning the commencement of this matter, then the consideration
concerning the commencement of this matter is first when the ship is
released and pushed in the water, and the commencement of the

matter for one who rides on it is first when the man places his foot in
38 it. If the ship and its people arrive at the land which you aimed for,
then it is necessary to consider concerning the commencement of the
arrival of the ship and its people if they are one.

39   Look concerning the commencement of a journey on land or sea;
if the man desires a journey on land when the Moon happens to be in
the seventh, not in a dry sign, but the signs in which the malefics
are or which they aspect are dry, and if he wishes a journey on the sea
when the Moon is not in a watery sign or in a sign whose nature is
the nature of water, while the malefics are in it or aspect it, then the
commencement of this journey on land or sea will not be good, but
40 discomfort and misery will reach him. If the Moon is injured while the
benefics are in the dry, earthy signs or aspect these signs, then it
indicates that misfortune will barely not reach them in this journey
of theirs, and if it does reach them, then it will be less than what I
41 mentioned. If the masters of this journey are some for whom death is
not judged and whose years are not determined, then they will depart
for their houses; if misfortune does reach them, then it will be less
42 than what I mentioned. The malefics from among the stars are the
worst of what is [possible] in damages, Mars if the traveler is a traveler
on the land, and Saturn [for a traveler] on sea and water; and it is the
worst of what is [possible] in damages if Jupiter and Venus do not
43
p. 128 aspect these two. The worst of what | is [possible] is the Moon in a
term or figure [decan] of the benefics with a malefic aspecting the
Moon from opposition or quartile and Jupiter and Venus not aspecting
the Moon either together or one of the two.

V-26   **Chapter 26.**

1   If a book or a message or a letter comes to a man, then consider
Mercury in the base of his nativity as, whenever the benefics aspect it,
or Mercury with the two luminaries aspects the benefics, or Mercury
is in a sign in which there is no malefic with it, then, if the situation of
these stars is in this way, it indicates what there is of good in the book
2 or letter. Concerning the report which arrives in the book or letter,
look at the Sun and the Moon in their motion as, if they are both free
from the malefics while the Moon is with Mercury in one of those signs
of which I wrote that [it is good if] they are free from malefics and the

benefics are in them or aspect them, then there are happiness and joy
in the book or message or letter which reaches the master of that
nativity at that hour. If, at that hour when the book or message or   3
letter arrives, the Moon is in one of those signs and a malefic is with it
while none of the benefics is with it or aspects it, then in the book or
message or letter which arrives at that hour [there will be] discord and
misfortune and injury. If Mercury is in some one of the places of the   4
benefics from among those signs and is eastern while the benefics and
the malefics aspect it together, then the message is good.

There were some of the scientists who considered concerning this   5
matter in another way. They said: they look at Jupiter and Venus in   6
their transit. If they reach the sign in which the two luminaries were   7
at the nativity of this man or are in quartile of that sign in which the
two luminaries were, or [if] the sign in which Jupiter and Venus are in
their transits, this is free from the malefics while Mercury is free from
the malefics and aspects Jupiter or Venus, then in this book or message or letter which reaches the master of this nativity at that hour
there will be joy and happiness and profit. If in this transit Saturn or   8
Mars or both of them are in the sign in which the two luminaries were
in the nativity or are in quartile of that sign while Mercury is with
them or aspects them, then the book or message or letter which at
that hour reaches the master of this nativity will be bad, and if he is a
traveler at that hour, injury will befall him.

| Chapter 27. Bondage and chains.

p. 129
V-27

If a man is bound because of the anger of kings or the anger of a   1
man against his slaves, then look at the Moon at that hour. If at the   2
hour at which he was bound the Moon was in Aries, then it indicates
that these chains will soon be loosened from him. If it is in Taurus,   3
then it indicates that these chains will stay a long time on him, and it
indicates that these chains are because of the property which he sought,
and it indicates that it was taken from him, but he will be saved from
this pain in his body after [his] misfortune. If the Moon is in Gemini,   4
then, if [the chains] are not loosened from him within three days, it
indicates that these chains will stay a long time on him. If the Moon   5
is in Cancer, then it indicates that these chains will stay a long time
on him. If the Moon is in Leo, then it indicates that these chains are   6
because of a man who has importance and power, [and] he will not

7 escape from the chains until they have been a long time on him. If the
Moon is in Virgo, then it indicates a mixture of good and bad, but that
8 is more abundant which benefits him, and there will be ease in him. If
the Moon is in Libra, then it indicates that the owner of these chains
9 will escape from them. If the Moon is in Scorpio, then it indicates that
these chains will stay a long time on him and he will be chronically ill
10 from them, but at its end there will be release from them. If the Moon
is in Sagittarius, then it indicates that these chains will stay a long
11 time on him. If the Moon is in Capricorn, then it indicates that he
12 will escape from these chains. If the Moon is in Aquarius or in Pisces,
then it indicates that these chains will cling to him [all] his life, and
he will be shackled in them and will not escape from them except with
13 death. The Moon alone indicates these situations when it is in these
signs, but the locations of the malefics [with it] or the aspect of the
Moon will change much of these situations and will alter them.

14   If Jupiter is with the Moon or in the ascendent or aspects them
both, then it indicates release from these chains quickly, and Venus
15 indicates similarly when it happens to be in these positions. If Mercury and Jupiter are with the Moon or aspect the Moon, then it
indicates that [his] power in escaping from these chains will increase
16 and it will hasten it, if God—be He exalted!—wishes. But if Mars is
with the Moon or aspects it, then it indicates that beating and difficulties and burning or bite[s] or sting[s] will reach him in these chains,
or a surgical operation with a piece of iron will happen to him from
17 this suffering and pain. If Saturn is with the Moon or aspects it,
then this misery will last a long time and will shackle him and he
18 will not be finished with it except after pain and misery. If Mercury
and Saturn and Mars together are with the Moon or the three of them
together aspect it, then it indicates that he will die in these chains.

19   Look at that hour in which is the commencement for this bondage
p. 130 at | the ascendent and what of the stars is in it and which of them
20 aspects it. The ascendent indicates something like that which the Moon
indicates of good or bad for the fettered [man] if the Moon is de-
21 creasing, and it will be worse for him if the Moon is increasing. This is
the hour of the Moon's weakness because of the Sun (its weakness is
22 when they conjoin in a sign in the same degree). Then the Moon moves
and becomes elongated from the Sun, and when it is in opposition to
the Sun in the seventh sign in a situation like that which I mentioned

with regard to the conjunction of these two, then this is an indicator
that these chains will be misery and trouble, [but] then he will be
freed from them.

If the Moon conjoins with Mercury while Mercury is western, then 23
it indicates release from these chains. If it is departing from the middle 24
of the equator, being taken towards the qibla [the South] with Mercury and Venus, then it indicates release from this soon. If Saturn and 25
Jupiter aspect the Moon from trine, then it indicates that the owner
of these chains will not escape until he has been a long time in them,
but he will be freed with a good reputation and profit.

They call from the region of midheaven to the cardine of the fathers 26
[the fourth] the region of descent, which is concealed; they call from
the cardine of the fathers [the fourth] to midheaven the region of
ascent, which is the region of the ascendent. If the Moon is in the 27
region of descent, which is concealed, and Mars also at that hour is
aspecting the Moon, then it indicates that the owner of the chains
will be set free of it quickly in death from it or [in] life. If the Moon is 28
in the region of ascent, which is the region of the ascendent, and Mars
aspects it from trine and Jupiter from quartile, then the owner of
these chains will escape from his chains and his bonds. If Saturn is 29
with the Moon in whichever region it is while Jupiter aspects it from
the tenth or from quartile, then it indicates release from these chains.
If Mars aspects the Moon from quartile and Saturn from trine, then 30
these chains will stay a long time on him and pain and misery will
happen to him in [his] escape from them. If Mars aspects the Moon 31
from trine and Saturn from quartile, then it indicates that misery
and effort will reach the owner of these chains, then he will break
these chains and bonds and will escape from them in flight. It is 32
necessary to look concerning the house of the fathers [the fourth] more
than the [other] cardines because in it is the clarification of every
outcome.

Chapter 28. Judgment about what may not be afterwards of a V-28
matter which one hopes for, or according to this of things.

Look at the conjunction of the Moon and its flowing away since 1
in whatever time [it is] it is necessary for it that you operate with its
flowing away and its conjunction. If the query is about what will not 2
be afterwards, but which is | existent, or a thing one hopes for or an p. 131

action on whose basis one has not yet commenced, then look concerning these subjects from the Moon's conjunction and its flowing away 3 in quartile in whatever star it is. If the query is about a pain or disease or imprisonment or flight from his land or his city whether he will escape from this or not, then look at the star from which the Moon 4 flows. Conjunction indicates what is to come of matters and flowing away indicates what has been and is passed.

V-29 **Chapter 29. Query about the sick.**

1 If a querist asks about a sick [person] at a time when the Moon is flowing from the benefics, then it indicates [his] recovery from this 2 illness. But if he asks when the Moon is flowing from Mars, then it indicates that this illness is from a fever which will exhaust him, or [that] one of his limbs will be cut from his body with an iron [knife], or [that] in cutting or phlebotomy he will be bled from his veins with 3 an iron [knife]. If the Moon is increasing in its light, then it will be 4 more hideous and worse for this illness. But if the Moon is flowing from Saturn, then it indicates a fever that shakes [him] and a hidden malaise in [his] diet, or some of this will reach him in [his] belly or in [his] body, or his spleen will swell, and sometimes it will bring down a miserable disease on him, and a wound and difficult sore will reach him so that his limbs will be wounded or will be dislocated, and sometimes [his] black bile will be stirred up in him until his intestines are cramped and burn, and it is an indicator that every illness which reaches him will stay in him a long time.

V-30 **Chapter 30. The commencement of all things.**

1 Look concerning each matter that you commence at the lord of 2 this action from among the stars. Sometimes one commences a matter when the benefics aspect the Moon and the ascendent and the lord of this action is under the [Sun's] rays or injured or does not aspect the ascendent and is in a bad place; then this action will be bad and 3 have no good in it. If you want to buy land or give power of attorney to someone, then look concerning this at the power of Saturn and 4 Jupiter. If it is a taking away or a gift or a quarrel or a practice or a partnership or an insult or love or trade or seeking culture or [something] like this, then look concerning this at the power of Mercury. 5 If it is a wedding or marriage or something pleasant of the acts of

Venus, then look concerning this at the power of Venus. If it is a fight 6
or arms or what is similar to this, then look concerning this at the
power of Mars. If it is a matter of the government | or a matter of 7
kings or a request before kings, then look concerning this at the power p. 132
of Jupiter. If it is one of the matter[s] evident and apparent in which 8
secrecy and a ruse and evil are not seen, look at the power of the Sun
also together with Jupiter. Every time Jupiter aspects a star it turns 9
it toward good. Venus does this [also], but not in momentous affairs 10
unless Jupiter is with it or aspects together with it. The power of 11
Venus is in the love which is between two [people] or food or perfume
or what is similar to this. In every time and in every situation Jupiter 12
is good because it increases the properness and good or diminishes
from the evil and misfortunes and destroys them.

Chapter 31.

If you want to know the condition of a sick [man] for whom death 1
and misfortunes are feared, then at the time of his taking ill look at
his nativity, in which sign[s] the benefics were and in which sign[s]
the malefics were. If the Moon in its course and its transit has arrived 2
at the sign in which a malefic was in his nativity and the malefics
aspect it from quartile while the benefics do not aspect it [either] in
his nativity or at its transit to this sign, then, if the commencement of
his illness was when the Moon in its transit arrived at that sign, then
it indicates that the illness will be hideous and he will not escape from
it; and it will be worse for him and more hideous if the time-distributor without the lord of the limit of that sick man has also arrived
at this sign. If the time-distributor has arrived at this sign or at a sign 3
like it from which in his nativity Saturn and Mars aspected this sign,
when the commencement of his illness is at this hour, then it indicates
a hideous illness, and he will not escape from it. One looks at these 4
signs according to which of the limbs of the man are [in] their power
like what I made clear in the introduction of this book as this also
indicates the disease of which I wrote that he will die in it, and you
will know from the pain of which of his limbs this loss will be. If the 5
Moon is in a sign possessing two bodies, especially if it is in Gemini or
Pisces, while Saturn and Mars are with it in this sign and it is squeezed
between them, then, if the time-distributor arrives at the aspect of

Saturn and Mars, then it indicates that gout will reach this native in his two hands and his two feet.

| **Chapter 32.**

1   If you want to know when the property of the native will increase or decrease, then look at the second sign from the ascendent which
2 was in his nativity called the house of property. If his time-distributor of what has passed of his life has arrived at this sign while the malefics are in it in the degrees which the time-distributor has arrived [at] or in opposition or quartile of these degrees, then it indicates that the
3 property of the native will diminish at this. If the benefics are in these degrees or aspect it while these degrees which the time-distributor has arrived [at] are the term of [one of] the benefics, then it indicates that the native's property and his happiness will increase.

4   Each time look at the Moon, and if in its transit and its course it is in the sign in which the malefics were in his nativity while the benefics do not aspect it, and the malefics are in the place in which they were [in] his base-nativity or its quartile or in its opposition or aspecting the Moon, then it indicates that at that hour pain and grief and
5 worry and misery will reach that native. If the Moon in its transit arrives in the sign in which it was in his nativity, and the benefics were in it and have arrived at this place in their motion and their transit while the malefics do not aspect it and the benefics do not aspect the Moon from trine, then joy and benefit and good will reach this native because of clothes or other than this because of [something] like what had not befallen this native before this, so that his happiness and his joy will be more intense in this.

Chapter 33. In which is the clarification of the matter of two adversaries, if they argue and plead before a judge, which of the two will be successful and which of the two will be defeated.

1   Look if you want to know this at the hour in which you are asked to the ascendent as the ascendent indicates the matter of incitements
2 and the commencements of quarrels. If you find the ascendent [to be] a hard [fixed] sign, then it indicates that the seeker of the right will be keen in his request and will not turn away from his argument.
3 If the ascendent is a sign possessing two bodies, then it indicates that the seeker of the right will be between two selves and that he will

regret his quarrel. If the ascendent is a tropical sign, then it indicates   4
that this quarrel will not be finished and will have no end.

If Mars aspects the ascendent or is with it, then it indicates that   5
grief and shame and disgrace will reach the seeker because of this
quarrel. If | Mercury is with the benefics in the ascendent or aspects   6
p. 134
the ascendent, then it indicates that the seeker of the right will attain
from his adversary dirhams and goods, and will turn from quarreling
with the defendent. If Saturn is the one which aspects the ascendent   7
or is with it, then misery will happen to the seeker because of this and
[because of] this quarrel.

If at the hour you are asked about it the malefics aspect midheaven,   8
then it indicates that this quarrel will not be cut off, but will come to
a second judge other than the first judge, and there will happen to the
judges because of this quarrel shame and a base reputation and disgrace, and the opinion[s] of the two adversaries will be in agreement
on amends and departure from the judges. If Saturn is in the cardine,   9
midheaven, it indicates that, because of their injustice in judging,
shame and misery and loathing will reach the judges. If the benefics   10
are in midheaven, then it indicates that the judge is just [and] will
not be unjust in his decision.

See the condition of the defendent in the seventh sign. If the ma-   11, 12
lefics aspect this sign or are in it, then misery and misfortune and pain
will occur to him. If Mercury is with the malefics in this sign or aspects   13
it, it indicates that the defendent will be deprived of his wish by injustice and false testimony.

Look at the outcome of this quarrel and at what the result will be   14
from the sign of the fathers, which is the cardine under the earth.
If the lord of the ascendent or the lord of midheaven or the lord of the   15
seventh sign is eastern and is with the lord of [the house of] the fathers
in the same sign, then it indicates that the victory is to the one who is
more suited to that cardine whose lord is eastern and is with the lord
of the house of the fathers in the same sign. If the lord of this cardine   16
is under the Sun's rays with the lord of the house of the fathers, then
[the planet] which is suited to this cardine will lose and be defeated
because it is with the lord of the house of the fathers under the Sun's
rays. If the lord of the ascendent and the lord of the seventh sign are   17
both of them eastern and are with the lord of the house of the fathers,
then it indicates that the two adversaries will become reconciled and

18 friendship will thrive between the two. If the lord of the ascendent and the lord of [the sign] opposite the ascendent are both of them under the [Sun's] rays with the lord of the house of the fathers, then their quarrel will be long and will linger and will have no termination.

19 The benefics indicate what there is of success and victory and a
20 just judgment. The malefics indicate, if they are western and are not in their house[s] in the cardines and are increasing, that the owner of this cardine will lose and be defeated, but if they are in their house[s] in the cardines and are increasing, then they indicate that the owner of this cardine will attain success by means of the injustice of the judge or because of bribes or forcibly or [by means of] favoritism.

p. 135
21 | The second sign from the seventh indicates the defendent's as-
22 sistance. If the lord of the midheaven and the lord of the ascendent are come together and conjoined in the same sign or are in the ascendent or the lord of the midheaven aspects the ascendent or the lord of the ascendent, then it indicates that the judge will help the seeker
23 and will be on his side. If the lord of the midheaven and the lord of [the sign] opposite the ascendent are as I wrote concerning the ascendent and its lord, then the judge's sympathy and assistance will be for the defendent, and he will attain success because of this.

24 Concerning all of these subjects—the condition of the seeker and the defendent and the matter of the judges and quarreling and sociability and who will succeed and [who] will lose and the rest of
25 what I wrote of these subjects—look to the Moon also. If you find it injured by the misfortunes of which I wrote in the introduction of this book or [if] the Moon before its entry under the Sun's rays is conjoining with the malefics and is in one of those cardines or one of the succedents, which are the second signs from the cardines, then it indicates that he whose condition is connected with one of these cardines or with the second [sign] from them will lose and be defeated, and misfortune and regret for this quarrel will reach him.

26 If two adversaries quarrel about a debt or money and bring it before the judges when the Moon is increasing in its light, then the Moon is an indicator of the matter of him who lent the money, who is the one who gave it, and the Sun indicates the matter of him who asked
27 for a loan, whose debt it is. If the Moon is diminishing in its light, then this characteristic is reversed so that it [the Moon] is the indicator of
294

him who asked for a loan and the Sun indicates him who lent [it].
According to this look at the Sun and the Moon, at the more power-   28
ful and the better of these two in [its] condition, and [its] power and
closeness in aspecting the ascendent. If the indicator of him who lent   29
[it] is the more powerful of the two, then success will belong to the
one who lent. If the indicator of him who asked for a loan is [the   30
more powerful], then success will belong to the one who asked for
a loan.

In all of these matters look at the lot of good fortune also as, if it   31
happens to be in the ascendent or in the second sign from the ascendent, then it indicates that success will belong to the seeker. If the lot 32
of good fortune happens to be in [the sign] opposite the sign of the
ascendent or in the sign which is the second from the seventh, then
success will belong to the defendent. If the lord of the lot of good   33
fortune is in the cardine of the fathers [the fourth] and aspects the
ascendent and [the sign] opposite the ascendent, then the two adversaries will be reconciled of their own accord. If the lord of the lot of   34
good fortune is in the midheaven and aspects the ascendent and [the
sign] opposite the ascendent, then it indicates the reconciliation of the
two adversaries, but the reconciliation of these two will be because of
the desire of the judges and their command.

| If the lord of the ascendent and the lord of the seventh sign are in   p. 136
                                                                            35
the same sign in their figure[s] [decans], then it indicates that the two
adversaries will be enemies. If the sign in which the lord of the ascend- 36
ent and the lord of [the sign] opposite it are is one of the houses of
Mercury, then it indicates that this quarrel will be stirred up between
these two because of children or one who is in the position of a child.
If this sign is one of the houses of Venus, then the quarrel will be be-   37
cause of women or sisters or daughters or one whose [position] is like
their position. If this sign is one of the signs of Mars, then it indicates 38
that this quarrel will be because of sisters or the children of sisters or
the children of brothers. If it is one of the houses of Saturn or the   39
Sun, then it indicates that the quarrel will be because of the fathers or
the grandfathers or one who is in this position. If it is the house of the 40
Moon, then the quarrel will be because of the mothers or because of
one having a relationship from the mothers. If it is one of the houses   41
of Jupiter, then it indicates that it will be because of the older brothers
or because of the brothers and the friends.

V-34   **Chapter 34.**

1   If you are asked about a man, whether he will depart from his land
and his city or travel from it or be exiled by a command from his
master or other than this, then look at the Moon at the commence-
2 ment of this. If it is flowing from the benefics while a benefic is in
the ascendent and is aspecting it [the Moon], then it indicates that he
3 will return to his home and his city. If the Moon is departing from the
malefics while the ascendent and the Moon are injured, then it indicates that misfortunes and misery will reach him and that he will not
be able to return.

V-35   **Chapter 35. If you want to know the matter of a theft that has been
committed or something that has been lost, whether he will possess it
[again] or not.**

1   Look, and if it is a time when goods are stolen or lost or gone astray
or if you are asked about this when, [as for] the two luminaries, each
one of them is aspecting its lord from trine, then it indicates that these
2 goods will be recovered quickly without pain or trouble. But if the
Sun aspects the Moon from quartile, then it indicates that these
goods of his which were lost will be found after a long time [and] with
trouble and that the thieves will have moved the goods from the first
3 place in which they put it when they stole it to another place. If the
Moon and the Sun are opposed, one of the two to the other, then it
4 indicates that it will be found after a time and trouble. If the Moon is
p. 137 with a star in the house which [belongs to] the star, then | it indicates
5 that it will be more proper that this be found. If the Sun is aspecting
this place and this star, then it will be more proper that it be found.
6 If the dodecatemorion of the Moon is in the ascendent or in the midheaven or in the sign in which the Sun is or in the sign in which the
lord of the Moon is or in the sign in which an eastern star is, then those
7 goods which were stolen or lost will be found. If the Moon is at the
end of [the sign] opposite the sign of the ascendent, or in the second
8 [sign] from it, then it indicates that it will not be found. But if the
Sun at that hour is aspecting the Moon from trine, then it will be
found because God made the Sun light and it is eclipsed from [his]
orders and it illuminates everything dark and overcomes it, if God
9 wishes. If the Moon is in the place which the learned from among the
masters of the stars name the "burned way", then it indicates that

he will not possess it or that he will possess it after trouble and delay. If both of the two luminaries are under the earth, then it indicates   10 that the thing which was stolen or lost will disappear so that he will not possess it. If the lot of good fortune is with the Sun or the Sun   11 aspects the lot of good fortune, it indicates that he will soon possess the thing which was lost or stolen. If the Moon is with the lot of good   12 fortune or it aspects the Moon without the Sun aspecting it or being with it, then it indicates that he will possess the thing which was stolen or lost, but it indicates that there will be slowness and trouble in it. If one of the two luminaries is not with the lot of good fortune   13 or they do not aspect the lot of good fortune, then it indicates that he will not possess the thing which was stolen or lost and it will not be necessary for its owner to search for it since he would toil without accomplishing anything. If the Moon is in the ascendent, then it   14 indicates that he will soon possess what was lost or stolen because, if the two luminaries are in the ascendent, they indicate that he will possess the thing that was stolen or lost as they both have superior power in this place. If the Moon is under the Sun's rays and is dimi-   15 nishing, then it indicates that he will not possess the thing which was stolen or lost perfectly because this is because of an unavoidable judgment. If the two luminaries are in [the sign] opposite the ascend-   16 ent, then it indicates that he will not possess the thing which was stolen or lost except with slowness and trouble or a quarrel and insult and fighting. If the Sun is alone in the ascendent, then he will possess the   17 thing which was stolen or lost unless the ascendent is Aquarius or Gemini or Libra and the Sun is in it, as these three signs are opposite the signs which are the Sun's triplicity. If the Sun is in one of these   18 three signs, then it will be bad and it will not be suitable for him to possess it. If the Sun is in | the ascendent and the thing which was   19
stolen belongs to someone whose nativity is known and it was lost or   p. 138 stolen at an hour in which the Moon was in the sign in which a bene- fic planet was in his nativity, then it indicates that he will possess the thing which was lost.

There were some of the ancient scientists who looked concerning   20 the matter of theft from the four cardines, and if one of them was asked about a theft or something lost he would look concerning what was stolen or lost from the ascendent, and at the midheaven for the owner of the goods, who is the one from whom these goods were stolen

and who is seeking them, and for the matter of the thief from [the sign] opposite the ascendent, and the shelter of the thieves [for] what they stole [and] where they put the goods from the cardine under the
21 earth. If the benefics are in the ascendent or aspect the ascendent, then they say that he will possess that which was lost or stolen, and [the slave] will return to his lords and the house from which he was
22 stolen. If a star is in the midheaven and this sign is one of its houses, then they say that he who asks about the theft will be sincere and will
23 seek it properly. If the midheaven does not belong to the star which is in the midheaven and it has no power in it, then they say that the
24 seeker calls upon other than truth. If the cardine under the earth is a sign possessing two bodies, then they declare that what was stolen or lost does not belong to one man, but [is shared] between two
25 partners. If the cardine under the earth is not [one] possessing two bodies but is a tropical sign, then they say that what was stolen or lost
26 belongs to one man and there is no partner in it. If the cardine under the earth is a masculine sign, then they declare that what was stolen or lost belongs to men, but if the sign is an effeminate sign they say
27 that it belongs to women. If the cardine under the earth is a moist sign, then they declare that what was stolen or lost is near a sea or a spring or a stream or a valley or a river or a canal or a place in which
28 there is water. If the sign, the house of the fathers, is a quadruped sign, then they say that what was stolen or lost is in the dung of sheep or the shelters of animals or in the place where animals are tied up or
29 the habitations of animals. If the cardine under the earth is one of the signs which resembles a man and Jupiter and Venus aspect it, then they say that what was stolen or lost is in a clean place and a
30 good place. If Jupiter and Venus do not aspect this cardine but Mars aspects it, then they say that what was stolen or lost is in places of
31 fires or in the forge[s] of blacksmiths or what is like this. If Mars does not aspect this sign but Saturn aspects it, then they say that what was stolen or lost the thieves have handed over to slaves, so that they received [it] from them and placed it in a dark house and a filthy
32 place open to [?] the wind or in a lofty, moist, dirty place. Even if
p. 139 Saturn aspects | this sign, if Jupiter is in it, then the slaves will not receive this theft from the thieves, but one who has a noble lineage will
33 receive it from them. If Jupiter is not in this sign but Mars is in it, then they say that he who takes these goods from the thieves will be in the

loathsomeness of his character a slave, or free for the day. If Mars is   34
not in this sign but Venus is in it from the first degree of this sign to
twenty degrees, then they say that the thieves will take what was
stolen from women, and they are women possessing properties and a
noble lineage. If Venus is in the remaining ten degrees of the sign   35
which is [the cardine] under the earth, then they say that slave girls
or those who do the work of slave girls will take what was lost or
stolen from the thieves. If Venus is not in the cardine under the earth   36
but Mercury is in that place in the ten degrees at the beginning of the
sign, then a man will take what was stolen from the thieves, and that
man will have wisdom and a noble lineage and a good reputation, and
[in the ten degrees] before [after] this he will be a poor man and will
be master of wealth and good fortune for the day. If Mercury is in the   37
remaining ten degrees of the sign, then they say that he who takes the
goods from the thieves is a slave or a man who does the work of
slaves.

If the Sun is aspecting the lot of good fortune, then they say that   38
he will soon possess what was lost or stolen. If the Moon is the one   39
which aspects the lot of good fortune and the Sun does not aspect [it],
then they say that he will possess these goods after a delay. If the two   40
luminaries do not aspect the lot of good fortune and do not aspect the
ascendent, then they say that they will not possess these goods except
after trouble and pain. They say that, if the Moon is in quartile of the   41
Sun or in its trine or [the sign] opposite the ascendent, then he will
possess [again] the slave who runs away at that hour or the goods
which are stolen at that hour or lost. If the Sun at that hour in which   42
I said that it was in trine of the Moon or quartile of it or opposition to
it is in the ascendent or in the cardine, midheaven, or with the lot of
good fortune, or aspecting the cardines and the places together, then
it indicates that he will properly possess these goods. If the Moon is in   43
the last degrees of the sign, in the third figure [decan], then it indicates that what was lost or stolen at that hour will be transported
from place to place.

If you want to know the condition of the goods which were stolen   44
or lost, and you want to know what they are, then the indicator of all
of this is the Moon. If at that hour in which you are asked about the   45
theft it is in a term of Saturn while Saturn is in the mid|heaven or in   p. 140
its exaltation, then it indicates that what was stolen is something

costly and is one of the things which are necessary in farming the
46 land or building or acquiring property. If Saturn is not in any of these
places but is under the earth, then it indicates that the goods are
47 filthy, shabby, [and] worn. If Saturn is in a sign cadent from a cardine, and is wherever [among] the signs it happens to be in [its] place
or is in Aries in its dejection, then it indicates that these goods are
48 vile, filthy, [and] broken. If Saturn is wherever it happens to be
among these places cadent from the cardines and aspects the Moon,
then it indicates that there is coarseness and roughness in what was
49 stolen or lost. If at that hour at which you are asked the Moon is not
in a term of Saturn but is in a term of Jupiter, then it indicates that
what was stolen or lost is of gold or silver or something having lustre
and [all] kinds of these or garments of silk brocade or costly goods,
which is something one will not get hold of except in the treasures of
50 the wealthy [and] rich. If at that hour the Moon is not in a term of
Jupiter but is in a term of Mars, then it indicates that what was stolen
is something worked in fire or in a kiln or the forge[s] of blacksmiths
51 or like that. If Mars and Mercury together aspect the Moon, then it
indicates that the thing which I mentioned as being worked in fire or
52 a kiln is something worked with a masterly work, a good method. If
the Moon is in a term of Mars but Mars does not aspect it while Venus
or Mercury does aspect it, then it indicates that that of which I wrote
that it is worked in fire and a kiln is something penetrated by a dye
53 or ring-stones or amulets or with all sorts of jewels. If you are asked
when the Moon is in a term of Venus, then it indicates that what was
stolen or lost is silver or gold or a jewel or a costly stone or garments
in which there is noble [and] beautiful cloth, or something whose co-
lors from the dye are like fire, perfume so that it receives from it the
odor of a scent, or a necklace, or the trinkets of women, or something
agreeable in [its] odor, whose nature is moist, which has a lustre, [and]
54 which women crave and are astonished at. If at the hour in which you
are asked the Moon is in a cardine of Venus and Venus is with the
Moon in an effeminate sign, it indicates that those goods which were
55 stolen belong to women. If Mars aspects Venus, then it indicates that
the thing which was stolen is some jewel which has no lustre, [but] was
56 worked with delicate workmanship. If at the time you are asked the
Moon is in a term of Mercury, then it indicates that what was stolen is
a book, or a ledger full of layers, or a ledger in which [there is] a book

of the learned, or what is necessary for women or men, or what is
necessary on journeys like denarii and dirhams and what has been
minted into coinage.

    I will make clear to you what the signs indicate with what I wrote   57
for you in the case of the terms as the power of the signs is mixed
with the terms so that they are more powerful for your science and
more learned | for your consideration. Look: if the Moon is in Aries at   p. 141
the hour you are asked about what was stolen or lost, then it indicates   58
that what was stolen is garments, suit[s] of clothes, or trinkets worn
on the head and face. If the Moon is in Taurus, then it indicates that   59
what was stolen is gold or silver or trinkets with which they are
adorned or something useful for vows and for mosques and deities. If   60
the Moon is in Gemini, then what was stolen is dirhams or denarii or
some of what is necessary in taking and giving [trade], or a ledger in
which is a book, or an idol useful for the deities. If the Moon is in   61
Cancer, then it indicates that what was stolen is a costly gem [or
something] moist. If the Moon is in Leo, then it indicates that it is   62
gold or silver or something fashioned from brass. If the Moon is in   63
Virgo, then it indicates that it is trinkets of women or denarii. If the   64
Moon is in Libra, then it indicates that what was stolen has a mixture
of things in it, or is something useful for the body, or something bought
[for its] weight, or trinkets useful for eternity. If the Moon is in Scor-   65
pio, then it indicates that what was stolen is gold or silver or brass
or a stone having a lustre. If the Moon is in Sagittarius, then it indicates   66
that what was stolen is something variegated, which is [all] sorts of
jewel[s], and something that is craved and competed for and is pre-
cious to its people. If the Moon is in Capricorn, then it indicates that   67
what was stolen is like what I wrote if the Moon is in Cancer or [some-
thing] like this or close to it. If the Moon is in Aquarius, then it   68
indicates that what was stolen is like what I wrote if the Moon is in
Leo or [something] like this or close to it. If the Moon is in Pisces,   69
then what was stolen is like what the Moon indicates when it is in
Sagittarius or [something] like this or close to it.

    If the Moon is increasing in computation and in light, then what   70
was stolen is something new, but if the Moon is decreasing in computation and in light, then it indicates that what was stolen is
shabby or worn. If you are asked the question when the ascendent   71
is a sign possessing two bodies, then it indicates that the thing

which was stolen is folded or something of which [one] part is joined
to [another] part; and if there is a conjunction of the Moon in a
72 sign possessing two bodies, then it indicates like this. If you wish
to know the quantity of the goods which were stolen, then count
from the first degree [of the sign] in which the Moon is to the degree
73 in which Mercury is. If they are in signs which are among those that
are double [even], then it indicates that what was stolen is tied to-
74 gether or more than one. If what is between the Moon and Mercury is
some of the single [odd] signs, then what was stolen is one.

75   If you are asked about a theft, then look at the ascendent at that
76 hour. If the two luminaries aspect it, then the one who stole these
goods is from the people of the house or the people of the dwelling,
77 and he did not enter from the outside. If one of the two luminaries
p. 142 aspects the ascendent and | the other of the two is distant from the
ascendent and does not aspect it, then it indicates that the thief is not
from the people of the house, but he has frequented them and its
78 people know him. If both of the luminaries are not aspecting the ascendent, then the thief is a stranger [and] has entered from the outside,
and there is no acquaintance between him and the people of the house,
and he has not frequented it before this.

79   If you want to know what is the decoration of the thief and his
figure and his color, then the stars which at that hour are in [the
80 sign] opposite the ascendent are the indicators of this. If you find
[that] this place has none of the stars in it, then look at the sign
cadent from the sign of midheaven, which is the ninth from the ascend-
81 ent. Then look at what of the stars is in it, as they indicate the cha-
82 racteristic[s] of the thief and his color and his decoration. If you find
this sign also empty with none of the stars in it, then look at the sign
cadent from the ascendent, which is the twelfth from the sign of the
83 ascendent. If you find any of the stars in it, then it indicates the
84 characteristic[s] of the thief and his decoration. If you find this place
also empty, then look at the Moon at that hour, with which star it is
conjoining, as it is the indicator of the characteristics] of the thief.
85 If the Moon at that hour is not conjoining with any of the stars, then
look at the Moon, from which star it is departing and at which star it
arrives as these two stars indicate the characteristic[s] of the thief.

86   If the indicator of the characteristic[s] of the thief is Jupiter, then
the thief will be white, fat, great in his eyes, the whites of his eyes

will be smaller than what is necessary for it to be because of the
measure of that eye; and their beards will be rounded [and] curly,
and their natures and their gentleness will be good. If the indicator of   87
the characteristic[s] of the thieves is Saturn, then it indicates that this
thief is repulsive in [his] face, black in [his] color; his gaze is toward
the ground, [and] he is broken [and] small in [his] eyes, slim, twisted
in [his] gaze; a pallor is upon him, [his] limbs abound in hair, [his]
eyebrows are grown together; he is a liar, sickly, and his gentleness and
his nature proceed in accordance with secrets and tricks; he is pro-
found and has idea[s] and contemplation. If the indicator of the   88
characteristic[s] of the thieves is Mars, then this thief will be red in
[his] color, reddish in [his] hair, lank-haired, sharp in [his] vision, fat-
cheeked in [his] face, [having] gaiety, a master of joking, capricious,
turning himself from [one] condition to [another] condition, sharp in
[his] glance; he rushes to injure men and to obliterate their thing[s].
If it is Venus which indicates the thief, then this thief is handsome,   89
abounding in hair on [his] head, fat, handsome in [his] eyes and the
black in his eyes is greater than their whiteness, white in [his] extrem-
ity and [his] color, [but] his whiteness is mixed with redness; and
he is fat, good in his gentleness and manner[s], [and] he submits
courteously to a command. If the indicator of the characteristic[s] of   90
the thief is Mercury, then it indicates that this thief is slim, emaciated,
good in [his] bones, powerful, bald, a man handsome in [his] beard,
pale, [and] not straight in [his] thinking. If the indicator of the charac-   91
teristic[s] of the thief is the Sun or the Moon, then his characteristic[s]
and his likeness is similar to the manner in which I wrote in one of
these situations if this [planet] is with the Sun or the Moon or aspects | p. 143
the Sun or the Moon. If the Sun and the Moon do not aspect the stars   92
and have withdrawn from them and have no aspect to any of the
stars and [they are] not with these two in the same sign, when the
Sun is the indicator of the characteristic[s] of the thief, then it indicates that the thief is fat [and] red, and yellowness is mixed in his
eyes. If the Moon is the indicator of the characteristic[s] of the thief,   93
then it indicates that this thief is comely in [his] appearance, white,
[and] fat-cheeked in [his] face.

Look also at the nature of the signs, what it is, as it is more suitable   94
if one of them agrees with the other or it is more appropriate if this is
known and the consideration about it is more learned. Its nature and   95

the figure of the sign indicate that that star which indicates the
characteristic[s] of the thief and his manner, if it [the sign] is with the
star which is the indicator of the characteristic[s] of the thief and his
96 manner, then mix the signs with the positions of the stars. Aries indicates that [his] limb[s] are full of hair, he is handsome in [his] stature,
his gaze is toward the ground, he is bald, joyful, gay in [his] face,
97 humorous, impudent in [his] speech. Taurus indicates that the thief
is sharp-nosed, broad in [his] forehead, protruding in [his] forehead,
elevated in [his] hair; his character is unknown because his character
is [of all] sorts, and he has power in what is hidden and deception and
trickery; he is broad in his nostrils, burly in [his] neck, fat, great in the
blackness of [his] eyes; his eyebrow[s] are smaller than the measure of
98 these two [eyes] and he is on the short side. Gemini indicates that the
thief is powerful in [his] stance, elongated in what is between [his]
shoulders; his gentleness and his character are good; there are some
of them who write and some who before this were trusted, and they
99 had a position among men, were pleasant in their view. Cancer indicates that the thief is large in [his] shoulder-blades, solid in [his] bones;
he has no hair, is stingy, glum-faced, black in [his] color, gag-toothed,
powerful in the stance of his lower limb[s], which are superior to the
100 higher of them [the limbs]. Leo indicates that the thief is blue, red-
haired, reddish in color, lank-haired, comely in [his] appearance,
superior in his higher joints which are more ample than his lower
[ones], slender in his legs, irascible, coarse, sharp-sighted; the sharp-
ness of his vision is like a lion's; there are some of them who are epi-
101 leptic [and] are recognized by it. Virgo indicates that the thief is
straight in [his] posture, handsome in [his] body, powerful in [his]
stance and [his] limbs, not excessive in [his] fatness or [his] slimness,
humorous, good in [his] gentleness, trustworthy, sincere, one of those
who is educated in writing and what it is useful for, coveted for this,
profitable in [his] uprightness and [his] friendliness in an affair.
102 Libra indicates that the thief is handsome in [his] face and color,
white, equal in [his] limbs; one of them does not differ from the other;
he was educated in beating on strings and singing and the rules of
tunes and of poetry; he is handsome in [his] face, good in [his] manner
in calculating [his] livelihood, learned in words; he tends toward what
is in the power of Venus and lust for women, [and] is greedy [and]
103 stimulated toward it. Scorpio indicates that the thief is thick in the

hair on [his] hand, elevated in [his] hair; there is no black in the pupil
of his eye; he has bluish-black eyes [and is] powerful in [his] eyes, fat-
cheeked in [his] face, narrow in his forehead, small in it, protruding
with [his] forehead, long-legged, large in [his] feet, | elongated in what   p. 144
is between [his] shoulders; his nature and his character are of embezzle-
ment; he has little diffidence or reflection on matters, but hastens
to his affair; he is not pleasing and his reputation is disgraceful.
Sagittarius indicates that the thief is long-legged, wide-thighed; if he   104
turns his back he is more comely than if he faces [one]; lank in [his]
beard, long in it [but] small in it, red in [his] color, clever, agile, delicate, a run-away slave, a marksman, he works with [his] hands; he is a
profiteer, a wastrel, a generous man; there are some of them whose
craving is for animals, and some who are bald or have no hair. Capri-   105
corn indicates that the thief is thin-legged, miserable in [his] two
[legs], slim, a male; the figure of his face resembles a goat's in the
dark; lank in [his] beard, sharp-eyed; his glance is toward the ground,
his opinion does not change from [one] situation to [another] situation;
he is trivial in [his] thought and consideration[s]. Aquarius indicates   106
that the thief is not tall in [his] stature nor slight, but powerful in
[his] stance, eager for ornamentation, eager for the gathering of properties, handsome in [his] beard, pleasing in [his] diet, good in [his]
gentleness in his meal[s] and in cleaning himself, abounding in ex-
penses ; one of his two legs is larger than the other and longer. Pisces   107
indicates that he is elongated in what is between [his] shoulders,
abounding in hair on [his] head, small-headed and small-faced, narrow
in [his] two sides; the blackness of his eyes is greater than their whiteness; he is bending down, he loves himself, he is twisted in his sight.

The stars and the signs are the indicators of these characteristic[s]   108
if one of them is mixed with the other. If the benefics aspect the   109
indicator which indicates the characteristic[s] of the thief, then the
thief will have a noble lineage. If the malefics are aspecting the indi-   110
cator, then the thief is a slave or a slave-girl or one who does service.
If Venus is the one which indicates the thief and his characteristic[s],   111
then he who stole is a woman or a lady stealing for women. If Mer-   112
cury is the indicator of the thief, then he is a boy or a youth, a
young man. If Mars is the indicator of the thief, then it indicates that   113
he is a young man. If Jupiter is the indicator of the thief, then it in-   114
dicates that the thief is [old age and youth] combined [i. e., middle-

115 aged]. If Saturn is the indicator, then it indicates that the thief has
years.

116   Together with what I wrote for you look at the positions of the
stars and mix them with what I wrote for you in the introduction of
117 this book. If a star is eastern, it indicates the thief [is] a young man.
118 If it is western, then it indicates that he has years. If it is very great
119 in its captivity [?]—I mean that it is in its first station— then it indicates that he is advanced in years and is closer to old age than to
120
121 youth. If it is in its second station, it indicates like this. If the indicator is one of the stars under the Sun's rays, then it indicates the
122 years of this thief. If the star comes out from under the [Sun's] rays,
p. 145 and becomes western or | eastern, the eastern [planet] indicates that
123 he is a youth and the western indicates that he is an elder. If Saturn
is the one that comes out from under the [Sun's] rays or becomes
eastern, then mix in his old age, and whenever its [Saturn's] position
is eastern, then according to this it indicates that the thief is mixed
124 [middle-aged], is not one abounding in years nor a youth. If the indicator is Mercury or Venus and they are both eastern, then they
125 indicate that the thief is a maiden or a young man, a youth. If they
both are western, then they indicate that the thief is mixed [middle-
126 aged]. If the indicator is in its exaltation, then it indicates that the
127 thief is healthy in [his] limbs. If it is in its dejection, then it indicates
128 that his limbs are not healthy. If this star is near its exaltation, it
129 indicates like what I wrote if it is in its exaltation or its dejection. [It
indicates also] thus if it conjoins with a planet in its exaltation or its
130 dejection. If there are between the indicator of the thief and that it
enters under the Sun's rays seven days, then the thief will have stolen
131 before that. If Mars is the one which aspects that star, then it indicates
that imprisonment and agony and misery and misfortune have reached
132 the thief before this on account of theft. Look at the lot of fortune
133 concerning this matter. If the malefics are not aspecting it, then it
indicates that the thief has not stolen before this.

134   If it is Saturn which aspects the Moon and the ascendent, then it
indicates that the thief has used tricks and has deceived and has mis-
135 led so that he might steal. If Jupiter is the indicator of the thief, then
it indicates that the thief did not desire the theft and entered the
house for [something] other than this, [but] then the theft happened
to him [and] it was determined for him after his entry into the house

that he should steal when he saw the deficiency. If Mars is the one   136
which aspects the ascendent or the Moon, then the matter comes to
theft so that he weakens or digs out the wall of the house in which are
the goods, or breaks the lock, or copies the key, or enters in the sky-
light of the house. If Venus is the one which aspects the ascendent or   137
the Moon, then it indicates that the thief has entered for conversation,
and there is friendship between him and the people of the house and
their trust is in this [man], [but] then he will steal. If Mercury is the   138
one which aspects the ascendent or the Moon, then it indicates that the
thief entered the house by a ruse and subterfuge and cleverness and
the wish for trouble for the people of the house in which he committed
the robbery.

Chapter 36. The runaway.   V-36

If a slave or a slave girl runs away or a fugitive flees and you want   1
to know whether you will get the better | of him or not, then look   p. 146
concerning the matter of the runaway at the ascendent and the
Moon, and [at] the Sun and the midheaven [concerning] the condition of his seeker and his master. If the ascendent and the Moon are   2
in a tropical sign, [one] of the signs in which the night and day are
equal, then it indicates that the runaway has travelled a distance on
land or on sea. If the ascendent is a sign possessing two bodies, then   3
it indicates that another has run away with the runaway. If the ascend-   4
ent is a sign crooked in rising, then it indicates that the runaway,
being confused, has strayed from the path or been seized in [his]
flight. If the ascendent is a sign straight in rising, then it indicates   5
that the runaway sticks to the street and does not stray and is not
confused so that he arrives at his place which he wishes. If the Moon is   6
not on the equator but is in a sign possessing two bodies in [its] first
degrees till it reaches fifteen degrees of that sign, then it indicates
that the running away of the runaway is his first running away, but
running away will be habitual [for him] after this. If the Moon is in   7
the remaining fifteen degrees of the sign, then it indicates that the
runaway was a runaway before this.

If the Moon is in the ascendent, then it indicates that the runaway   8
is headed towards the East. If the Moon is [in] the midheaven, then it   9
indicates that the runaway is headed towards the qibla [the South].
If it is opposite the ascendent, then it indicates that he is headed   10

11 towards the West. If the Moon is in the cardine of the fathers [the fourth], then it indicates that the runaway is headed toward the seas
12 [the North]. If the Moon is not in any of the cardines but [is] in one of the signs which [are] between the midheaven and the ascendent, then
13 it indicates that the runaway is headed toward the East. If the Moon is in [one of] the signs which [are] between the midheaven and [the sign] opposite the ascendent, then it indicates that the runaway is
14 headed toward the qibla [the South]. If the Moon is in [one of] the signs which [are] between [the sign] opposite the ascendent and the cardine of the fathers, then it indicates that the runaway is headed toward the
15 West. If the Moon is in what is between the cardine, the fourth, and the ascendent, then the runaway is headed toward the seas [the North].

16   If the Moon is conjoining with Mars while Mars is in its station or from its place in which it is in its station aspects the Moon, then it indicates that the runaway has shed blood in the city which he came to so that because of this he has fallen in chains or was seized by force
17 so that he might be sent back to his master. If it is Saturn which aspects the Moon as I wrote for you of the aspect of Mars, then it indicates that the runaway has caused suspicion and committed a ruse
18 so that because of this he has fallen in chains. If Saturn is stationary when the Moon conjoins with it, then it indicates that the runaway
19 will strangle himself. If at that hour any of the benefics aspects the
20 Moon, then it indicates that this misfortune will leave him. If Saturn is not in its station when the Moon conjoins with it, then it indicates that the runaway has lost the goods which he stole when he ran away, he wandered away from them, and the runaway will be seized and sent back to his master, and misery and chains will reach him in this running away of his.

p. 147
21 | If the benefics are in the ascendent or aspect the ascendent or are with the Moon, then release from slavery truly [and] certainly is
22 determined for the runaway who has run away at that hour. The best of the benefics in this matter [is] Venus when it aspects the ascendent or the Moon or is with the Moon or in the ascendent, as, if Venus happens to be in this position, then, if the runaway who ran away at that hour escapes, he will not be caught, and if he is caught and sent back to his master, then he will be content with him and will grant him his rule.

If the Moon is increasing, then he [the master] will not catch the   23
runaway and will not be his equal in speed. If the Moon is decreasing,   24
then he will soon be caught. If the Sun is in [the sign] opposite the   25
ascendent while Saturn is in the sign which sets after the Sun, which
is the eighth sign from the ascendent, then it indicates that the master
of the runaway will die before the runaway is caught. If a malefic is   26
[in] the midheaven or with the Sun, then it indicates that the seeker
of this runaway will have no good in his search, and if he catches him
and gets the better of him, then misfortune and misery will happen to
him. If he runs away when the Moon at that hour [is] in [the sign]   27
opposite the ascendent while Mars is in the sign which sets after [the
sign] opposite the ascendent, which is the eighth from the ascendent,
and there is no aspect to it from the benefics and no relief, then it
indicates that misfortune and difficulty will reach the runaway in
this running away of his, and its outcome will be that he will die with
respect to this. If the Moon is in [the sign] opposite the ascendent and   28
it is not Mars which sets after it but Mercury which sets after the
Moon while Mars aspects Mercury from trine, it indicates that evil
will reach the runaway in this running away of his, and its outcome
with respect to this [is] that he will die. If the Moon is under the Sun's   29
rays and has no light while Mars aspects it at that hour, then destruction from the burning of fire or death by a knife will reach the runaway
in this running away of his.

Look at the nature of the sign in which the Moon [is] under the   30
Sun's rays, that is diminished in its light, as this sign indicates from
what cause his death will be. If the nature of this sign is like a human,   31
then misfortune will reach him from men. If the nature of this sign is   32
the nature of animals who walk on four [feet], then this misfortune
will reach him from animals. Look concerning the nature of the rest   33
of the signs in which the Moon is diminished in its light. If this sign is   34
one of the signs of earth, then it indicates that a building will be
demolished upon the runaway so that he perishes.

If the Moon is in [the sign] opposite the ascendent under the [Sun's]   35
rays while Saturn aspects it from a watery sign, then it indicates that
the death of this [runaway] will be [from] drowning in a flood of
water. If Mercury is with Saturn in the way of which I wrote, then it   36
indicates that the runaway will kill himself. If Jupiter and Venus are   37
together in this location or aspect the Moon, then the two of them will

dispel this misfortune from him, if God wishes, especially if Jupiter and Venus are in their light and their power.

38   If the Moon conjoins with Mars in longitude, then beating and im-
p. 148 prisonment will reach the runaway at that hour | in this running away
39 of his. If the Moon is conjoining with Mars in latitude while Jupiter aspects Mars, then it indicates that misfortune will reach the runaway because of the Moon's conjoining with Mars and fear of death will be immoderate in him, but he will escape from this death because of
40 Jupiter's aspect of the Moon. If the Moon is with the malefics in one of the cardines, then an unpleasant death will reach the runaway at that hour in this running away of his, and his hand[s] and his feet will
41 be cut off. If the Moon is [in] the midheaven while Mars is in another sign on the right of the Moon and Saturn on its left so that they squeeze the Moon in between them or squeeze the Moon with [their] aspect, then it is an indicator that the runaway at that hour will be strangled
42 so that he dies. But if Mars is on the left of the Moon and Saturn on its right squeezing the Moon between them, then it indicates that the runaway who runs away at that hour will be crucified and will die
43 with respect to this. If the Moon is in the cardine of midheaven or [the sign] opposite the ascendent or in the cardine of the fathers while, in another sign on the right of the Moon and on its left, in one of the two is the Sun and in the other Mars, squeezing the Moon between them, then the runaway who runs away at that hour will be burned alive in
44 a fire. If it is the sign in which the Moon is under the [Sun's] rays and the lord of the sign in which the Sun is does not aspect the Moon, then it indicates that the master of the runaway who runs away at that
45 hour will die before the runaway is caught. If he runs away at an hour when the ascendent or the Moon or the lord of the sign in which the Moon is is in a tropical sign, then it indicates that the runaway will
46 return to his master submissively. If the Moon is aspecting the benefics and the malefics together, if they are in one sign or in diverse signs, then he who runs away at that hour will be caught, especially if this malefic is in quartile of the Moon or in opposition to it, or rather he
47 will catch him when the Moon reaches the position of this malefic. If this runaway is not caught also at this time, then whenever the Moon reaches the position in which this malefic was, then difficulty and
48 misfortune will reach him. If the Moon and the ascendent are injured while the benefics do not aspect the ascendent or the Moon, then it

310

indicates that a return will be difficult for him who runs away at
that hour, and if he does return, calamity and misfortune will reach
him. If the benefics aspect the ascendent and the Moon and the bene- 49
fics which aspect the ascendent and the Moon are in a fixed sign
while the ascendent and the Moon are free from the aspect of the
benefics, then this runaway has escaped and made his get-away, and
he [his master] will not get the better of him. If the benefics which 50
aspect the Moon and the ascendent are not in a fixed sign but are in a
tropical sign or a sign possessing two bodies, then it indicates that the
runaway will return or will be caught, but evil and suffering will not
reach him from his master because of this running away of his, and
his master's anger with him will be shattered.

If the Sun aspects the ascendent and the Moon, then it indicates 51
that, whoever runs away or steals goods at that hour, [his master]
will triumph over the runaway and the goods and get the better of
him. If Mars aspects the ascendent and the Moon, then it indicates 52
that he will get power over him soon. If Saturn aspects | the ascendent 53
and the Moon, then it indicates that [his master] will not get power p. 149
over him except after a delay or trouble. If Jupiter is in [the sign] 54
opposite the ascendent, then it indicates that the anger of his master
with the runaway at that hour will subside and be dissolved, and
disgrace and evil will not reach him from his master. If Venus is in 55
[the sign] opposite the ascendent, then it indicates that the runaway
[is] in a place in which the deities are worshipped.

If the lord of the ascendent is in the first decan of a sign or aspects 56
it, then it indicates that the runaway is not in a place which it is
thought that he is in, and he has not come to a distant place, but is
near by. If a retrograde star is with the lord of the ascendent or aspects 57
its house from its place, then it indicates that the runaway [is] near
by and is not distant.

I will make clear to you the matter of the runaway from the ascend- 58
ent and the sign in which the Moon is if no star is with these two or
aspecting them. Look, and if the ascendent is Aries, or [if] the Moon 59
is in Aries and the runaway runs away at that hour when the ascendent is Aries or Gemini or Leo or Sagittarius or Pisces, then it indicates
that [his master] will soon have power over the runaway, or rather
that he will return submissively of his own accord. If the Moon is in 60
Aries while the ascendent is in another than the signs which we

mentioned, then it indicates that, even if his seeker wears [himself]
out and is concerned about his search, he will not get power over him

61 who runs away at that hour. If the Moon or the ascendent is in Taurus,
then it indicates that [his master] will get the better of him who runs
away at that hour, but this [will be] after effort and trouble and delay.

62 If the ascendent or the Moon is in Gemini, in the first fifteen degrees,
then it indicates that, if [his master] does not get the better of him
who runs away at that hour within two days, then he has escaped and
[the master] will not get power over him, but he has reached a distant

63 land and a report that he is alive will come to his masters. If the
ascendent is in the remaining fifteen degrees of Gemini, then it indi-

64 cates that he who runs away at that hour will soon be caught. If the
ascendent or the Moon is in Cancer, then it indicates that [his master]
will get the better of the runaway [who] runs away at that hour after

65 a delay in a place in which the deities are worshipped. If the ascendent
or the Moon is in the first half of the sign of Leo, then it indicates that
[his master] will get the better of him who runs away at that hour in the
house of one mighty in importance, who has power and strength and
nobility, and because of the strength of this man [his master] will

66 not reach him except after delay and trouble. If the ascendent or the
Moon is in Virgo, then it indicates that capturing the runaway at that
hour will be troublesome to his seeker, as he [is] swift in motion and

67 will not stay in one place. If the ascendent or the Moon is in Libra,
then it indicates that [his master] will get the better of the runaway
at that hour, but the runaway will return after this when he sees the

68 severity of his master's anger. If the ascendent or the Moon is in
Scorpio, then it indicates that [his master] will get the better of the
runaway soon in a place in which the deities are worshipped, and

69 sometimes he will return of his own accord, submissively. If the
ascendent or the Moon is in Sagittarius, then it indicates that, if [his
master] does not get the better of the runaway at that hour within
five days, then he will die and will not get power over him and will

70 not know where he has gone. | If the ascendent or the Moon is in
p. 150   Capricorn, then it indicates that the runaway at that hour will turn
from place to place and [his master] will not get power over him except

71 after delay and trouble. If the ascendent or the Moon is in Aquarius in
the first ten degrees, it indicates that [his master] will get the better of

72 the runaway at that hour. If the ascendent or the Moon is in the re-

maining degrees of Aquarius, then [his master] will not get power over the runaway at that hour and will not hope to get the better of him. If the ascendent or the Moon is in the first degrees of Pisces, then it indicates that the runaway at that hour will not be caught. If the ascendent or the Moon is in the remaining degrees of Pisces, then [his master] will get the better of the runaway at that hour.

73
74

If the Moon is in a sign possessing two bodies, in the first half, then it indicates that the runaway was not a runaway before this, which is his first running away. But if the Moon is in a sign possessing two bodies, in the second half, then it indicates that the runaway has run away before [this] time, and this is not disclaimed by him.

75

76

This is a hidden chapter because, [if his master] does not possess the hour at which the runaway ran away, then look concerning the commencement of this matter at the hour in which the report of the running away of the slave or slave girl reached the slave's master, {and look concerning all of these things at the conjoining of the Moon also. If the commencement of an action [is] when the Moon first conjoins with the benefics, then with the malefics, then it indicates that the beginning of this action will be good and its end bad. If it is opposite to this situation, then according to the opposite of this—that is, if the Moon is first conjoining with the malefics, then with the benefics, the beginning of the action will be bad and its end fortunate. If there is a planet in the ascendent, in the first ten degrees, then it indicates that the action and the thing which is commenced at that hour will be easy. If a planet is in the remaining degrees of the ascendent, then it indicates that in the thing which is commenced at that hour there will occur delay and difficulty. If Jupiter is in the ascendent while the Moon conjoins with Saturn or Mars, then the beginning of the action which is commenced at that hour will be easy, simple, but its end troublesome, bad. If what I mentioned is opposite to this situation, then predict the opposite of this.} If the Moon is under the Sun's rays, then he who runs away from his master at that hour will not be caught, and if he is caught, then [it will be] after a delay. {Every commencement of an action or thing that is at that hour [will be] bad.} If the Moon is with a star, [one] of the malefics, in the same degree in the ascendent or in other than this of the places, then [his master] will not get the better of him who runs away at that hour, and will not get

77

(77a)

(77b)

(77c)

(77d)

(77e)

(77f)
78

(78a)
79

(79a) power over what is stolen or lost of [his] goods. {Every action or thing that
is commenced at that hour is successful.

(79b)   ... or boarding a ship at sea is bad, and it indicates that misfortune
(79c) and terror will reach him who boards a ship. If it is at conjunction or at
opposition [of the Sun and the Moon] while the malefics aspect the
p. 151 luminaries from opposition and Mercury is with the malefics | which
injure the luminaries, then it indicates that, whoever boards the ship
at sea at that hour, the ship will sink and its people and what is in it
80 will be lost.} ... whoever runs away at that hour will soon die in this
(80a) running away of his. {Conjunction and opposition kill and harm everyone and every action, especially if the conjunction or opposition hap-
(80b) pens to be [at] his nativity. If Mercury is with the malefics, it increases
the power for the malefics in what there is of calamities and evil from
the malefics.}

V-37   **Chapter 37. The treatment of spirits.**

1   If something like the devil is in the house of a man, or what you
want to expel from him, or you see in him bad, bumping signs, or a
demon, and you wish to expel this from him with drugs and incan-
tations or appeal to it concerning this or treat [him] with a remedy
from religion or entreaty or by another stratagem in order to purify
this place and house, then you should commence this when the
2 ascendent and the Moon are in Aries or in Taurus or in Gemini. Avoid
commencing it when the ascendent and the Moon are in Cancer or Leo.
3 It is good when the ascendent and the Moon are in Virgo or Libra.
4, 5 There is no good in it when they are in Scorpio. It is good in Sagitta-
6 rius and Capricorn. If they are in Aquarius, then there is no good in it.
7, 8 If they are in Pisces, then it is good. It is better for it and this is
stronger if Jupiter and Venus are with the Moon or in the ascendent.

V-38   **Chapter 38. Someone wishes to retain [his food] or to drink a medicine
for diarrhoea, and the rest of what is a remedy, with which he is cured
from vomiting and diarrhoea.**

1   If someone wishes to retain from his satiety or [to take] medication for the nose and the rest of that with which are treated those
who are among those sick in the head [and] he wishes to suppress it,
then commence this when the Moon is in Aries or in Taurus and the
Moon is diminishing as these two signs magnify and are called the

314

"region of the ascent", and this is the best of what is [possible] when
the benefics aspect the Moon. If you want to commence drinking the   2
medicine for diarrhoea or something that eases the stomach or an
enema or a drink of what is equal to this from among the drugs which
ease, then the commencement of it is the best of what is [possible]
when the Moon is in Libra or Scorpio as these place[s] compress and
are called the "region of lowness", and it is the best of what is [pos-
sible] when the benefics aspect the Moon.

| **Chapter 39. Someone wishes to out something from his body with** _{p. 152}
knife or scalpel, or to bleed a vein.   _{V-39}

If you wish to cut a vein or cupping or what is like this of what is   1
cut from the body with iron, then you should avoid this when the
ascendent or the Moon is in Taurus or Virgo or Capricorn or in Pisces
as there is no good in it. You should avoid this also when the new Moon 2
appears until the Moon has risen from the Sun's rays by thirteen
degrees. You should avoid this also when the Moon is [away] from the   3
Sun in opposition and decreases as it is bad. Avoid Mars and beware of 4
it with the greatest of precautions that it is not in the ascendent and is
not with the Moon or does not aspect the ascendent or the Moon. If   5
Mars with Saturn aspects the ascendent or the Moon when someone
cuts something from his body at that hour, then it indicates that this
man is not about to escape from it or he will soon become accustomed
to this cutting. It is the best of what is [possible] when you wish a   6
treatment of this if the Moon is diminishing in its light and the malefics are not in the succedent of the Moon, that is when they are behind the Moon. Let the Moon and the ascendent be with Venus or   7
[let] Jupiter or Venus aspect the ascendent while the Moon is among
them free from the malefics. Avoid the treatment, cutting with a knife   8
or scalpel from the limb whose government belongs to the sign in
which the Moon or the ascendent is at that hour. If the Moon is in a tro- 9
pical sign or in a sign possessing two bodies, then this commencement
is not good in it unless the benefics are with the Moon or aspect it.

Chapter 40. If there is an infection in the eye or a covering over it _{V-40}
or something of what is treated with iron.

You should commence this at an hour in which the Moon is increasing in computation and in light while Jupiter or Venus is with

it or aspects the Moon and Mars does not aspect the Moon and it is free from Mars, as Mars is most injurious of what is [possible] to the Moon if the Moon is increasing in its computation and its light.

V-41   **Chapter 41. Illness as Qitrinus [Cedrenus?] the Sadwali [?] says. I took this statement from him.**

1   He says: Whoever desires to know the condition of the patient [at] the beginning of when he is ill, how long he will endure [it], let him look at the ascendent and the Moon and the lord of the ascendent and
p. 153 the lord of the Moon's house and the Moon's conjoining | with a star,
2   whatever it is, and the Moon's dodecatemorion. If the lord of the Moon and the lord of the ascendent are from among the benefics, or the benefics aspect the ascendent and the Moon and the Moon's dodecatemorion, or the Moon conjoins with the benefics, then, if the patient became ill at that hour and it is the beginning of his illness, it indicates recovery from his illness and his being healed of this illness
3   quickly, if God wishes. But if Mars or Saturn happens to be in the situation of what I wrote, then it indicates that the illness will remain
4   a long time in him. If the lord of this illness is Mars, then he got this
5   illness from heat. From Saturn it indicates [that] the disease will remain a long time in its owner, and there has reached him from it
6   consumption and coldness and swelling. If there is injury to the Moon from Saturn and Mars but they do not harm the ascendent, then it
7   indicates that this illness will harm his body. If these two harm the ascendent but do not harm the Moon, then it indicates that it [the illness] will harm his soul and overwhelm his understanding and blind him, or [something] like this of disasters because of which his soul
8   will be ruined. If Saturn and Mars injure the ascendent and the bene- fics do not aspect these two, then the patient will die because of this illness of his, and grievance and pain will be in the limb which the
9   sign in which the Moon or the ascendent is governs. If any of the malefics is in this sign or in [the sign] opposite it, then this pain and agony will be harsher in him.

10   If you want to know [whether] he will escape from this disease or not, then look concerning this from the aspect of the planets as it will
11   teach this. If you want to know the condition of the patient, when it will be heavy and when it will be light, then the indicator of this is
12   the Moon. When the Moon in its transit or its motion first reaches the

malefics or they aspect it, then, as for the patient, [his] pain at this
time will be the heaviest of what is [possible] and the most severe.
Whenever the Moon reaches the place of the malefics and their aspect   13
of it is in the term[s] of the malefics, then it indicates that the patient's
condition is the worst of what is [possible] at that time. The patient is   14
released as long as the Moon remains in a place and term away from
death as, when it reaches the benefics or they aspect it, his pain is
lightened and he is helped from agony. The Moon after seven days   15
reaches its left quartile, and after nine days its left trine, and after
fourteen days its opposition, and after eighteen days its right trine,
and after twenty-one days its right quartile, and after twenty-eight
days is when it attains its place in which it was. If the Moon reaches   16
any of these places which I named on those days [that it reaches]
them, then these are the days on which a judgment of the patient is
best. Whenever the Moon on one of these days reaches one of those   17
places and a malefic conjoins or aspects it, then the pain will be harsher in him and will be heavy. If the Moon on these days arrives in   18
these places and the benefics aspect it or are with it, then it is lightened
from the patient [and there is] much from which he is helped.

| I will name the days in which judgment is best. They are when the   p. 154
Moon has passed its place in which it was when there was the first   19, 20
beginning of the patient's illness by ten degrees or by forty degrees
as those days on which the Moon in its motion reaches ten degrees and
forty degrees are from among the days on which judgment is best.
When the Moon in its motion reaches these two places and the bene-   21
fics have stopped in this place or aspect it, it indicates that he will
be released from his illness and recover from it, if God wishes. If the   22
malefics are in this place when the Moon reaches it or aspect [it], then
it indicates that [his] pain will increase and he will die from this illness
of his. If the malefic which the Moon reaches is Mars and the beginning   23
of this illness is by day, then it is worse for his pain and more hideous.
If the beginning of the illness is by night and the Moon reaches Saturn   24
at this place, it indicates like this of the severity of the illness and its
hideousness.

If the beginning of this illness is at an hour in which the ascendent   25
or the Moon is in a tropical sign, then it indicates that it will be easier
with respect to this illness, or rather that he will recover from it, but
sometimes he will also relapse. If the beginning of the illness is at an   26

hour in which the two luminaries [are] under the earth, then it indicates that this illness is hideous, severe, but this situation alone does
27 not indicate loss and death. It is necessary from this situation that you look at the aspect of the malefics and the two luminaries' reaching the benefics or the malefics as it is more suitable for your learning the condition of the patient and where his circumstances will wind up.

28   If on those days which were named the days of judgment the Moon reaches Saturn in one of these places, then the illness will increase because of fevers and chills and stretching and extension of the
29 nerve[s]. If Mars is in this situation, it indicates that the patient's illness will increase and it will be harsher in him from a fever [which is] hot, strong, sharp, and this illness will be from excitement [and] heat, and sometimes he will pour forth blood, but it is not necessary that he tend to the outflowing of this blood and its pouring forth as sometimes he will benefit from it and the patient will be helped from his illness, it will make him comfortable.

30   If the patient [becomes] a patient and the beginning of his illness is when the Moon is increasing in its calculation and is with the Sun or with Mars in the same sign, then on the day that the Moon reaches its left quartile or its opposition loss and death are feared for the patient.
31 But if the Moon is in its quartile or its opposition and is increasing in computation while Saturn aspects it, it indicates his recovery and
32 his good health, if God wishes. If the Moon on that day is diminishing in its calculation and is with Saturn or [Saturn] aspects it, then it is in another than this situation and he will not benefit from Saturn's
33 aspecting the Moon. If it is with the Sun and emerges from the Sun's position, then, as for him who becomes ill at that hour or whose illness has its beginning [then], when the Moon reaches that sign or [the sign] opposite the sign in which the Moon was while benefics aspect
p. 155 it or reach it, then it indicates his recovery with certainty on that day, |
34 if God wishes—He is exalted! If the Moon is in this situation and reaches malefics or they aspect it, then it indicates that his death and loss will certainly be on that day.

35   Look concerning the matter of the patient from these four cardines.
36 The ascendent indicates the doctor, the midheaven indicates the patient, [the sign] opposite the ascendent indicates the cause of his illness, from what thing it is, and the cardine of the fathers [the fourth]
37 indicates his recovery and his medication, if God wishes. If the patient

first becomes ill when the malefics are in the ascendent at that hour, then it indicates that he will not benefit from any of the doctor's drugs and his exertion and his treatment; this is because everything from the doctor becomes an injury. If the benefics are in the ascendent 38 at that hour, then it indicates that he will benefit from the doctor and that he will be pleasant in this treatment. If a benefic is in the mid- 39 heaven, then it indicates that this patient will be treated with a medicine from which he will benefit, if God—He is exalted!—wishes. If a benefic is in [the sign] opposite the ascendent, then it indicates 40 that this patient will recover from the power of the drug which he drinks, but it will treat him not at all, and it will not be an illness for which he will be afraid, but its treatment will be easy. If you see a 41 malefic in the ascendent and a benefic in opposition, then it indicates that, as for the doctor who begins to treat the illness, even if he is kind [and] learned, he will not benefit from his kindness and his treatment, but the reputation of this [man] and his praise will fall to another than this doctor.

If you want to know the condition of the patient and his death and 42 he is one of those whose nativity is known, then look at the Moon, if it transits in its motion in the sign in which Saturn was in his nativity. If when he becomes ill Saturn also is with the Moon in its transit or 43 aspects it, then this illness will be severe [and] one will fear for him from it. If the Moon in its transit is at that sign in which Mars was in 44 his nativity, and Mars is with it or aspects it [at the beginning of his illness], then this patient will be [ill] from excitement [and] intense heat, [and] one will fear for him from it. If the Moon in its transit and 45 its motion is in that sign in which Saturn and Mars were in his nativ- ity, and one of them is with the Moon while the other aspects it, then it indicates that his illness will be harsher in him and will be heavy and one will fear for him from it. If the Moon in its transit is in 46 that sign in which the malefics were in his nativity and reaches a benefic star in its motion when it reaches this sign in it or it [the benefic] aspects it [the Moon], then it indicates that this illness will last a long time in him and will be harsher upon him, but he will be released from it, if God wishes.

Every patient whose nativity is known is one who was born in seven 47 months or in nine months [from conception]. Count for him from the 48 day he was born till the day in which he became ill and the beginning

of his illness occurred, then subtract from the total of this calculation,
if his birth was for nine months, nine after nine, and for whom his
49 birth was [in] seven months, seven after seven. If there is nothing
[left] from the computation for him for whom you subtracted nine
after nine or for whom you subtracted seven after seven, then it indicates that the days of this patient are completed and his years are
50 finished and he is dead. Because the years of the people of Egypt
[contain] three hundred and sixty-five days, when you subtract from
them seven after seven there is left one, [and when you subtract from
51 them nine after nine there is left five]. Count for him whose nativity
was for seven months one day for each year that has passed of his life
p. 156 till the day he became ill, | and if his nativity is for nine months
52 [count] five days for each year that has passed of his life. Take what
has passed of the days equal to the years, then add these together as
it is easier for you than if they were all of the days in what has passed
53 of the years. Then look in which sign are the place[s] of the Sun and
the Moon in his nativity, and count the signs which are between the
Sun and the Moon, and also [between] the sign[s] in which the Sun
54 and the Moon are [now]. See how much this reaches, and keep its
55 number. Then subtract the number of those signs which are between
the Sun and the Moon from the days which have passed of his life till
56 the day in which he became ill. If nothing is left of the number of
these days, then it indicates that this illness is a severe illness or he
does not hope to recover or be released from it.

57 　　If the Moon in its transit is in the sixth sign from the ascendent
(this place is called the house of illness) or the Moon in its transits
reaches the eighth sign from the ascendent or the sign which was the
house of the fathers [the fourth] in his nativity or the sign in which
the Moon was in the nativity, this native attains an illness; when the
Moon is in one of these places, then it indicates that this illness is not
58 negligible [and] easy, but is severe [and] hideous. If in this transit in
these places the Moon aspects the benefics, then it indicates that this
59 illness will leave him and he will escape from it, if God wishes. But if
the malefics are aspecting it in this situation, then it indicates that
60 one will fear for him from the illness. The illness is the worst of what is
[possible] when the beginning of the illness is at an hour in which the
Moon is in the sign in which the deadly star was in his base-nativity.
61 The deadly star is that which at the start of the nativity was the first

lord of the triplicity of the cardine of the fathers [the fourth], because
the first lord of the triplicity of the house of the fathers indicates
death and the second illnesses and sickness. Some of the lords of the   62
triplicity are called "evil" [dushisah]. They are "evil" when the com-   63
mencement is by day and the lords of the triplicity are diurnal star[s]
and when the commencement is at night and the lords of the triplicity
are nocturnal star[s]. If none of the lords of the triplicity of the house   64
of the fathers is "evil", then it indicates illnesses and a chronic
disease. This is the most hideous of what is [possible], that according   65
to the transit of the stars the deadly star is with the Moon or aspects
the Moon.

Concerning the matter of the illness consider how the positions of   66
the Sun and the Moon are at the start of his nativity and when the
beginning of his illness occurs. If you find the Moon has preceded the   67
Sun to its left quartile from where its place was in his nativity or has
reached the transit of the Sun at the beginning of his illness, then it
indicates that this illness will leave him and he will soon recover from
it. But if it does not reach the transit of the Sun before it reaches its   68
left quartile, then this is an indicator that this illness will stay a long
time in him and will not leave him except after misery and delay.

| Chapter 42. The will.

p. 157
V-42

If a man wants to make his will, let him commence this when the   1
ascendent or the Moon is in a tropical sign as it indicates that the
will and the legacy will be changed. Let him make his will when the   2
Moon is increasing [in latitude], decreasing in computation and increasing in light, and its motion is from the middle of the ecliptic
ascending toward the seas [the North], and conjoining with a star in
its station, and not under the [Sun's] rays. If it is under the [Sun's]   3
rays [but] not in this sign but in another sign and emerging from
under the rays, then it does not indicate immediate death. Avoid   4
making your will in the hour in which Mars is with the Moon or in the
ascendent as if one makes his will at this hour it indicates that the
will will not be changed, and the patient will die from this illness of
his, and the will will not be executed after his death, but someone after
him will refute him in his will and write in the will or steal the will.
You should not make any will when Mars is with the Moon or in the   5
ascendent or in the quartile of the ascendent or in its opposition or

6 aspects the Moon or the ascendent. If Mars is not in this position but
Saturn is with the Moon or with the ascendent, then it indicates that
[there will be] a delay in the time at which he makes the will, and the
will will be removed afterwards and will not be executed in his life-
7 time or after his death. If Saturn is not in this position but Venus or
Jupiter is with the Moon or in the ascendent, then, [after] some of
the life of the owner of the will has passed, he will change the will.

V-43   **Chapter 43. On clarifying the phases [fasis] of the Moon and the head
of the dragon and its tail, which indicate selling and buying and
cheapness and expensiveness.**

1   The head is called the "ascending" and its tail the "descending",
and the signs which those learned in the stars call "obscured" are
from Leo to Capricorn, which is the region of descent, while from
2 Aquarius to Cancer is the region of ascent. Look, and if the Moon is in
the region of ascent increasing in computation, then he who buys at
this time will buy dearly and at an increase in its price over what is
3 right. If the Moon is in the region of descent and is diminishing in
computation, then he who buys at this time will buy cheaply and at a
4 price less than what is right. Look concerning the phases of the Moon.
5 Its phases are when it emerges from under the Sun's rays till it reaches
left quartile of the Sun, and he benefits from this whose intention it is
to buy and to sell sincerely and faithfully as he who buys at this time
buys the commodity for a price that is right [and] in which there is
6 neither cheapness nor expensiveness. When the Moon goes from left
p. 158 quartile | of the Sun till it reaches opposition to the Sun, then selling
7 benefits from this and commencing a litigation. When it moves from opposition to the Sun till it reaches right quartile of the Sun, then buying
8 benefits from this and what is properly sought. When the Moon moves
from right quartile of the Sun until it reaches the Sun's position,
then the people whose intention is proper and just benefit from this.

The fifth book of Dorotheus is completed, and with its completion
the whole book ends. Praise to God Whose praise is true, and His
prayers upon His servants whom He chooses and [upon] all His
prophets and His messengers.

Collated against the base-copy one [word] by one and corrected in
the measure of [my] ability and diligence. In God is success.

Appendix 1: Charts

According to James Herschel Holden (**A History of Horoscopic Astrology**, AFA, 1996, pg. 34), the charts in Dorotheus are among the earliest known. We do not know how Dorotheus originally presented them in his text, nor do we know anything about the original chart data used to cast them. What has come down to us are the Arabic versions which Pingree copied. With one exception, the data used for these modern constructions are as speculated by Pingree. I have used whole sign houses, mean node and day/night Lot of Fortune. Times given are approximate. Taking a hint from Book V (pg. 308), the location used is Alexandria, Egypt, but this, also, is speculation.

In his Praefatio, Pingree ordered the charts by date. I have set them here in the order they appear in the text. I have kept Pingree's numbering. Differences between Dorotheus and modern calculations are noted.

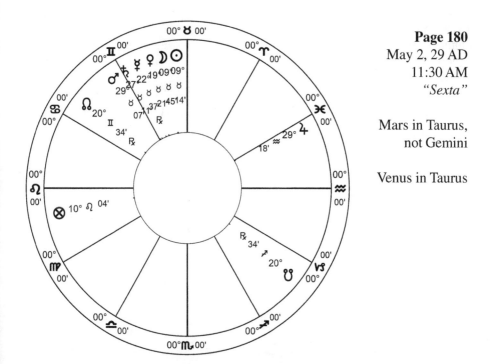

Page 180
May 2, 29 AD
11:30 AM
"*Sexta*"

Mars in Taurus,
not Gemini

Venus in Taurus

Page 184
August 2, 43 AD
2:00 AM
"Octava"

Mars in Scorpio,
not Aquarius

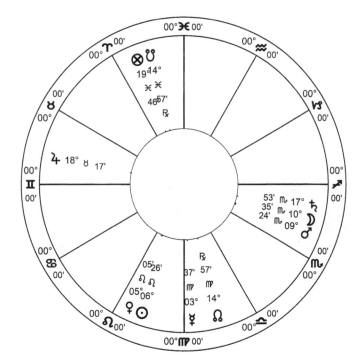

Page 185
January 26, 13 AD
10:00 AM
"Tertia"

Venus in Capricorn,
not Pisces

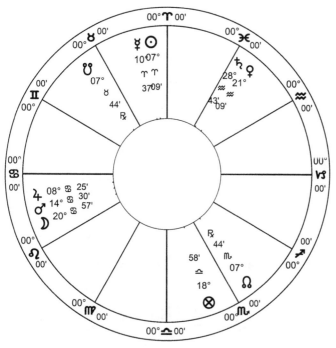

Page 186 - *top*
March 30, 22 AD
11:00 AM
"Quinta"

Saturn in Aquarius,
not Pisces

Mars in Cancer

Venus in Aquarius,
not Virgo

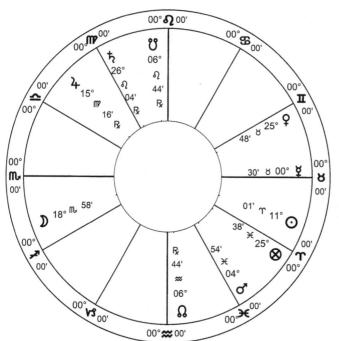

Page 186 - *bottom*
April 2, 36 AD
8:00 pm
"Septima"

Saturn in Leo,
not Virgo

Mars in Pisces,
not Aquarius

Mercury in Taurus,
not Pisces

Page 187
October 31, 12 AD
10:00 PM
"Secunda"

Mars in Virgo,
not Leo

Venus in Libra,
not Virgo

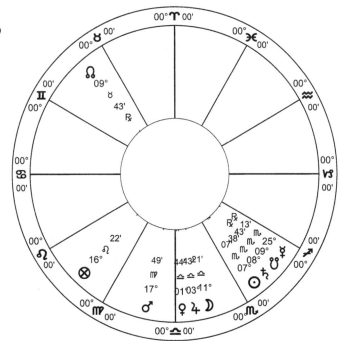

Page 188 - *top*
March 29, 7 BC
9:00 AM
"Prima"

Venus in Aries,
not Taurus

Mercury in Pisces
not Aries

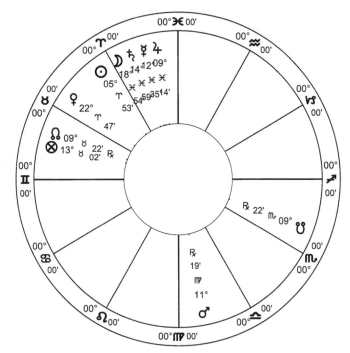

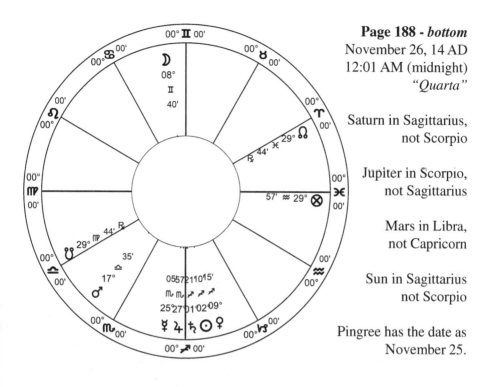

Page 188 - *bottom*
November 26, 14 AD
12:01 AM (midnight)
"Quarta"

Saturn in Sagittarius,
not Scorpio

Jupiter in Scorpio,
not Sagittarius

Mars in Libra,
not Capricorn

Sun in Sagittarius
not Scorpio

Pingree has the date as
November 25.

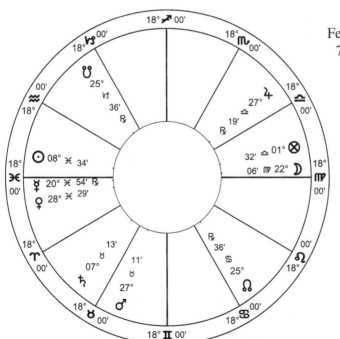

Page 238
February 26, 381 AD
7:01:18 AM (LMT)
Alexandria

In Pingree's
reconstruction,
the planets are
correctly placed in
the signs,
their exact degrees
differ somewhat
from Dorotheus.

See the discussion
on the next page.

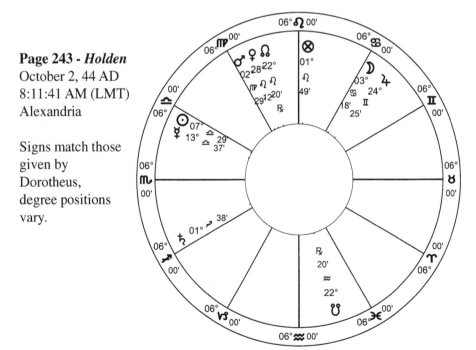

Page 243 - *Pingree*
October 20, 281 AD
6:54:44 AM (LMT)
Alexandria

Venus in Libra,
not Leo

Mercury in Scorpio,
not Libra

Degree positions
vary from
Dorotheus

Of the chart on page 243, Holden writes, "*Pingree dates this chart to 20 October 281, since he wishes to ascribe it to the Persians, but a better fit to the positions given in the text is 2 October 44, which is also consistent with the dates of Dorotheus's other example charts.*" (**A History of Horoscopic Astrology**, pg. 34, footnote 83) **Carmen Astrologicum** survives in Greek excerpts, and an incomplete and interpolated Arabic version (c. 800 AD), which itself was made from a 4th century Pahlavi (middle Persian) translation. Pingree speculates the final two charts were added later, by other hands. Holden disagrees, but, presuming the signs given for Saturn and Jupiter for the chart on page 238 are accurate, the chart cannot be placed for any date between 120 BC and 380 AD - *Publisher.*

Page 243 - *Holden*
October 2, 44 AD
8:11:41 AM (LMT)
Alexandria

Signs match those
given by
Dorotheus,
degree positions
vary.

Appendix 2: Tables

Signs	The Triplicities of the Signs: Day	The Triplicities of the Signs: Night	Houses of the Planets (R = Rejoice)	Exaltation	Descent			Lords: Day	Lords: Night	Lords: Associate	The Terms of the Planets ("Egyptian")				
♈	☉ ♃ ♄	♃ ☉ ♄	♂	☉ 19	♄ 21	Eastern	Diurnal	☉	♃	♄	♃ 6	♀ 12	☿ 20	♂ 25	♄ 30
♉	♀ ☽ ♂	☽ ♀ ♂	♀ R	☽ 3		Northern	Nocturnal	♀	☽	♂	♀ 8	☿ 14	♃ 22	♄ 27	♂ 30
♊	♄ ☿ ♃	☿ ♄ ♃	☿			Western	Diurnal	♄	☿	♃	☿ 6	♃ 12	♀ 18	♂ 24	♄ 30
♋	♀ ♂ ☽	♂ ♀ ☽	☽	♃ 15	♂ 28	Southern	Nocturnal	♀	♂	☽	♂ 7	♀ 13	☿ 20	♃ 27	♄ 30
♌	☉ ♃ ♄	♃ ☉ ♄	☉			Eastern	Diurnal	☉	♃	♄	♃ 6	♀ 11	♄ 18	☿ 24	♂ 30
♍	♀ ☽ ♂	☽ ♀ ♂ ☿	☿ R	☿ 15	♀ 27	Northern	Nocturnal	♀	☽	♂ ☿	☿ 7	♀ 17	♃ 21	♂ 28	♄ 30
♎	♄ ☿ ♃	☿ ♄ ♃	♀	♄ 21	☉ 19	Western	Diurnal	♄	☿	♃	♄ 6	☿ 14	♃ 21	♀ 28	♂ 30
♏	♀ ♂ ☽	♂ ♀ ☽	♂ R		☽ 3	Southern	Nocturnal	♀	♂	☽	♂ 7	♀ 11	☿ 19	♃ 24	♄ 30
♐	☉ ♃ ♄	♃ ☉ ♄	♃ R			Eastern	Diurnal	☉	♃	♄	♃ 12	♀ 17	☿ 23	♄ 27	♂ 30
♑	♀ ☽ ♂	☽ ♀ ♂	♄	♂ 28	♃ 15	Northern	Nocturnal	♀	☽	♂	☿ 7	♃ 14	♀ 22	♄ 26	♂ 30
♒	♄ ☿ ♃	☿ ♄ ♃	♄ R			Western	Diurnal	♄	☿	♃	☿ 7	♀ 13	♃ 20	♂ 25	♄ 30
♓	♀ ♂ ☽	♂ ♀ ☽	♃	♀ 27	☿ 15	Southern	Nocturnal	♀	♂	☽	♀ 12	♃ 16	☿ 19	♂ 28	♄ 30

Signs straight in rising: Cancer, Leo, Virgo, Libra, Scorpio, Sagittarius
Signs crooked in rising: Capricorn, Aquarius, Pisces, Aries, Taurus, Gemini

Dodecatemoria

Table of Degrees

Planet's degree	Sign	Degree	Planet's degree	Sign	Degree
1	00	12	16	06	12
2	00	24	17	06	24
3	01	06	18	07	06
4	01	18	19	07	18
5	02	00	20	08	00
6	02	12	21	08	12
7	02	24	22	08	24
8	03	06	23	09	06
9	03	18	24	09	18
10	04	00	25	10	00
11	04	12	26	10	12
12	04	24	27	10	24
13	05	06	28	11	06
14	05	18	29	11	18
15	06	00	30	12	00

Table of Minutes

Planet's minute	Degree	Minute	Planet's minute	Degree	Minute	Planet's minute	Degree	Minute	Planet's minute	Degree	Minute
1	00	12	16	03	12	31	06	12	46	09	12
2	00	24	17	03	24	32	06	24	47	09	24
3	00	36	18	03	36	33	06	36	48	09	36
4	00	48	19	03	48	34	06	48	49	09	48
5	01	00	20	04	00	35	07	00	50	10	00
6	01	12	21	04	12	36	07	12	51	10	12
7	01	24	22	04	24	37	07	24	52	10	24
8	01	36	23	04	36	38	07	36	53	10	36
9	01	48	24	04	48	39	07	48	54	10	48
10	02	00	25	05	00	40	08	00	55	11	00
11	02	12	26	05	12	41	08	12	56	11	12
12	02	24	27	05	24	42	08	24	57	11	24
13	02	36	28	05	36	43	08	36	58	11	36
14	02	48	29	05	48	44	08	48	59	11	48
15	03	00	30	06	00	45	09	00	60	12	00

0 Aries	4 Leo	8 Sagittarius	
1 Taurus	5 Virgo	9 Capricorn	
2 Gemini	6 Libra	10 Aquarius	
3 Cancer	7 Scorpio	11 Pisces	

The signs are numbered in base 12. 11 + 1 = 12, e.g., 0. i.e., Pisces + 1 = Aries.

To find the Dodecatemorion of any planet:

In the Table of degrees, find the degree of the planet & take the sign & degree you find there. Do the same in the Table of minutes, to find degrees & minutes. To these, add the natal sign, degree & minute. The result is the Dodecatemorion of the position.

Example: The Dodecatemorion of Saturn at 8^0 31' Capricorn (09 08 31):

8 degrees is	03	06		
31 minutes is	00	06	12	
Natal position	09	08	31	
Sum:	00	20	43	e.g., 20^0 43' Aries

Adapted from page 29 of **On the Judgement of Nativities**, by Johannes Schoener. Translation copyright © 2001 by Robert Hand. Used by permission.

(adapted from Pingree)

Note that the first four books are primarily devoted to the topics of the octotopus, but not in the canonical order.

The remainder of the work consists of:

INDEX OF SUBJECTS

CPSIA information can be obtained
at www.ICGtesting.com
Printed in the USA
BVHW082152090620
581038BV00003B/178

9 781933 303147